Riots

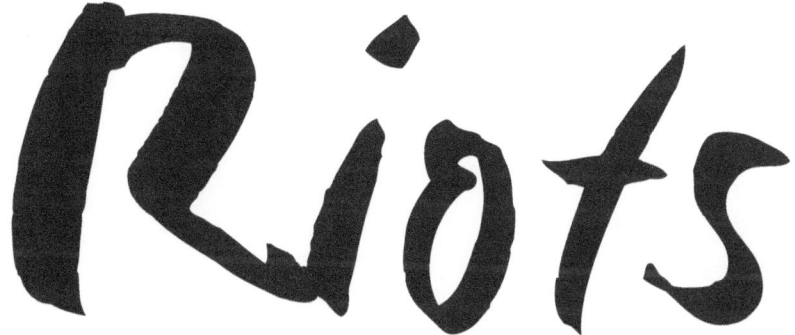

Riots

Returned soldiers and public disorder in Australia at the end of World War I

FIONA SKYRING

UWA PUBLISHING

First published in 2025 by
UWA Publishing
Crawley, Western Australia 6009
www.uwap.uwa.edu.au

UWAP is an imprint of UWA Publishing
a division of The University of Western Australia

This book is copyright. Apart from any fair dealing for the purpose of private study, research, criticism or review, as permitted under the *Copyright Act 1968*, no part may be reproduced by any process without written permission. Enquiries should be made to the publisher.

Copyright © Fiona Skyring 2025

The moral right of the author has been asserted.

ISBN: 978-1-76080-309-4

 A catalogue record for this book is available from the National Library of Australia

Cover image: excerpt from 'Cartoon of the Red Riot on Merivale Street, South Brisbane, 1919', State Library of Queensland.
Cover design by Hazel Lam
Typeset in 11½ point Bembo Book by Lasertype
Printed by Lightning Source

 uwapublishing

For my mother
Fay Skyring OAM
1932–2019

CONTENTS

	Acknowledgements	ix
	Introduction	1
1	Riots on Peace Day, November 1918	11
2	'Taking Matters Into Their Own Hands'	43
3	'Dulce et Decorum Est': Remembering Soldiers' Sacrifice	69
4	When The Boys Came Home: Riots in Fremantle and Melbourne, 1919	99
5	The Internal Enemy and Diggers 'Uphold the Law'	133
6	Vigilante Violence and the Beginnings of Secret Armies	163
7	The Loyal Nation	183
	Notes	191
	Index	217

Acknowledgements

This book started life as a PhD thesis. My supervisor Stephen Garton provided guidance and incisive critique, as well as showing a lot of patience, and I thank him for that. Some busy decades intervened, but I knew this history of riots involving returned soldiers was too good and important a story to stay gathering dust on a shelf. Like most theses it was not publication-ready, so after a major restructuring and further research the book started to take shape. I am grateful to the team at UWA Publishing for accepting the manuscript and steering the project through to completion. I felt like I had a strong advocate for the book in UWAP managing publisher Kate Pickard, whose support I very much value. Editing the manuscript has been a completely positive experience for me, with many thanks to editor Kirstie Innes-Will. Her insightful comments and questions helped me sharpen the focus in the text. Any errors are of course mine. I would also like to thank Lauren Pratt at UWAP and Hazel Lam for her wonderful cover design.

I am indebted to many librarians and archivists across Australia. Staff at the offices of the National Archives of Australia in Canberra, Brisbane and Melbourne have provided invaluable help to me over years of research. The increasing digitisation of archival records in recent decades makes it easier for historians like me to explore government archives from my desk, but there remains a huge number still in their old paper files. I have relied on the knowledge of archivists in navigating these collections. This applies to the National Archives as well as to the State Records Office of Western Australia, the Queensland State Archives, and state archives offices in Victoria, New South Wales and South Australia. I would like to thank especially the staff at the Queensland State Archives and the State Records Office of Western

Australia for helping me find some illusive references, and for keeping the doors open while I worked on the archival files up to the final minute of office hours. Similarly, librarians at the National Library of Australia, the State Library of New South Wales, John Oxley Library in Brisbane and the State Library of Western Australia have helped me considerably in finding resources. For reference checks and photograph reproductions in the final months of editing I am very thankful to librarians at the State Library of South Australia, the State Library of Victoria and the State Library of Western Australia, and to staff at the Australian War Memorial and the National Library's digitisation on demand service. Also, many thanks to the Army Museum of Western Australia and to the Legislative Assembly of Western Australia for giving UWAP permission to reproduce photos from their collections.

Finally, special and wholehearted thanks to my father Graham Skyring and sisters Sally and Melissa, for their support and encouragement over the years to get this book done.

Introduction

In late October 1919, nearly a year after World War I had ended, a group of unemployed returned soldiers was sent from Sydney to Newcastle to look for work. When they arrived in Newcastle, officials at the local Repatriation Department told the men there were no jobs available. This 'caused resentment among the men' according to a newspaper report, and a few days later all but three of them returned to Sydney. The three returned soldiers who stayed then went to the Newcastle Repatriation office. They had been drinking and the Repatriation branch secretary, Birch, told them to come back when they were sober. They started yelling abusive language at the clerks and 22-year-old returned soldier Robert Kelly hit Birch across the jaw. The police arrived and the returned soldiers challenged the officers to arrest them. What followed was described in the press as 'wild scenes' and a 'free fight' between the returned soldiers and police on the street outside the department office.[1]

Kelly was charged with assault, using improper language and damaging a police uniform (Constable March's uniform was torn in the fight). He pleaded not guilty and was fined a total of £5 5s 16d (five pounds, five shillings and sixpence), which at the time was substantially more than the weekly minimum wage. If Kelly was unable to pay the fine, he faced a term of nearly two months in prison as a default. In court, Kelly said that he had gone to Newcastle to find a job and had no place to stay, and that he had been drinking on the day of the event. He had no memory of what had happened during his arrest.[2]

'Wild scenes' and returned soldiers fighting with police on the streets were features of the postwar landscape in Australia. Incidents like those in Newcastle were not isolated outbursts, and many events posed much more serious threats to public order. Large-scale riots involving returned soldiers – sometimes numbering in their thousands – exploded in regional towns and cities across Australia, starting in 1918 and reaching a peak in the middle of 1919. The riots that occurred in Australia from 1918 to 1920 were more widespread, numerous and serious than has been acknowledged in the millions of words written about Australia and the Great War so far. They occurred at a time when the nation, far from being united by the experience of war, was deeply divided.

Returned soldier riots varied in terms of severity and context but there are some connecting themes, which I explore in the chapters ahead. The central importance of returned soldiers' sacrifice and what it meant for soldiers' place in postwar society is a familiar part of current day celebrations of the Anzac legend. But the anger, violence and resentment that returned soldiers expressed through the riots, and which the soldiers themselves always stated was based in their sacrifice, does not fit with a celebratory legend, not now and not then. The riots also helped to define the parameters of membership of the 'loyal' nation versus its 'disloyal' enemies. This was contested terrain, with many Australians opposing those who called themselves loyalists and who sought to control the meanings of patriotic allegiance.

The conflicts within white Australian society at the end of the war were a series of interconnected crises. But the schisms within the divided nation were not clearly drawn and, as Gavin Souter has argued, were instead a series of overlapping divisions 'which all drew their acrimony from the war'.[3] Probably the most well-known of these conflicts is that over conscription. The conscription referendums in October 1916 and December 1917 failed to introduce compulsory enlistment into the Australian defence forces. The campaigns for and against conscription polarised Australian society and fuelled existing class divisions. But the depth and concentration of opposition to conscription needs more explanation.

At a national level the defeat of each referendum was close. In 1916, 51.6 per cent of voters were against conscription and in 1917 it was 53.79 per cent. But the results at a regional level showed a more varied picture. In Western Australia, just over 64 per cent voted 'yes' to conscription in the 1917 referendum, whereas in New South Wales that year only 41 per cent of voters supported the introduction of conscription. In Queensland the 'yes' vote was 44 per cent. When we look at results by electorate, there is a clear link between working-class areas and the 'no' vote. In the inner-city electorate of South Sydney, then solidly working-class, 75 per cent of people voted 'no'. So did nearly 76 per cent of electors in the seat of Cook, in the southern suburbs of Sydney, which was not an affluent area in 1917. In contrast, voters in North Sydney were 68 per cent in favour of conscription.

It was a similar story in suburban Melbourne, with the working-class, inner-city electorates of Melbourne Ports and Yarra voting 'no' by substantial margins – 69 per cent and 72.6 per cent respectively. These results show just how divided urban communities in Australia were over the issue of conscription.[4]

The class divisions over conscription were also clear in regional areas. In the vast rural electorate of Kennedy in Queensland, which in 1917 was home to shearers in the Australian Workers' Union (AWU) and other unionised rural workers, 67 per cent of electors voted 'no' to conscription. In the neighbouring electorate of Capricornia the 'no' vote was nearly 63 per cent. Queenslanders generally were opposed to conscription. Out of the ten electorates then in Queensland, the majority of voters in all except one electorate were opposed to conscription. The electorate of Lilley in the northern bayside suburbs of Brisbane was the only one in Queensland that voted 'yes', and this was by a majority of 53 per cent.[5]

The referendum results were also close among soldiers at the front and on troopships. In the 1916 referendum they voted 'yes' by 54 per cent, with 2,520 soldiers casting informal ballots. In 1917, based on figures by state, the national average for soldiers at the front and crews on transports was a 'yes' majority of 53 per cent. But this national average masked some extremely slim margins at a state level. Soldiers and sailors from New South Wales voted 'yes' to conscription by only 50.58 per cent, and there was an even smaller margin for soldiers from Tasmania, who voted 'yes' by 50.51 per cent. Soldiers from Queensland gave a muted endorsement of conscription in 1917, with a 'yes' vote of only 51.76 per cent.[6]

A few days after the first failed conscription referendum in 1916, the government introduced regulations prohibiting the publication of ballot results from Australian soldiers at the front, so these referendum results from 1916 and 1917 were never made public at the time.[7] In November 1917, just weeks before the final referendum, Horace (Barney) Allen of the Universal Service League, a pro-conscription organisation, was visiting injured soldiers at a military hospital in England. Allen reported that he

> hardly met a man yet who will vote for conscription. They allege all sorts of queer reasons, but the commonest by far is that they would not ask their worst enemy to go to France – France is Hell. The next is that the Australians do not get a fair deal, and are shoved into all the most dangerous shows...as the first storming troops. 'The Australians and the Scotties never come back', is the saying...the result of camp-life...is certainly to make a man feel a fool to have come, and that he is wasting his time in a ludicrous farce. And then he steps from farce suddenly to grim tragedy.[8]

Allen was dubious about the claim that the casualty rate for Australian troops was higher, but it was. Among soldiers of the Australian Imperial Force (AIF), the casualty rate was 64.8 per cent, one of the highest of any army in the war.[9]

The debate over conscription was a bitter conflict that helped to split the Australian Labor Party and change the government. In 1916, Labor Prime Minister Billy Hughes and his followers were kicked out of the Labor caucus for their support of conscription. Hughes had already been expelled from the NSW Labor Party for the same reason. Hughes and his followers formed a minority government with a coalition of conservative MPs. Similar splits among Labor-elected representatives occurred in state legislatures across Australia, and one of the outcomes was that the only state in which Labor remained in government was Queensland.

There was a lot more to the Labor Party split than the issue of conscription alone, but the result was depleted parliamentary Labor representation across the country. The pro-conscriptionist Labor MPs joined forces with conservative MPs to form the Nationalist Party. The non-Labor political landscape at the time included the very new Commonwealth Liberal Party under Alfred Deakin (not the same as the Liberal Party of Robert Menzies decades later), the Free Traders, and a group called the Anti-Socialist League. Combined, these were generally referred to as 'Tories' by Labor supporters and the union movement, after the British nickname for conservatives. Stuart Macintyre called the Nationalist coalition 'that fragile child of unlikely parents, ex-Labor and anti-Labor'.[10] The Nationalists under Billy Hughes held government on their own federally until 1922, after which they governed in a coalition with the support of the newly formed Country Party.

The union movement and those who remained in the Labor Party campaigned against conscription, though many supported voluntary enlistment. Those who opposed conscription did not necessarily oppose Australia's involvement in the war, although the anti-war movement grew as the war dragged on over four years. Opposition to Australia's involvement in the war came not only from parts of the union movement but from some church groups as well. The sectarian division in Australian society that drew heightened hostility from the failed conscription campaigns was that between Protestants (for) and Catholics (against), although this dichotomy blurred the variations within that divide. Some Protestant clergymen declared themselves opposed to the war and some Catholic spokesmen supported conscription or campaigned for recruitment to the AIF.

Sectarian bigotry towards Catholic Australians was commonplace and open in 1917, and 'Papist' was used as a term of derision. The Republican uprising in Ireland in 1916, also known as the Easter Rising, was represented on the pages of the mostly conservative Australian newspapers as a treacherous betrayal by the Irish. Many retained this stance even after the British military authorities executed by firing squad fifteen of the leaders of the uprising, in an act of brutal retribution that was widely condemned. For many Protestant Australians, suspicion of Irish Catholic Australians remained. Archbishop Daniel Mannix in Melbourne was an opponent of conscription and Prime Minister Billy Hughes sought to make political capital out of it, accusing him of sedition. This heightened already high sectarian animosities. Edmond Campion wrote that an outcome of the conscription debates was 'the typecasting of any Catholic as potential disloyal'.[11] In response to this, many Catholic Australians emphatically defended their religious identity, claiming it had no relevance in determining wartime loyalty.

The depth and ubiquity of sectarian hostility were features of wartime Australian society that have been completely removed from contemporary celebrations of Anzac. But communities were divided and the government blamed Catholic Australians for the defeat of the conscription referendums. In secret official correspondence from January 1918, George Steward, then private secretary to the Governor-General, Sir Ronald Munro Ferguson, wrote to Frank Hall in London. Hall was private secretary to Major General Vernon Kell, who was the first director of the British Security Service, the precursor to MI5. This is what Steward wrote about the defeat of the 1917 conscription referendum:

> As a personal opinion, also an official opinion…I attribute the defeat almost entirely to the Roman Catholic element resident in this country; particularly do I attach the greatest blame to Dr Mannix…It is true that a number of Roman Catholics have expressed their disapproval of Dr Mannix's utterances and general attitude, but these merely counted for the value of their individual votes. Nothing more. It may be accepted without the slightest hesitation that ninety percent of Roman Catholics in this country voted 'No', and did all they could to induce others to do likewise.[12]

After sheeting home the blame to Catholics, Steward also suggested that women influenced the 'no' vote against conscription. As an immigrant from England himself, where women did not have the vote, Steward noted the novelty of women's suffrage in Australia. He suggested it was too much to expect women to vote to send their sons to war. The devastating impacts of war were all around them:

> Week after week transports arrive here and deposit wounded and broken men…one can never pass through any of the leading streets of

the cities and towns here without meeting men in more or less crippled condition…to ask any country where all the women and all the men have votes to conscript itself, was asking a great deal more than one had any right to expect from humanity.¹³

After the wartime years of deep community divisions, the year 1919 brought more upheaval. In January 1919 cases of 'pneumonic influenza', or 'Spanish flu', were reported almost simultaneously in Melbourne and Sydney. The first cases of what became a worldwide pandemic were reported among military bases in western Europe in 1918. It was dubbed 'Spanish flu' because in Spain, a neutral country during World War I, there was no press censorship to limit news of the spread of the virus. By the end of 1918, populations on every continent except Australia and Antarctica were infected. Australia's distance from Europe was initially an effective quarantine, but once the virus arrived the pandemic raged across the country in early 1919, with a repeat outbreak in June. It claimed the lives of an estimated 12,000 to 15,000 Australians. Troopships were quarantined, schools, churches and theatres were closed, and meetings were disallowed. Each state government closed their borders to most travellers and separately imposed a range of restrictions, but these uncoordinated efforts had little impact on the spread of the disease.¹⁴

Add to this the return in 1919 of approximately 167,000 soldiers and sailors of the AIF who were still overseas when the war ended in November 1918. From a country of just under five million non-Indigenous people, close to 60,000 Australian men had been killed in the war and 155,000 were wounded in action. This was a story of departure, loss and return of dramatic proportions. Little was known at the time about shell shock, but families, co-workers, fellow soldiers and magistrates all recognised that many otherwise healthy men had been severely damaged by their war experiences. Violent assault increased, and as early as 1915 military authorities warned that rowdy returned soldiers considered themselves to be 'beyond the reach of law and order'.¹⁵ In giving lenient sentences to two returned soldiers charged with the brutal murder of a man in Sydney in March 1920, the magistrate described their crimes as 'war products' but warned against the continued use of deadly weapons by soldiers.¹⁶

First Nations men joined the AIF and fought alongside their non-Indigenous 'cobbers' or 'comrades'. An estimated 1,000 Aboriginal men enlisted in the First AIF, and their wartime contribution has only recently been recognised in historical representations of Australia during the war.[17] The major difference with their story, and part of the reason that these returned soldiers were never mentioned in the accounts of riots, was that many returned to closed and poverty-stricken missions and town reserves. These places and their Aboriginal residents were under the control of the Chief Protectors. Each state and the Northern Territory had its own version of this unelected official role, though Torres Strait Islanders did not officially come under the control of the Queensland Chief Protector's Office until 1917. In the aftermath of World War I, Aboriginal soldiers were not acknowledged as citizen soldiers who had fought for their country.

While Aboriginal men who served in the First AIF could have expected to be rewarded for risking their lives for the country, the opposite occurred. These returned soldiers and their families continued to be denied citizenship, and were subject to a range of racially discriminatory and oppressive laws that threatened every aspect of their working and family lives. Very few were given access to postwar repatriation schemes such as land grants for returned soldiers.[18] Indeed in the first three decades of the twentieth century, the racially discriminatory legislation governing First Nations communities across Australia became more authoritarian, and included greater numbers of people within the malevolent reach of so called 'protection' regimes.[19] Then the role of First Nations soldiers was 'excluded from the digger legend'.[20] While the story of First Nations soldiers was remembered within their communities, published research about and acknowledgement of their contribution is relatively recent.

The story of the riots from 1918 to 1920 is one in which white Australian men were the main actors. In the riots sometimes women were involved in the violence. On occasions, returned soldier spokesmen referred to the presence of women in the crowd as a factor that should be restraining rough conduct. But for the most part it was men who did the rioting.

At its centre the idea of the Anzac was exclusively masculine. Women were confined to limited and secondary roles, with severe censure for women who did not fit the stereotypes of grieving mother, grieving widow or loyal sweetheart. While the surviving court statistics are not complete, there appears to have been an increase in femicide and assaults on women and girls in the postwar years. Like other examples of assault by returned soldiers, this gendered violence was treated leniently by the courts. By reasserting the distinction between public and domestic spheres, rigid definitions of masculinity and femininity were reinforced. Any place that women had in the post-Gallipoli task of nation building was based on their kinship links with soldiers, at least according to returned soldier 'loyalists' who claimed the right to determine what that nation would look like.[21]

The Bolshevik revolution in Russia in 1917, socialist uprisings across Europe in 1919 and Ireland's War of Independence further reinforced social and political divides among white Australians. While they were on the winning side of the war, in 1918 and 1919 many Australians were preoccupied with fears of internal threats and anxiety about the future. The cost of living had risen dramatically and people on average wages were suffering. One of the outcomes of the split in the Labor Party was that the labour movement was more militant than it had been before the war, and strikes were widespread. Two of Australia's 'Bloody Sundays', when demonstrating workers were injured and some were killed in violent conflicts with police, occurred in 1919: at Fremantle in May and Townsville in July.

The fears of internal threats to the nation were amplified through the Commonwealth Government's use of emergency wartime powers, which identified disloyal and seditious menaces everywhere. The intelligence services that are now a regular part of government had their origins in Australia in World War I. The Nationalist government of Billy Hughes used the military intelligence networks and emergency powers against their political opponents.[22] Under the *War Precautions Act* and its regulations, a range of activities and public statements were made offences, punishable by potentially heavy fines or imprisonment. Residents deemed 'enemy aliens', even if they were naturalised, could be interned or deported. Personal mail was opened and censored, as were all newspapers. According to John Hilvert, censorship in Australia during World War I was the 'harshest of any country in the British Empire'.[23] In a telling anecdote, when asked 'Would it be an offence under the *War Precautions Act…*', the Commonwealth Solicitor General Robert Garran replied 'yes' before the question was finished.[24] Opposition to the continued use of the *War Precautions Act*, and what was effectively government rule by decree, intensified after the war ended in November 1918. The Act was not repealed until December 1920.

Returned soldiers participated in riots across Australia, and their actions exposed the conflicts and social devastation engendered by Australia's involvement in the war. The riots also highlighted disputes between soldiers themselves over their political role in postwar society, about what their sacrifice and that of their dead comrades meant and how it was to be acknowledged by civilians. The Anzac legend did not emerge fully formed from the battlefield at Gallipoli; it was generated and developed through conflict in Australia on the streets. What was done in the riots, and the way they were represented at the time, articulated the tensions, fears and disputes that shaped the postwar nation.

The image popularly associated with the term 'riot' is that of a mindless mob acting on irrational impulses under a force beyond the control of the participants. But each episode of returned soldier riot had its own internal logic, a dynamic that followed clear patterns. Further, the word 'riot' was applied selectively by contemporary commentators. When returned soldiers in Melbourne battled police over a period of four days in mid-1919, newspaper editors called the events riots. When returned soldiers attacked union activists and socialist speakers, the anti-Labor press did not name their actions as riotous. The use or not of the word 'riot' was a political tactic in the contest over representation of returned soldiers' regular threats to public safety, which happened with increasing severity over the course of 1918 and 1919.

1

Riots on Peace Day, November 1918

On 11 November 1918, the guns finally stopped. The Turkish army had already surrendered on 30 October, and the German forces were defeated in France. The Kaiser had abdicated and fled to Holland (which was neutral during World War I) and Germany sought an armistice with the Allied forces. The news of its signing was officially released in the United States. On 11 November, President Woodrow Wilson announced to Congress the terms of the armistice, which included cessation of military operations and the withdrawal of German troops from France and Belgium. President Wilson declared 'this tragical war, whose consuming flames swept from one nation to another until all the world was on fire, is at an end'.[1]

In November 1918, Europe was at the beginning of another grim winter, but in Australia it was nearly summertime. Official war historian Ernest Scott described how, when the news of the Armistice was confirmed on the morning of 12 November, 'all business seemed to stop; one great sigh of relief went up'.[2] On 14 November, street processions, church services and civic ceremonies were planned in towns and cities across Australia. But what was intended to be a day of celebration and thanksgiving became, for the people of Broken Hill, Adelaide and Townsville, a day marked by riot and public disorder.

In Adelaide, angry crowds led by returned soldiers pelted tramcars with stones and attacked the drivers, and later in the day forced theatres and cafés to close. In Broken Hill in western New South Wales, Sergeant Roy Inwood VC threatened to drive 'the Bolsheviks', as he called local unionists, out of town by firing at their feet with a machine gun. On 14 November, there was fighting in the main streets in Broken Hill between unionists and returned soldiers and their supporters. The violence did not stop until around 8 pm when 5,000 workers marched from the Trades Hall through the streets of the town, in a show of force. On the same day in Townsville, in northern Queensland, a fight at a pub between unionists and returned soldiers escalated to a riot in the street. Police were initially unable to disperse the crowd, who used broken bottles and furniture as weapons. One policeman and six soldiers were injured, mostly with head wounds.[3]

These events were not revelling crowds getting a bit rowdy. While the street fight in Townsville lasted only about half an hour, the riots in Adelaide and Broken Hill were serious threats to law and order. Riotous crowds wreaked havoc in inner-city Adelaide in the morning and shut down the tram system, with one tramcar so badly damaged it was never returned to the depot. In Broken Hill, the street fighting lasted for about eight hours, and the local force of thirteen police made seven arrests. Returned soldiers were participants in all these episodes of public disorder; as the Adelaide *Register* proclaimed, 'khaki was in the forefront of the riots'.[4]

Naming soldiers as rioters was a radical departure for the predominantly conservative media. In the Australian press, returned soldiers were always represented as heroes. This was the case for conservative daily newspapers like the Adelaide *Register* and for the small minority of newspapers that were owned and operated by worker organisations, such as Brisbane's *Worker* and the Adelaide *Daily Herald*. While the labour movement after 1916 was staunchly opposed to conscription, men who enlisted voluntarily were lauded. Returned soldiers were men who had sacrificed for King and Country and towards whom a grateful civilian nation owed a blood debt. This was the way the economy of sacrifice was supposed to operate, as a consensual exchange between the citizen soldier and civilian society, which in turn underpinned the triumphant commemoration of Australia's role in the war. Through this schema, soldiers' sacrifice was made meaningful, and dying for one's country was a noble and decent thing to do. Investing soldiers' deaths with exalted and widely recognised meaning was supposed to ensure a peaceful transition from warfront to civilian society.

But when soldiers did not behave like heroes, when they were angry and violent, rioted in the streets and smashed property, the economy of sacrifice did not work. The Peace Day riots exposed interpretations of the meaning of sacrifice by soldiers themselves that challenged the idea of a consensus. While the three riots addressed in this chapter had their specific origins and contexts, and returned soldiers played different roles in the violence in each instance, these events articulated the competing voices at the end of the war about how soldiers' sacrifice should be remembered. It was through the narrative of riots that this terrain was exposed and acknowledged as fragile and disputed.

Conflict over commemoration of soldiers' sacrifice was central to the Adelaide Peace Day riots. In the lead-up to the celebrations and public holiday on 14 November, tram workers were told by their bosses at the Municipal Tramways Trust that they had to work on the holiday, transporting people from the suburbs into the city for a day of processions and festivities. Members of the tramway workers' union had been in negotiations with the privately owned Tramways Trust over award wages. Their minimum wages were the lowest of all tramway workers in Australia, and the South Australian branch secretary of the Federated Tramway Employees' Union argued in September 1918 that dissatisfaction over low pay was 'seething' among the members of the union.[5] At a late-night meeting on 13 November, tramway employees voted to defy the order to work on the holiday.

But in defying the order to work on a holiday, wages were not the main issue; the tramway men considered this *their* time for commemoration and remembrance, along with everyone else. Union president Lionel Hill, also a member of the Legislative Assembly in South Australia, argued that tramway workers had been 'most loyal to the cause of the Empire' throughout the war, and that about 300 of them served at the front.[6] The press reported on the meeting of the tramway employees and their unanimous decision that

> in honour of the tramway men who have fallen in the war and those who are absent on active service, they desired to take part in the celebrations and did not intend to work on the following day.[7]

Hill stated: 'The men have decided that no trams will run, and if any do they will be in charge of "scab" motor men and conductors.'[8] Which is what happened.

No employees turned up for the first shift at 5.17 am on 14 November at the Hackney Road tram depot east of the city, nor for the rest of the day.[9] The trouble started just after 9 am, when some of the Tramways Trust managers and men called 'volunteers' tried to break the strike by driving thirty-one tramcars from the depot. The city was already crowded with people who had travelled by train or car, or had walked, from the suburbs. Some enterprising Adelaideans charged a fare of sixpence to transport people in their private cars. A huge victory procession involving thousands of schoolchildren, soldiers and civilians was taking place at Adelaide Oval on the northern edge of the city centre.

The strike breakers who ran the trams, but who weren't named in the newspaper reports, were identified as businessmen and lawyers, and a former mayor of Adelaide.[10] They acted as conductors while the

'Commuters alighting from a Model 'T' Ford...in King William Street, Adelaide, being used as transport during a tramway workers' strike'. State Library of South Australia: PRG 280/1/29/300.

Trust managers and officials drove the trams. At North Terrace, one of the trams heading north was pelted with stones, road metal and missiles by a crowd who jeered the volunteer drivers and conductors. All along the route to the northern suburb of Enfield, the tram was attacked with stones, so that by the time it returned to the city, all the windows were broken. A lawyer acting as a conductor recounted that 'we received such a hostile reception that we applied the accelerator and ran the gauntlet'.[11]

The centre of the riot, at the corner of Grenfell and King William streets in the city, was only a block away from Parliament House. Trams were attacked and their volunteer drivers punched. Men from the crowd unhinged trams from the cables, and some of the 'volunteer' conductors climbed onto the top of the trams in an effort to keep the poles attached to the cable. Then the men used knives to slash the cables. They lodged chains in front of the wheels to halt the trams and broke the signal levers. Some of the crowd cheered the Trust managers and others who manned the trams, but it seemed they were outnumbered by those intent on stopping the trams from conveying passengers.

'A tramcar which fared badly in the riotous scenes on Thursday'. State Library of South Australia: *The Observer*, 23 November 1918.

Under the headlines 'Disgraceful scenes in the streets' and 'Violent vagaries of the mob', the editors of the Adelaide *Register* reported that, 'returned soldiers appeared to be the leading spirits in the disturbance'.[12] Some were in uniform, and others were in civilian clothes wearing their returned soldier badges. *The Observer* identified the 'ringleaders' who rushed the trams and attacked the strikebreaking drivers at King William and Grenfell streets. They were 'a one-armed soldier, a number of returned men in civilian clothes, and many young fellows who obviously had ignored the call to serve the Empire through the war'.[13]

This reference to young men who had not served in the armed forces contrasted with all the other newspaper coverage of the riots of the morning. The consistent story was of returned soldiers leading the attacks on the trams and their drivers. None of these soldiers were identified by name. The reports in *The Daily Herald*, a local newspaper describing itself as 'owned and controlled by the workers', provided more detail about where and how returned soldiers participated in the riots. Under the headline 'Blacklegs mobbed by returned soldiers', *The Daily Herald* reported that in one attack on a Dulwich tramcar and its 'volunteer' driver, a returned soldier jumped on the car and punched the driver.[14] When the police went to apprehend the soldier,

> fully a dozen returned men threatened that if he interfered there would be serious trouble. One of the soldiers shouted, 'This is Peace Day! We have fought a lot of scabs and have beaten them, and we don't want any here in Australia'. Another backed him up by saying, 'Yes, and Australia is not going to be a scabby country'. A dozen mounted Policemen came upon the scene and tried to disperse the crowd, but their efforts were useless. Thousands of persons were leaving the celebrations on the oval and were joining the combined effort to prevent the cars running. The motorman of the Dulwich car scrambled on board and endeavored to run along Grenfell Street to the depot, amid the hoots of the people. A soldier rushed at the back of the car, seized the rope and pulled the trolley pole off the wire. At the same time another soldier attempted to climb on top of the car with the same object, but he saw that there was no necessity for his action and jumped to the ground, where he was cheered.[15]

At one stage during the riot, Colonel Stanley Weir addressed recently returned soldiers and enlisted men from Mitcham Camp. Weir asked for more 'volunteer' strike breakers, this time to keep the way open along King William Street to allow women and children to board the trams. There were a few 'antagonistic voices' from the soldier audience who supported the striking tramway workers, but Weir persuaded a group to follow him to the city centre. There were a few fights and 'exciting scenes', but by this time all the trams were being recalled, so the soldiers disbanded.[16] In *The Daily Herald*'s coverage of the same incident, a returned soldier called for three cheers for the boys at the front, which was done, and then hoots for the men driving the trams, and they were booed 'with as much vigour as the cheers'.[17] In another exchange, a returned soldier approached South Australian military commandant Brigadier General Antill and, after saluting him, asked whether there was anything the Brigadier General could do to stop the trams from running. The returned soldier said it was 'causing disharmony on this, our Peace Day'. Antill replied that no, it was a matter for civilian authorities. The returned soldier then organised a large group of civilians and returned soldiers, along with soldiers from the Mitcham camp, who 'threatened to deal severely with any man who attempted to drive a tramcar'.[18]

Soldiers also attempted to stop the violence. *The Daily Herald* reported on one soldier who intervened when one man punched another in the jaw. The returned soldier said, 'This is Peace Day. I'm for the trammies, but we don't want any fight over it.'[19] Around midday, on the advice of the military authorities and the police, the Tramways Trust ordered that the trams be returned to the depot. Police Superintendent Edward Priest was quoted as saying that the Trust's decision to run the cars that day was 'absurd', given that 'serious trouble' could result. The superintendent said he had 'advised the Trust not to run the cars'.[20]

There were no figures published on the extent of casualties in the Adelaide riots on 14 November, but instances were reported of passengers on the trams being injured by broken glass, and some of the volunteer drivers being punched and kicked by the rioters. The police did not use their batons, and that probably had the effect of minimising casualties among the crowd, as Superintendent Priest argued. Of the thirty-one trams that were driven from the depot that day, all were badly damaged and one, it appeared, was destroyed completely and never returned to the depot.[21]

The police were criticised in the press for not doing enough to stop the riots, and when asked, Police Commissioner Edwards refused to comment. Defending the actions of the police, Superintendent Priest reported they did not want to endanger the many women and children in the crowd by moving in with mounted troopers.[22] Superintendent Priest reported to his superiors, blaming soldiers for the violence:

> The police had to act with great caution or a regular riot would easily have been precipitated, and the general consensus of police opinion is that anything really serious had happened it would in a great measure been due to a section of Returned Soldiers and others in Military Uniform.[23]

The riots in the morning in Adelaide were not the end of the story. In the afternoon, after all the trams were recalled, a crowd of around 500 men, led by about 200 returned soldiers, went from one theatre and café to the next, forcing the businesses to close. They started at the Wondergraph picture theatre on Hindley Street in the city in the late afternoon; a crowd pushed their way into the building and demanded that the show stop immediately. At the Theatre Royal on Rundle Street, men demanded free admission and were told by the manager that all the tickets were booked. The police were called to usher the paying customers into the theatre and the show proceeded under police guard.[24] Proprietor Myers of the Theatre Royal offered to show a free matinee to all returned soldiers, including wounded ones, the following Monday. With the force of foot and mounted police outside the theatre, and Brigadier General John Antill there to 'subdue the riotous spirits', the crowd agreed to this offer and moved on to the next place. At the Majestic Theatre, returned soldiers took over the stage and threatened they would 'smash the place up' if the evening show was not cancelled.[25]

They returned to the Wondergraph theatre around 7 pm and told the manager, Finkelstein, that he 'would not be allowed to open'.[26] He replied that he would not close the theatre, but so as not to undercut every other theatre in town that had been forced to close, Finkelstein offered a free show 'in commemoration of Peace Day'. Some in the crowd jeered, others cheered, and the show went ahead with police protection.[27] Finkelstein was quoted in a returned soldier magazine as saying that returned men were not to blame, and that there were 'only a few' returned soldiers in the crowd who wanted him to close, along with cadets and members of the AIF in uniform. The crowd told Finkelstein that 'it was not a day for making profits'.[28]

Newspaper reports described returned soldiers leading the crowds. Returned soldiers and their supporters closed the Grand, the Pav, the Central and the Empire theatres with similar threats of violence. The Tivoli theatre manager promised to admit enlisted soldiers and returned men for free on Tuesday of the following week, but this theatre was also forced to shut on Thursday night. Cafés and other businesses open in the city were similarly targeted. The newspaper coverage of these events was very brief, and this was all that was reported of the crowd's motivation:

> Representations were made to the management that it was not a working day, and the shows could not go on, or if they did there should be free admittance...During Thursday afternoon practically every refreshment shop in the city which had opened its doors was shut up by a crowd that went from place to place. In some instances the proprietors were given ten seconds to close under threat that the windows would be smashed.[29]

As with the riots of the morning, the newspaper reports of the afternoon's and evening's events on 14 November in Adelaide did not provide details of who the returned soldiers were who led the crowd around the city, threatening business proprietors and their civilian customers. Maybe they were the same men who had led the riots in the morning and were emboldened by their success in stopping 'volunteers' from breaking the tramway workers' strike. The central theme of honouring fallen comrades connected the riots of the morning with the forced café and theatre closures of the afternoon.

By the end of Thursday, only four men had been arrested. Three of them were charged with drunkenness and the other with riotous behaviour. Superintendent Priest reported that a 'well-known' returned soldier named Evans was seen assaulting someone, but he was not arrested. At the time the police decided it was 'was injudicious to them to convey offender through the excited crowd'.[30] The police themselves had only just in the previous week resolved a long-running dispute with the South Australian Government over their pay and conditions, and 350 police constables had resigned in protest. These men (there were only five policewomen in the entire force in 1918) had returned to work, but only after the Police Association secured assurances from the Premier that their members would not be victimised for their industrial action.[31] It was possible that on Peace Day the police on duty were not sympathetic to the Tramway Trust managers and volunteers who were acting as strike breakers.

The newspaper reports did not detail explanations for the soldiers' actions, but the deliberateness of the returned soldiers' path on the afternoon and evening of Peace Day showed a pattern. Returned soldiers went to sites of leisure where people could enjoy a movie or dine with their friends. The returned soldiers insisted that civilians were not allowed to regard this special holiday as a time for entertainment. The leaders of the roving gangs resented civilians apparently oblivious to the real meaning of Peace Day – which was to honour soldiers' sacrifice – and took as their rightful reward the promise of free shows to be enjoyed later. The returned soldiers' message seemed to be that you should show due respect and reverence on a day of commemoration towards those men who had won the victory or have your trams or your business attacked by returned soldiers.

It was not uncommon around this time at the end of the war for branches of the Returned Soldiers' Association (RSA) and the Returned Sailors' and Soldiers' Imperial League of Australia (RSSILA) to coexist at a local level, and they shared membership and clubrooms. The RSAs had started forming in 1915 when the first invalided soldiers were repatriated home. At a meeting of RSA representatives in June 1916, plans were made to establish a national organisation, and the first federal congress of the Returned Sailors' and Soldiers' Imperial League of Australia (RSSILA) was held in September 1916.[32] It was the RSSILA that was the precursor to today's Returned and Services League (RSL).

There was no specific time when the RSSILA took over from the RSAs as the main organisation for returned soldiers. The Western

Australian RSA branches were the last to officially amalgamate with the RSSILA in August 1918, but even after this time the RSAs in many places continued to operate and speak on behalf of returned soldiers. In 1918, in the public's mind and in the reporting of returned soldier organisations, the RSA and the RSSILA were usually interchangeable. For instance, the *Returned Soldiers' Association* magazine in South Australia was subtitled 'the official organ of the Returned Sailors and Soldiers' Imperial League, South Australian branch'.

In the December issue of the *RSA magazine*, the riots were the topic of the lead article. The editor asserted that 'returned soldiers as a body are exonerated from all blame'.[33] An RSSILA executive committee meeting was held the day after the riots, and its members distanced themselves from the riots. The branch president was Captain Arthur S. Blackburn VC, who was also a Nationalist member of parliament in South Australia. Branch secretary Aubrey Fearby, who had served as a sergeant both at Gallipoli and in France, referred to the 'wicked poisoning of the public mind' and stated that their organisation had 'neither sympathy nor any connection whatsoever with Bolshevism'. In his article in the *RSA magazine*, Fearby claimed that the returned soldiers who lead the riots (he alluded to two unnamed men) were not members of the League, and that the other rioters in uniform were members of the Citizen Forces who had 'not see fit to defend their country'.[34]

The aftermath of the violent events of Peace Day in Adelaide exposed conflicts between returned soldiers that roughly fissured along class lines. While the executive committee of the South Australian RSSILA tried to deny the involvement of their members in the riots, a full meeting of the League held on Monday, 18 November revealed that the story was more complex. About 1,200 men attended the meeting, which was chaired by Captain Blackburn. The men attending passed a resolution condemning as 'untrue' the claim that returned soldiers were the 'ringleaders' in the riots, as well as a resolution denying the 'rumour' that the RSSILA had 'undertaken to supply the necessary men to run the trams', effectively acting as strike breakers.[35] They also passed a resolution expressing confidence in the executive committee, though the reasons for this resolution were not explained in the reports of the meeting.

Press reports of the 18 November RSSILA meeting showed that there was considerable dissent between some of the returned men and the executive committee. One newspaper headlined its report: 'Not "scabs", returned heroes support tramway men'.[36] There were arguments and 'considerable disorder' at the meeting. When one speaker asserted that the Returned Soldiers' Association was 'not a political one and it had nothing to do with party politics', someone interjected 'We have!'[37] Private Edwin Corboy told the meeting that the South Australian Attorney-General, Henry Barwell, had stated that the Returned Soldiers' Association would 'supply all the men needed to run the trams'.[38] Corboy was the youngest member of the House of Representatives; at twenty-two years old he was elected the Labor member for the electorate of Swan in Western Australia. His claim was rejected by the meeting chairman, Captain Blackburn, as an 'absolute lie'. Corboy went on to say that 'coercion was being used by the Repatriation Department', and that the department was sending returned soldiers to work at the Tramways Trust, threatening that their repatriation assistance would be suspended if they refused. Corboy was given a standing ovation when he rose to speak, and created an 'uproar' with his allegations about the Repatriation Department. An employee of the department also spoke to the meeting and denied that they were forcing men to seek work at the Trust, but Corboy said he was 'absolutely sure of his facts'. The audience gave Corboy 'three rousing cheers'.[39]

Some returned soldiers at the meeting attested to the Repatriation Department's threats. Men at the meeting were told that an RSA member stopped six men who had been told to go and apply for work at the Tramways Trust or their maintenance payments would be stopped. Private Asplin told the meeting that it had happened to him as well and said he had seen a returned soldier's card showing that repatriation payments had been discontinued. One of the vice presidents of the South Australian branch, Dr Charles Duguid, promised to investigate.[40]

There appeared to be conflict between some members of the executive committee over the stance of the RSSILA towards the union and the strike. Vice President E. V. Martin said that the RSSILA 'should not in any way try to break up unions, but returned men should try and get into as many unions as possible'. A returned soldier member who was also a member of the Tramway Employees' Union wanted to address the meeting and explain the reasons for the strike on Peace Day, but Chairman Blackburn would not let him speak. Blackburn opened the meeting with a statement that they had gone away 'to fight to keep in existence law and order', and a returned soldier from the audience interjected, 'and freedom!'[41] Vice president Duguid proposed a resolution that they had 'neither sympathy nor any connection with Bolshevism' and were on the side of 'properly constituted law and order'. The newspaper report of the meeting recorded the following exchange:

> Dr Duguid: Some men had returned from the front and had a distinct spirit of Bolshevism in them. They had to decide whether the association was to be ruled by Bolsheviks or anti-Bolsheviks.
> A Voice: The men will rule.
> Another Voice: And not by the heads.[42]

Lieutenant Price, who had been awarded a Military Cross and was vice president of the South Australian branch of the RSSILA, then spoke to the meeting. He argued that it was not returned soldiers who were prominent in the 'demonstrations' of Peace Day, but 'coldfooters', a term that referred to men who had not enlisted. Then,

> There was much disturbance at the rear of the meeting at this stage, and the words 'Not dishonorable' were heard. Lieutenant Price said if there was a member of the association [the RSA] who said that such a demonstration would not be dishonorable to it, then the association would be far better off without him than with him. They would not in any way uphold men who demanded free entrance to picture shows. The returned soldiers were not responsible for the trouble.[43]

There was 'further uproar', and a speaker was 'counted out'. The practice of counting out – shouting 'one', 'two', 'three', and so on, at increasing volume – was a popular strategy used at public meetings around this time to silence speakers.

Other returned soldier meetings across Australia in 1918 and 1919 were similarly rowdy, with yelling and fights. A recurring conflict was about the political direction of the returned soldier organisations, the RSA and the RSSILA. Always the central issue was the relationship between returned soldiers and the union movement. Most of the executive officials of the RSSILA were former officers, and some were publicly allied with conservative politics. Captain Blackburn VC was a Nationalist politician, and the federal president of the RSSILA, William Kinsey Bolton, was a Nationalist Senator for Victoria. The links between the Nationalist government and the RSSILA executive were further strengthened when the Defence Minister, Senator George Pearce, declared in October 1918 that the RSSILA would be recognised by all government departments as the 'official representative body of returned soldiers'.[44]

At the 18 November meeting in Adelaide, vice president Duguid stated that 'they could have nothing to do with politics'.[45] Yet, in branches across Australia in 1918 and 1919, while the former officer executive members of the RSSILA publicly condemned 'party politics' and 'class division', they were busy trying to win the class war within their organisation. Two days after the riots, at a 16 November meeting of striking tramway workers held at the Trades Hall, a returned soldier claimed that the RSSILA condemnation of the Peace Day demonstrations 'emanated entirely from the Executive'. There were about fifteen returned soldiers at the meeting of approximately 700 union members, and the membership records showed that about sixty-nine returned soldiers were members of the tramway employees' union.[46] The returned soldier spokesman at the Trades Hall meeting said that the RSSILA's statements from their executive committee

> did not represent the views of the rank and file…If the true feeling of members had been asked for it would have been totally different. A meeting of the League [the RSSILA] had been called for Monday night, and the 69 men mentioned above would give their views.[47]

As shown in the reports of the RSSILA meeting on 18 November, returned soldier unionists were denied a platform to speak. The Adelaide Peace Day riots were an illustration of how the creation of an

Tramway men at a meeting at the Trades Hall, 15 November 1918, the day after the riots.
State Library of South Australia: *The Observer*, 23 November 1918.

apolitical Anzac brotherhood, one in which pre-war class allegiances no longer mattered, was generated through dispute between political and class factions among returned soldiers themselves. Interwoven with conflicts over allegiance was a more multifaceted dispute about soldiers' sacrifice and what it meant. The riots and the forced closure of theatres and cafes by returned soldiers showed that there was no clear agreement between them and civilian society about how soldiers' sacrifice should be remembered, or how the moral exchange between soldier and civilian should operate once the war was over. Some soldiers said that they were not being 'dishonourable' through their actions on Peace Day. But angry crowds of returned soldiers shocked a civilian public and unsettled the RSSILA leadership. RSSILA Vice President Duguid, who was a medical practitioner and had served as a captain in the AIF Medical Corps in the Middle East, said he 'got the severest shock' reading about returned soldiers being blamed for the riots.[48]

On the day of the strike, 14 November, the Tramways Trust sacked 750 employees and demanded they return their uniforms. No trams operated in Adelaide on Friday, 15 November, or for the next few days.[49] The matter was eventually mediated by no less than the South Australian Premier and Leader of the Opposition, with representatives from the union and the Trust. On 19 November, the workers were reinstated. There was no mention of a pay rise, but the conditions of return to work were that no employees would be victimised for their involvement in the strike, and they could return to their old jobs and existing roster.[50]

The allegations that the Returned Soldiers' Association would supply men to work the trams during the strike continued to attract attention after the strike was resolved. Questions were asked in the Legislative Assembly, and on 21 November, MLA and union leader Lionel Hill repeated his assertion that during the dispute, the

'A crowd at the tramway meeting in the Botanic Park on Sunday afternoon' [17 November]. State Library of South Australia: *The Observer*, 23 November 1918.

Attorney-General, Henry Barwell, had said that 'the Association [the RSA] was going to find men to man the cars'. The leader of the Opposition, John Gunn, had been at the conference as well and he endorsed Hill's recollection.[51] Barwell was under pressure in parliament, and while he did not completely deny the allegations, he was reported to have said,

> no communication had passed between himself and the RSA on the matter. He had heard that some men might be supplied by the Association – merely that returned soldiers might be available to fill the vacancies. He had stated that it was only hearsay.[52]

The involvement of returned soldiers in the riots of 14 November was not mentioned again, and the assertion by South Australian RSSILA president Captain Blackburn that 'returned soldiers never would lead riots' became the way the Peace Day riots were described in the local press.[53] By early December, the Tramways Employees Association had been 'kindly' forgiven by the Adelaide public for their 'desertion of duty' on 14 November.[54] No further reference was made to returned soldiers rioting. The link between the Tramways workers' strike and the angry assertion of soldiers' honour, and the unambiguous connection between the closure of theatres and soldiers' demand for civilian gratitude, were apparently forgotten. A violent and coherent expression of returned soldiers' resentment at the inadequate functioning of the economy of sacrifice was reinvented by the conservative media and the executive of the RSSILA as an event which had nothing to do with genuine returned soldiers.

∞

The riot in Broken Hill on 14 November was different in several ways to the Adelaide Peace Day riots, but again returned soldiers played a major role in the violence. In 1918, Broken Hill was referred to in some newspapers as 'that Gibraltar of Unionism'. An estimated ninety-five per cent of all workers in the town were union members at the start of World War I, belonging to either the Amalgamated Metalliferous Affiliation of the Australian Coal and Shale Employees' Association

(AMA) or the Federated Engine Drivers and Firemen's Association (FEDFA), or other unions. Broken Hill was a solidly anti-conscription town during the war.[55] And by 1918, union members in Broken Hill, like many unionists across the country, opposed Australia's involvement in the war itself.

The Labor Volunteer Army (LVA) was formed in Broken Hill in July 1916. Led by local Labor members of parliament and union leaders, members of the LVA pledged that they would not serve as conscripted soldiers even if it meant being sent to prison; LVA members would not be 'crushed into subjugation by the Capitalistic Military Oligarchy'.[56] In 1918, the LVA had between 1,200 and 1,500 members, and in a police report they were described as 'late members of the IWW [International Workers of the World], socialists and a large number of the militant section of the unionists of Broken Hill'.[57] The police reported that the LVA made no attempt to acquire guns; their main activities were weekly meetings and dances at the Trades Hall. They also ran a Sunday school where children sang union songs instead of hymns. The LVA had very little money and closed its bank account in late 1918, handing over its meagre funds to the union for strike relief.[58]

On 10 November 1918, a day before the Armistice was signed, members of the LVA joined with the local branch of the Socialist Party to celebrate the first anniversary of the Bolshevik Revolution. The event was described as a picnic, with girls from the Sunday school acting as 'charming and energetic little waitresses'. A cricket match was held between teams calling themselves the Bolsheviki and Mensheviki (the Menshiviks were among the opponents of the Bolsheviks in Russia).[59] The flying of the Red Flag, then the socialist standard, was prohibited under the regulations of the *War Precautions Act*, so one person dressed up in red in lieu of a flag. People sang 'The Red Flag' and other socialist anthems, and after the picnic at Stephens Creek, twenty-five kilometres north of the town, they continued with an evening of speeches and songs at an open-air meeting outside the Trades Hall. Police, who had prevented them from meeting inside the Trades Hall, watched but no arrests were made.[60]

Below is a copy of the music and words to 'The Red Flag', from an original published by the Socialist Party of Victoria, Melbourne.

'The Red Flag' words by Jim Connell, sung to the tune of 'O Christmas Tree'. National Library of Australia.

This is a transcript of the opening lines:

> The People's flag is deepest red/ It shrouded oft our martyred dead/ And ere their limbs grew stiff or cold/ Their heart's blood dyed its every fold.

> Chorus: Then raise the scarlet standard high!/ Within its shade we'll live and die/ Though cowards flinch and traitors sneer/ We'll keep the red flag flying here![61]

News of the Armistice on 11 November was greeted with little fanfare by the residents of Broken Hill. The editors of the *Barrier Daily Truth*, the paper published by the Broken Hill branch of the AMA, declared that the main reason for celebration was that 'no more workers will be sacrificed'.[62] The conservative daily, *The Barrier Miner*, was more effusive about the Allied victory, but by all reports the public response in Broken Hill was muted compared to other places. At picture shows, once the news was announced in the evening, the orchestras played 'Rule Britannia' and 'God Save the King', but there were only a few 'isolated' cheers in the audience.[63] At another place after the audience rose and sang 'God Save the King', someone in the audience said, 'Now give us 'The Red Flag'.'[64] At the time, local unionists were boycotting Broken Hill hotels that were selling half pints of beer for four pence (the previous price was three pence), and the ongoing dispute over the high prices charged by hotels was referred to as the 'beer strike'. One resident, on hearing the news that the Armistice had been signed, queried, 'What, with the brewery?'[65]

A gathering was held outside the Soldiers' Club rooms on the evening of 12 November, and local returned soldiers addressed the crowd. *The Barrier Miner* reported the crowd to be several thousand people, but in the *Barrier Daily Truth* the editors estimated only 1,500 people.[66] Such disparity in numbers was a feature of newspaper reports not only in Broken Hill but across the country. The pro-Labor or pro-union papers tended to downplay the size of loyalist crowds, and in the anti-Labor newspapers this practice was usually reversed. Because of this, it is sometimes difficult to establish numbers unequivocally. Nevertheless, the crowd that gathered on the evening of 12 November was considerable.

Among the speakers outside the Soldiers' Club was James Hebbard, president of the Barrier Returned Soldiers' Association, who before the war had been president of the Mine Managers' Association and after the war was manager at Central Mine.[67] In alluding to the LVA commemoration of the Bolshevik revolution two days earlier, Hebbard stated to the crowd's applause that 'very soon the returned boys would have an opportunity of kicking out the Bolshevik element'. He was followed by returned soldier George Dempster, who told the crowd that the 'stunt' of two days earlier, when the socialist anthem 'The

Red Flag' was sung by LVA members and others, was 'a disgrace to the citizens of Broken Hill'. In referring to the workers of Broken Hill, Dempster used language strategies that were repeated across the country by conservatives around this time, arguing that striking or militant workers were being hoodwinked by manipulative leaders. In the *Barrier Miner*'s report, which also described the crowd's responses, Dempster was quoted as saying,

> The so-called worker – they were all workers – but he particularly referred to the mine worker – was loyal, but he was badly bluffed by a few men who were not even decent scum. (Laughter) It was no laughing matter, and the sooner the people realised it the better for all concerned. It should be stopped by the loyal workers themselves. (Applause) The Bolshevik element should not only be put out of the jobs they held, but also out of the town. (Hear, hear and applause) He would be one who would help the workers to do it…The men were nothing but disloyal rebels. (Hear, hear).[68]

The next returned soldier to speak at the 12 November gathering was Reginald Roy Inwood, VC. He had been a miner before the war and returned to a hero's welcome in Australia in late October 1918. First there was the civic welcome for him and fellow Victoria Cross winner Corporal Jensen at Adelaide train station, followed by an official reception at the Town Hall.[69] Travelling on to his hometown of Broken Hill, Inwood was welcomed at the train station by a 'guard of honour' of members of the local RSA, along with cadets and boy scouts. The mayor addressed the crowd, and then after 'band playing, cheers and reply', Inwood went home to rest before a welcome reception that evening.[70] A couple of weeks after his return to Australia, Inwood was promoted from corporal to the rank of sergeant.[71] He had been awarded the Victoria Cross for capturing an enemy post at Polygon Wood on 20 September 1917, during the battle of Menin Road. Inwood killed several of the enemy and took nine prisoners. The following day he and another soldier virtually wiped out a German machine-gun station, taking the sole survivor as prisoner.[72] Roy Inwood was one of three brothers who had joined the AIF. His brother Robert was killed in France in 1916, and the third brother, Harold, was wounded and invalided home to Australia in 1917.[73]

'Corporal Reginald Roy Inwood VC 1918'. State Library of South Australia: B 74907.

At the 12 November meeting, Inwood addressed the crowd and condemned the 'dirty mongrels' who he said had 'stoned' him at the train station when he enlisted in 1914. Unionists and 'dirty mongrels' were the same for Inwood, who suggested that 'the sooner they pull down their hall [the Trades Hall] the better'. He continued:

> If the boys stick together like they did in France there will be no Bolshevikism [sic] in this town. (Applause) We want to do the same with them as they did in Queensland. We should drive them from town to town…I would like to be at one end of the street with a machine gun and have them at the other end. I would drive the mongrels out and make them dance some as they went. (Applause) I am surprised at you people allowing them to hold a picnic on Sunday…I will give some of these fellows a kick in the neck yet.[74]

Inwood's comments about 'mongrels' and wanting to shoot at them were published as far afield as Adelaide and Barcaldine, in northern

Queensland, under the headline 'VC's views on mongrels'.[75] Neither in these newspaper reports nor at the 12 November meeting was Inwood censured for his threats of violence towards socialist activists in Broken Hill. On the contrary, people cheered.

The following day, 13 November, there was a procession through several blocks in the centre of town, led by local marching bands and flag bearers and between forty and fifty returned soldiers, some of whom travelled in motor cars. The march was followed by a patriotic concert at the Pictureland theatre. Again, RSA president Hebbard addressed the audience. He was supported by H. O. Whitford, who was president of the Broken Hill branch of the RSSILA.[76] The Barrier RSA had formally amalgamated with the local branch of the RSSILA in December 1917, though the Barrier RSA was still referred to as a distinct organisation.[77] The RSA shared a clubhouse with the RSSILA in Chloride Street, usually referred to as the Soldiers' Club, or the BRSA rooms.

It was at the Soldiers' Club that a meeting was reported to have been held on the night of 12 November, where returned soldiers agreed to attack the Trades Hall as well as the house of W. D. Barnett, secretary of the local AMA branch. The premises of the *Barrier Daily Truth* newspaper were also allegedly threatened.[78] On the morning of 13 November, after the meeting outside the Soldiers' Club, some returned soldiers went to a house off Oxide Street, near the centre of town, and pulled down some Red Flags that were flying there.[79]

On the evening of 13 November there was another Thanksgiving celebration, this time at the skating rink. When a member of the audience refused to take off his hat for the singing of the national anthem, 'God Save the King', returned soldier George Dempster challenged him. In the ensuing scuffle, Dempster was knocked to the ground and fractured his elbow.[80] The threats against union leaders and property had been circulating around the town during the day, so the AMA ordered members to leave the afternoon shift at three of the mines; other workers could not be notified in time. The editors of the AMA newspaper reported that the police had offered to protect union property, but the AMA office replied that they did not need help and 'that if the unionists of this town could not defend their own property it could go up'.[81]

A meeting at the Trades Hall on the evening of 13 November was attended by a large crowd, and AMA president George Kerr told the audience that the Red Flag that had been torn down by returned soldiers was in the yard of a 'harmless widow'. This was greeted with cries of 'Shame! Mongrels!' from the audience.[82] Kerr told the crowd that

> They did not again intend to be kicked by dirty, patriotic mongrels and dirty, jingo profiteers, who had during the last four years been fattening upon working men and working women and the wives of soldiers who were fighting for them.[83]

Kerr urged against unprovoked violence against the 'dirty, jingo crowd that started this trouble', but warned that 'if they come here looking for trouble they will get more than they ever dreamt of'.[84] One eyewitness report claimed that armed unionists were stationed on the second floor of the Trades Hall, ready to defend it against attack.[85] There were some fights between returned soldiers and unionists, referred to as a 'street row', but police made no arrests.[86] AMA officials told the police inspector to 'devote his energies to the drunken soldiers and the mine managers who were filling them up with beer'.[87] The lights at the Trades Hall were not turned off until midnight, by which time the crowd had gone home. Only the vigilance committee stayed at the Hall.[88]

On 14 November, the *Barrier Daily Truth* published a 'coldblooded warning' that if there were any 'pranks', the perpetrators 'will be faced by organized Broken Hill'. The editors referred to 'boasting blackguards' but qualified their condemnation and said they were not referring to 'soldiers generally, but upon such as the cap fits'.[89] They also suggested that it was the 'patriots' who had been filling some of the young men with whiskey.[90] Meanwhile, an advertisement from the executive committee of the Barrier RSSILA published on 14 November in *The Barrier Miner* stated that they had 'no designs' against the Trades Hall or other union property, and that such reports were 'malicious mis-statements'.[91] President Whitford and branch secretary W. J. Stagatich wrote that

> We are not opposed to unionism or to unionists...We are against all those who flourish disloyalty in our faces and who insult us or the British flag

we have fought for…we are up against all who insult soldiers, and who, by doing so, insult the relatives of those who have died for Australia and for the women and children of Broken Hill…The Returned Sailors' and Soldiers' Imperial League of Australia is purely non-political and non-sectarian, and is not connected in any way with any capitalistic or employers' association…To sum up, returned soldiers are against all disloyalists, whether unionists or not.[92]

In this context of published threats and challenges, fights broke out on the streets of Broken Hill on 14 November. A delegation of French officials was hosted at a reception at the Town Hall, and there were a lot of people gathered for the event. One eyewitness account referred to 'a few fights…things were fairly lively at times'.[93] But despite being downplayed by some newspaper accounts, the violence took the local police force of thirteen men several hours to control. The street brawls had started during the day around lunchtime, but the worst of the violence was in the evening. Seven men were arrested, including one returned soldier, and charged with assault or riotous behaviour.[94]

The fighting was between unionists, many of them wearing red LVA ribbons on their coats, and returned soldiers and people calling themselves 'loyalists'. At one stage, a returned soldier pulled a revolver but did not fire it. Sergeant Inwood was reported to be involved in the fighting, knocking out five of the men who attacked him.[95] After one retreat by returned soldiers to one of the hotels in town, there was a resumption of the street fighting, and the riot finally ended around eight o'clock in the evening when 5,000 unionists (*The Barrier Miner* estimated only 3,000), including returned soldier unionists, marched through the streets from the Trades Hall and back again, singing 'The Red Flag' and 'Solidarity Forever'.[96] By this stage, the police had ordered all hotels in Broken Hill be closed.

The events of 14 November in Broken Hill were referred to as riots in most newspapers and were reported across the eastern seaboard and in Adelaide. Nearly all the press reports represented it as a fight between loyalist returned soldiers and their supporters, and those variously referred to as 'red raggers', 'Bolsheviks' and the LVA. But as with the Adelaide riots, the allegiances of soldiers were varied. At a Labor Peace Celebration held that weekend in Broken Hill on Sunday 17 November, returned soldiers in uniform crowded onto the speakers' platform. One unionist who attended the Sunday rally commented that many were surprised that the soldiers knew all the words to 'The Red Flag'. He wrote that contrary to other reports, there were 'dozens' of uniformed soldiers in the crowd.[97] A letter from a returned soldier published in the *Barrier Daily Truth* on 15 November condemned the 'soolers and profiteers who masquerade in the guise of patriots'. The writer claimed that soldiers would not quarrel with their fellow unionists, and even though the so-called patriots could 'dope a few of my shell-shocked comrades with cheap grog', returned soldiers would not be fooled.[98]

Reports of returned soldiers being affected by alcohol during the riots were repeated in several accounts. Others suggested a diminished responsibility because of soldiers' war experiences. *The Australian Worker* newspaper condemned as dangerous the 'bombastic' talk of soldiers such as Inwood. The editors suggested that 'the rigors of warfare have mentally unstrung some of the men who talk like Inwood', and that they deserved pity rather than blame.[99] In Federal Parliament, the Labor MP for Broken Hill, Michael Considine, stated that the events in Broken Hill were a case of 'interested individuals provoking [trouble] between returned soldiers and the working class', and that

> when men have passed through the trials of warfare their nerves are not in a normal state, and no doubt Sergeant Inwood's feelings were played upon by other individuals.[100]

Considine condemned the incitement to violence, and laid the blame on 'such persons as mine managers' for making inflammatory public speeches.

The editor of *The Barrier Miner*, J. Smeshurst, blamed the LVA for the riots. In a letter to the Prime Minister, he warned of 'serious results' if the government did not stop the 'grossly offensive behaviour' of members of the LVA.[101] Smeshurst wrote that the LVA

> flaunted their red badges in the faces of the loyal citizens and the soldiers…We think it is a crying shame that loyalists are either to suffer insult and humiliation or defend themselves by mob law…when there

are more returned soldiers here than now (not crippled ones) the trouble will begin.[102]

Smeshurst's assertion that 'insulted' loyalists had little choice but to respond with violence was by this time a familiar refrain, and would be repeated over the following two years. Loyalists were 'taking matters into their own hands', and this phrase was used by returned soldiers in one of the riots addressed in the following chapter. A central theme when loyalist riots involved returned soldiers — which they always did — was that any sort of anti-war or socialist or pro-union expression was transformed into 'disloyalty', and an insult against soldiers' sacrifice. As RSSILA leaders Whitford and Stagatich wrote, an insult to the British flag for which soldiers fought was the same as an insult to soldiers who had fought under the flag on behalf of everyone, as far as they were concerned.

In this way, the criminal and disorderly nature of loyalist riot was denied. As an example, in relation to the riots in Broken Hill, the magazine of the NSW RSSILA was outraged that a returned soldier had been arrested at all, and condemned the law rather than the riotous behaviour by the returned soldier.[103] The idea that returned soldiers were compelled to respond violently was often expressed in terms of soldierly action on the battlefield. A Broken Hill correspondent, described as a 'comrade from the city of red-raggers', wrote that when the 'gauntlet' was thrown down to a returned soldier by 'calling him filthy names and waving a red flag in his face', then

> If forced to, we who have seen the field of battle can take it again if we are compelled to do it.[104]

In several events in the following chapters, the loyalist rioters claimed they were acting 'above the law' out of necessity and were responding to a 'higher law' of the loyal nation. But the notion that loyalists were a beleaguered minority constrained by the legal system was a fabrication. There were conservative governments federally and in all States except Queensland at the end of the war. The sweeping powers of the *War Precautions Act* and the military authorities meant that any criticism of the government, the King or the war effort was dangerous. Many of these offences under the *War Precautions Act* carried a jail sentence; political activists and unionists risked imprisonment for things they said in public against the war. In January 1918, the Governor General's private secretary, George Steward, was confident that

> We killed absolutely the IWW. Every one of its leaders is in gaol, mostly with from ten to fifteen years' hard labour to serve. The few that were left were mortally scared with the introduction of the Amending Bill which gave us power to deport them upon conviction of being members of an unlawful association. The IWW is a thing of the past, and there is no other society at present in sight which looks like filling the bill in its place.[105]

The outcome of the riots in Broken Hill was not the loyalist victory that editor Smeshurst and mine managers like Hebbard had hoped for. There was no 'driving out' of socialist activists and the union movement remained as strong as ever in Broken Hill. Sergeant Inwood left for Adelaide, and in 1919 was charged with assaulting a police constable. In pleading guilty, Inwood said he'd 'had a few beers', and in his defence said that the constable had 'made an insulting remark'.[106] Inwood travelled around for the next few years, working in various jobs in South Australia and Tasmania, until he married his second wife in 1927 and secured permanent employment as a labourer with the Adelaide City Council.[107] The Barrier RSA was subsumed within the Broken Hill branch of the RSSILA, and by 1921 they had 795 members on their books, but it seemed the overwhelming majority were not financial members. Only forty men turned up to RSSILA branch meetings in April and May 1921, down from seventy in July 1920.[108]

∞

In Townsville on 14 November 1918, returned soldiers and others calling themselves 'loyalists' attacked men in a pub known locally as a worker's drinking place, and the fighting spilled out onto the street. Like the riots in Broken Hill on the same day, the riot in Townsville occurred in the context of industrial action, in this case a strike by drivers of the sanitary trucks that collected household garbage and waste from pre-sewerage toilets. The strikers wanted an increase in wages and some changes in conditions (such as airtight lids on the waste pans), and the matter had been discussed in the Queensland parliament in late October 1918.[109] The Leader of the Opposition, William Vowles, had claimed that the government was leaving the northern town at risk of disease by not forcing the strikers back to work.[110] The Labor Premier, Thomas Ryan, had denied it was the fault of the government. There seemed to have been some arguments over who should fund action by the health commissioner, with the local Townsville council not wanting to incur expenses. Meanwhile, toilet pans had not been collected for four weeks.[111] When the public health commissioner arrived in Townsville on 29 October, he declared it an emergency and offered to pay the workers £6 per week to start cleaning up the streets of the town. The sanitary workers accepted the offer (which was the wage they had asked for at the start of the strike) and resumed work for a fortnight.[112]

A network of Military Intelligence officers throughout regional Queensland reported regularly to head office in Brisbane, which was in the Victoria Barracks. It was a similar story across Australia. The International Workers of the World (IWW) was a focus of much of their attention. Local military spies compiled lists of suspected members of this organisation that campaigned for a One Big Union (OBU) for all workers, rather than what they regarded as ineffectual craft-based unions and the system of government-controlled arbitration. For instance, from Townsville, Captain Willis reported to Captain C. N. Wood in Brisbane in December 1918 with a list of 'alleged IWW men' who worked at the meatworks.[113] Willis regularly attended street meetings of unionists in Townsville in order to report on what was said, and he considered that local union leaders were 'mostly importations from other States and towns', and were in Townsville 'to spread the doctrine of IWWism'.[114]

In a report from October 1918 to Military Intelligence in Brisbane, Captain Willis identified several local union leaders, including Michael Kelly, president of the Townsville Industrial Council, Pearce Carney, secretary of the Australasian Meat Industry Employees Union (AMIEU), and Archie Eastcrabb of the Queensland Railway Union (QRU). Willis described the unions in Townsville as a 'seething mass of discontent' and sought advice on whether to impose Regulation 17(1) under the *War Precautions Act*. This regulation enabled military authorities like Willis to order out of an area any person who was acting, or about to act, 'in a manner prejudicial to the public safety…of the Commonwealth'.[115] There were an estimated 15,000 union members in Townsville, and around this time the idea of the One Big Union was discussed at open-air meetings. Davis, the secretary of the Ross River branch of the AMIEU, argued that One Big Union could free the workers 'from the tyranny of the employers'.[116] With the Bolshevik revolution a relatively recent event, and before the murderous purges, the idea that workers could control the means of production was spoken of with enthusiasm by some union leaders. Davis finished his speech by declaring: 'We are not ready to run the meatworks yet, but when we are ready, we shall take it and we will run it, and the profits shall go to the workers.'[117] The next speaker, Kingston of the Bakers Union, disagreed with such direct action and considered that industrial problems could be solved by 'constitutional methods'.

With the declaration of the Armistice, the RSSILA branch in Townsville advertised a 'grand procession' on 14 November to celebrate the Allied victory, and asked all employers to give their employees time off work to attend. The RSSILA exhorted, 'Roll up and give us a fair spin. The diggers deserve it.'[118] The procession stretched for seven kilometres down Flinders Street in the centre of town and included most of the adults and children in Townsville. Returned soldiers and unionists were represented, and a report described the crowd as 'practically the whole community who had any conveyance whatsoever'.[119] In the same report, Captain Willis of Military Intelligence wrote,

> During the forming up of the procession it was quite evident that a large number of returned soldiers and working men of the town were more or less suffering from the effects of alcohol, and a section of the returned men even had a fight amongst themselves before moving off.[120]

The day passed without incident, but in the evening, at around 8.30 pm, a group of about fifteen men paraded up Flinders Street singing 'The Red Flag'. They ended their march at the Palace Hotel, which was

'Mounted troops leading servicemen in Armistice Day Peace Parade, Townsville, 1918.'
John Oxley Library, State Library of Queensland.

known as a workers' drinking place. Some soldiers ran into the hotel and tried to drown out the singers with a rendition of 'Rule Britannia', and fights broke out. The licensee at the Palace Hotel had already closed the doors when returned soldiers and others 'smashed their way into the bar'.[121] Men used bottles and chairs in the fight and, according to several reports, boy scouts rushed to the picture theatres to alert returned soldiers that 'returned soldiers were being ill-treated by the IWW men'. It was 'diggers to the rescue', but according to the reports of injuries sustained, the returned soldiers were outnumbered.[122] Six returned soldiers were injured with cuts on the head, a police constable was injured and another 'dazed' by a missile to the back of the head.[123]

A huge crowd had gathered outside the hotel. The police came but had trouble controlling the fighting. They arrested three of the 'disloyal element' from the hotel. One man had to be escorted to a waiting ambulance and the police had difficulty protecting him from the crowd.[124] According to the report from Captain Willis, people were by this time 'very excited and angry'.[125] The doors and furniture in the hotel were wrecked. There was another fight later in the night, but Captain Willis dismissed this as a 'drunken argument' between a returned soldier and a civilian.

In his report on the incident, Captain Willis of Military Intelligence said that in hindsight he should have recommended licenced premises be shut earlier in the day since 'drink had a lot to do with this incident'.[126] That night, the Police Commissioner ordered the hotels closed in Townsville until further notice. Hotelkeepers reacted with affront and blamed the police for not intervening earlier, when the 'red raggers' were marching through the streets.[127] The streets of Townsville were quiet over the weekend following the riot on Thursday night. Unionists continued to hold their Sunday night street meetings. Captain Willis reported 'consistent rumours of fresh outbreaks', with thousands of people in the streets, but these did not occur. Willis credited the secretary of the local RSSILA branch with having a 'restraining influence' on the returned soldiers who threatened further violence.[128]

∞

The riots in Adelaide, Broken Hill and Townsville all occurred on a day of thanksgiving set aside to commemorate peace. They exposed the deep fractures in Australian society at the end of the war, and the way in which the significance of peace was interpreted differently by returned soldiers and civilian society. The Adelaide riots in particular exposed the differences between what soldiers themselves felt their sacrifice meant and the role they would play in society now the war was over. The riots in Townsville and Broken Hill illustrated how local industrial disputes could turn violent with the introduction of threatening loyalist rhetoric and a lot of alcohol.

2

'Taking Matters Into Their Own Hands'

Before the riots on Peace Day in November 1918, there were riots in Sydney, Brisbane and the town of Hughenden in northwest Queensland. The events in Sydney in June 1918 escalated into a major threat to public order, with mounted police blocking city streets to stop the progress of an angry and armed crowd. In Hughenden in October 1918, over two days of violence, union organisers were beaten up and forced to leave town, with one man threatened with being tarred and feathered. I begin this chapter, though, with a smaller event in the regional town of Orange in New South Wales, which illustrated some of the recurring themes in the riots of the final months of the war.

First was the intensity of hostility between pro-war and anti-war factions within Australian society; even suggesting a negotiated peace was interpreted by self-styled loyalists as an intolerable threat. The disloyalty that loyalists claimed to fight against had a fluid definition, depending on the context, and could include people who supported a negotiated peace or called for an end to a capitalists' war. Disloyalty could also include being a member of a labour union or being a socialist activist. Others who were often implicated in the broad sweep of disloyalists were Irish Catholics, or sometimes Catholics in general.

Then there was the idea that returned soldier violence against anti-war activists was an understandable response to criticism of the conduct of the war and was therefore justifiable. Anti-war dissent was transformed into a moral transgression against the memory of fallen comrades, and in this way political difference was reduced to a simple dichotomy of rejection or endorsement of Anzac sacrifice. Debate was silenced, and the supporters of violent loyalist soldiers claimed that their actions were legitimate, even though the actions were assault and riotous behaviour. This style of representation was shown in the newspaper coverage and government response to the riot in a church in June 1918.

The Reverend Thomas Roseby led the Congregationalist Church (then a breakaway faction from the Church of England) in Orange, New South Wales. He was well known for his anti-war stance. His father, Dr Thomas Roseby (Snr), a former clergyman himself, described his son as 'perfectly sincere and honest', and said his only flaw was that he was a 'fanatical pacifist'.[1] In 1918, after having been active in the anti-conscription campaign of 1917, Reverend Roseby held weeknight meetings in the church on the topic of 'war and peace'. Reports in the local newspaper described how Roseby was heckled by members of the audience who 'had hard work to keep their tempers, and refrain from committing personal violence to him'.[2] At the end of one meeting, Reverend Roseby led the congregation in the singing of a hymn but did not join in the singing of the national anthem, 'God Save the King'.

At the meeting the following week, on 5 June 1918, the front pews of the church were occupied by a group of returned soldiers, who continually interjected and asked whether the Reverend would sing 'God Save the King', to which he replied that he would not. In Orange, *The Leader* reported what happened next when the returned soldiers

> burst through the railing surrounding the platform, and ejected Mr. Roseby from the pulpit, at the same time informing him in no mild manner that they were men who had fought and bled for their country, and would brook no interference or disloyalty from persons like Mr. Roseby. Pandemonium reigned for a brief period, women screamed and rushed for the doors, while blows were interchanged between the soldiers, their civilian supporters, and the partisans of Mr. Roseby. When the church was cleared fighting again took place outside, but the police took a hand and quelled the disturbance.[3]

The fight was widely reported in the press, as far away as Launceston and Kalgoorlie, Melbourne and Sydney, with most editors headlining their articles 'Riot in a church'.[4] The local paper in nearby Bathurst called it a 'brawl' and added that at one stage in the fight there were seven men on the dais, and one man was knocked behind the church organ.[5] There were no reports of injuries, but the pulpit railings were smashed.[6] The incident prompted questions in Federal Parliament about 'sacrilege', and Acting Prime Minister William Watt was asked by Labor MP Samuel Nicholls what he intended to do about preserving 'law and order in the House of God'.[7] Reverend Roseby was reported as saying that the fight was

> pre-arranged by a certain section of the Orange people, who have been against his opinions, and have thought it necessary to resort to violence in order to prevent discussion.[8]

Roseby also argued that he did not consider 'God Save the King' to be the national anthem, since 'the throne does not symbolise a nation's greatness or character'.[9] Roseby said that his opposition to the continued war was to save the soldiers 'of all nations' who were 'being sacrificed on the altar of Mars' [the ancient Roman God of War].[10]

In a letter to the Bathurst *National Advocate*, a correspondent expressed astonishment that a Protestant clergyman like Roseby would refuse to sing the national anthem, stating that such action would not be surprising if Roseby was 'a Jesuit, a Priest or an Irishman'. The correspondent warned Roseby to 'thank his lucky star' that he was Protestant, otherwise the violence towards him may have been worse.[11] In the wake of the Easter Rising, anti-Catholic bigotry intensified in Australia. On the same night that Reverend Roseby was attacked in his church at Orange, about ninety kilometres away the Cowra branch of the Catholic Federation held a community meeting to protest 'religious bigotry' and the 'campaign of lying abuse and slander' towards their religious leaders and the Catholic laity in general.[12]

Sectarian hatreds in Australia were already deep and drew further hostility from wartime conflicts. Some Protestant leaders claimed loyalty to King and Empire as their own, and characterised Catholics as inherently disloyal. The Church of England Synod in 1916 endorsed support for conscription in Australia and the conviction that a Protestant God was on the side of the Allies.[13] Sectarian schisms were not uniform (Roseby, a Protestant clergyman, was staunchly anti-conscription), but they were a feature of a divided nation.

Back in Orange, rather than any of the rioters being arrested, it was Reverend Roseby who was investigated by authorities. The riot prompted a visit by the Reverend Cocks of the Pitt Street, Sydney, Congregationalist Church. He and Police Inspector Lewis interviewed Roseby. *The Leader* also reported that the Department of Defence was analysing what Roseby said in the meetings to see whether his words could be considered a hinderance to recruiting, which was an offence under the *War Precautions Act*.[14] Roseby's father, Dr Roseby, wrote to the NSW Chief Secretary, George Fuller, pleading for Fuller's help to prevent any government prosecution of his son.[15] No one was charged with offences relating to the fights in the church on 5 June and the damage to church property. There was no further newspaper coverage of the story, but *The Leader* suggested it would be a good thing if 'Mr Roseby and his class' left town, since all they did was stir up 'strife and enmity in the community'.[16]

What was not reported was that government employees were opening Reverend Roseby's mail, including a letter from his sister Amy, the founder and headmistress of Redlands School in Neutral Bay, Sydney.[17] This letter has survived in the archives of the censor's office, highlighting just how extensive was the network of secret government surveillance of Australian citizens. The personal correspondence of anti-war activists was targeted by the censor's office, even though letters such as that from Amy to her brother Thomas had no details of anything that could be construed as a threat to national security. She disagreed with Thomas on his political stance against Britain in the war (Amy Roseby herself became a peace advocate a decade later), though acknowledged that there were 'injustices done to Ireland' by England. Amy urged her brother several times to consider the feelings of their distressed and anxious parents. At the same time Amy professed sisterly affection towards Thomas, calling him 'dear'. She finished her letter 'Your always loving Amy'.[18] Yet someone employed by the censor's office in Sydney decided that the letter should be intercepted, a copy was typed by a secretary, then recorded on an index and filed with other censored mail.

In the middle of 1918, when the war had been going on for nearly four years, political conflict regularly turned violent. Public parks, called the Domain in both Sydney and Brisbane, were popular places for public debate, and crowds gathered there each Sunday. The Sydney Domain was at the harbour end of the city, near Parliament House, and remains a large open green space today. In Brisbane, the Domain was on the river, next to the Botanical Gardens in the city, where the Queensland University of Technology campus is now. At both the Sydney and Brisbane Domains in 1918, speakers against Australia's involvement in the war vied with AIF recruiting campaigners for the crowd's attention. The anti-war speakers had to choose their words carefully, as regulation 28 under the *War Precautions Act* made it an offence to make statements likely to prejudice recruiting. In 1917, an amendment to regulation 28 made it an offence to make 'a statement advocating or encouraging any omission of action' which could prejudice or discourage recruiting.[19] Opposition to the war was regularly interpreted by the courts as being prejudicial to recruiting.

On most Sundays in the Sydney Domain, there were plain clothes policemen in the crowd taking notes of what was said in the speeches, and reports were sent each week to state and Commonwealth governments.[20] Anyone criticising this use of police powers risked being charged under the *War Precautions Act*, such as when Percy Brookfield, the Labor Legislative Assembly representative for the electorate of Sturt, around Broken Hill, addressed a crowd of about 2,000 people in the Domain in July 1917. Brookfield complained that 'civil laws had gone by the board' and that for a man to even mention peace, he risked being called a traitor. He continued,

> Intolerance reigns supreme even in this vast audience; there are pimps and spies here with the object of doing their best to place working-class agitators behind the prison bars.[21]

Although Brookfield denied calling the police 'pimps', he was convicted and fined £6, with 8 shillings in costs, and put on a good behaviour bond for twelve months. Brookfield paid over £700 in fines and forfeited bonds during 1916 and 1917 for similar offences.[22]

Portrait of Percy Brookfield, c 1915. State Library of South Australia: B 69875.

There had been riots in the Sydney Domain earlier in the war. One such incident was on Sunday 13 August 1916, when soldiers and pro-conscription groups attacked anti-conscription speakers. There were an estimated 80,000 to 100,000 people in the Domain at the time, and reports of the riot (downplayed as 'lively proceedings' in *The Sydney Morning Herald*) indicated that the opposing groups were evenly matched in terms of numbers. The 'soldiers and their friends', according to the report, tried to 'count out' the anti-conscription speakers. In turn, their voices were drowned out by cheers for the speakers, who were mainly Labor MPs, socialists and union officials. There were several attempts to rush the cart that served as a makeshift speaking platform, and this only stopped when the police mounted the platform and became targets of violence themselves. Three men were arrested, two of them for assaulting police, and one policeman was injured with two broken ribs.[23]

It was a similar story in the Sydney Domain on 16 June 1918, except this time the violent affray took over an hour for the police to quell. Another central difference between the two events in 1916 and 1918 was the public threats by returned soldiers in the lead-up to the riot. On 10 June 1918, the *Evening News* reported that 'returned soldiers are daily growing more and more restive regarding disloyal utterances', and that the RSSILA was planning, with other returned soldier organisations, to take 'concerted action'.[24] In the NSW Parliament on 12 June, during a debate about 'seditions and disloyal speeches' in the Domain, Nationalist MP Charles Oakes warned 'if the authorities do not take action…the Returned Soldiers' Association intends to take matters into its own hands.'[25] The *Sunday Sun* repeated the threat on the Sunday morning of the riot, and wrote that soldiers

> will not stand by and listen to seditionists vilifying the memory of their dead mates, and that, if necessary, they will take matters into their own hands.[26]

An unnamed soldier was quoted as saying, 'We have stood it about as long as we can. If someone does not interfere we will go down and clear them out ourselves.'[27]

These published threats before the June 1918 Domain riot showed that returned soldiers were intending to use force to silence alleged disloyal speakers 'if necessary', as if the soldiers themselves had some official authority to act. Many of the riots that occurred from 1918 to 1920 followed a similar pattern: a threatening prelude by returned soldiers, followed by riotous attack, all within a context where violence by soldiers was reinvented as justified. It was represented by the RSSILA and RSA and their supporters in the conservative press as a soldierly response to insult against dead mates. But these events were episodes of serious public disorder, as the eyewitness accounts and police reports show.

On 16 June 1918, a troopship carrying about 200 soldiers, mostly invalided men returning from France, docked at Woolloomooloo. After a procession through the city the soldiers finished with tea at the Anzac Buffet, set up on the edge of the Domain. When 100 soldiers in uniform and between 200 and 300 wearing returned soldier badges began to break up various anti-war and socialist meetings in the Domain, a tumult began which lasted for over an hour. Speakers were knocked off platforms, and there were fights among the crowd. Soldiers were not the only ones breaking up the meetings; civilians joined them in rushing the speaking platforms. There were 150 police on duty in the Domain that day and, of these, nine officers were there to take notes of the anti-war and socialist speeches, which Metropolitan Superintendent Tait described as 'disloyal utterances'.[28] According to their own reports, the police did not try to stop the speaking platforms being overturned, but told the socialist, Labor and anti-war speakers to shut down their meetings. They did not arrest any of the soldiers, and P. Evans, the General Secretary of the NSW Labor Party, later complained that although the police had the capacity to maintain law and order, 'the only menace to the public peace was the soldiers'.[29]

At the meeting of pacifist women in the Domain on 16 June, seaman Frank Melburn was reported to have called for 'three cheers for the IWW and God damn the King of England'; for this he was arrested.[30] At the Labor Party meeting, one of the speakers, Vincent Jeffries, jumped off the platform that was being rushed by soldiers and civilians and offered to fight them. He too was arrested and charged with riotous behaviour.[31] Arnold Holmes was speaking at the Social Democratic Party meeting, and he condemned the soldiers trying to break up their meeting, saying they were 'the sons of the Squatters who would put us in the Capitalistic jails'. He added that the soldiers there that day were 'the pups of the squatters'. Vance Marshall, who had just been released from a prison sentence after being convicted under the *War Precautions Act*, got up to speak, but was pulled off the platform before he could begin.[32] Marshall was recorded as saying that the soldiers were a 'rabble hired by capitalists'.[33]

Socialist Ernest Judd told the crowd that the soldiers who were trying to break up the meetings were law breakers. He said he had seen soldiers holding down his brother while two others punched him. Judd added that while good men went to the front, he had 'nothing but contempt for the men who got as far as Cairo, and the Egyptian women put them out of action.'[34] Here Judd was referring to a notorious riot in Cairo in April 1915, where about 2,500 Anzacs stationed in camps near the city had smashed up and set fire to the brothel district and fought with military police into the night. The consensus of subsequent investigations was that the rampage was in retaliation for the spread of venereal disease, and the soldiers blamed the Egyptian prostitutes whose sex services they used.[35]

At the Sydney Domain on the afternoon of 16 June 1918, fighting was widespread, but only four arrests were made by police. They included Jeffries, Melburn and a 16-year-old boy, Ernest Vincent, who was arrested for hitting several people, including a one-armed soldier. The fourth man arrested, Anton Kluge, pleaded guilty and was given a small fine of £2.[36] Ernest Judd and Vance Marshall were later charged with offences under the *War Precautions Act* for prejudicing recruiting and making 'statements likely to cause disaffection to His Majesty'. Marshall was jailed again – this time for six months – and Judd was fined £50.[37]

There were no official reports of injuries, although journalist Sam Rosa later reported he was poked in the eye by a woman wielding an umbrella.[38] Ernest Judd's brother was held down and punched, and there were reports of several speakers being dragged off the speaking platforms. Inspector Charles Turbet witnessed a returned soldier named Muncaster (he was a well-known recruiting officer) hit a man, but Turbet considered this a 'minor assault'.[39] Senior police made it clear that they thought the socialist and Labor speakers attacked in the riots had it coming to them.

In his summary report, Metropolitan Superintendent Tait blamed the 'insidious, disloyal propaganda' of the Domain speakers, and offered his opinion that they should be banned otherwise it could 'lead to bloodshed'. Tait argued that 'our depleted Police Force cannot be held responsible for the preservation of law and order when such disloyal red-raggers are permitted to hold forth with impunity to the detriment and danger of the whole Empire.'[40]

On the evening of 16 June, the soldiers and their supporters – maybe including the same men who had rioted in the Domain that afternoon – marched through the city. First, a group of about 200 soldiers in uniform disrupted a meeting in Darlinghurst. Labor General Secretary Evans reported that the soldiers 'invaded' the meeting and that their actions were 'calculated to cause a riot'.[41] The soldiers then headed towards the Trades Hall in Sussex Street, where a meeting was being held, but a force of police blocked their path. Inspector Bannan reported that the soldiers were after Ernest Judd, who they claimed had said that 'soldiers were only the companions of prostitutes and rotten with the pox'.[42] At the police blockade, the soldiers gave three cheers for the British flag and the King, and then left, but returned via another street.

By nine o'clock in the evening on 16 June, the soldiers had been joined by a large crowd of civilians, and the police sent in mounted troopers to stop them from storming the Trades Hall. The police eventually 'induced' the crowd to disperse, and the soldiers headed to Central Railway Station, where police were on duty until 10.30 pm. The uniformed soldiers then went back to their camp.[43] Inspector Drew reported that no damage was done and that the soldiers were 'good humoured and easily handled'.[44] Even though it took a force of mounted police to stop the crowd, and a garrison of military police had been brought into Central Police Station in case there was a full-scale riot.[45]

Inside the Trades Hall that evening, the police had asked the chairman of the meeting to adjourn 'in the interests of public safety'. He refused and told the police it was their job to maintain order.[46] Sam Rosa was at the Trades Hall meeting, and he said that the crowd of soldiers outside the hall were armed with stones, sticks and bottles, and he suspected some were carrying guns.[47] When the crowd outside increased to about 500, the police again asked the chairman to close the meeting because the police 'could not guarantee the safety of the women and children, nor the building'. This time the chairman agreed to close the meeting. The following day, ALP General Secretary Evans wrote to the Defence Minister, George Pearce, that,

> it would appear that the people are to be terrorized by the undisciplined soldiery - some say with the connivance and encouragement of those in higher authority.[48]

In the wake of the riots of 16 June 1918, Premier William Holman tried to introduce legislation disfranchising people convicted under regulations 28 and 43 of the *War Precautions Act* and prohibiting them from holding office. This would have affected many of Holman's

'A study in hats at a meeting in the Domain yesterday', *The Daily Telegraph*, 24 June 1918, National Library of Australia.

political opponents, and it was going too far, even for members of his own conservative Nationalist Party.[49] The editors of *The Sun*, usually solid Nationalist supporters, warned against 'monkeying with the franchise'.[50] While Holman tried to make political mileage out of the events on 16 June, his police chiefs were concerned about more violence. The following Sunday, all leave was cancelled for metropolitan constables. Police were stationed shoulder to shoulder on the edge of the Domain, as well as forming a guard around each speaker.[51]

In the newspaper headlines about the Sydney Domain riots, the violence was rarely described as a riot. The major Sydney dailies described the events as 'Domain scenes' or 'Domain orators', with the *Evening News* headlining it 'Domain disturbance'.[52] *The Daily Telegraph* started their report with reference to 'a mild demonstration' at the Domain and later in the evening outside the Trades Hall. The reporter used the language of soldierly conduct in describing how, after the crowd had threatened to storm the Trades Hall in the evening, the soldiers 'formed up and marched' to Central station.[53] In *The Sydney Morning Herald*, the report of the Domain riot described how soldiers 'fell into orders' before rushing the meetings and pushing the speakers

'Police drawn up to protect speakers' and 'The speakers' reserved space', *The Daily Telegraph*, 24 June 1918, National Library of Australia.

off the platforms.⁵¹ *The Mirror* called it a 'peaceful demonstration' by soldiers, under the headline 'Disloyalists of the Domain; State police cannot deal with them.'⁵⁵

With this style of representation, the threat that returned soldiers posed to public order – a threat real enough to have foot and mounted police stationed in the city until late at night – was denied. The weekly journal of the NSW branch of the RSSILA, *The Soldier at Home and Abroad*, did not report on the riot at all. In the 21 June issue, in the regular 'Shrapnel' column of short pieces, the editors wrote that 'Iodine Lancers' should be ready in the Domain each Sunday to stop the spread of 'skeptic [sic] poisoning'. This was a reference to the Queen's Lancers which were a British cavalry unit.⁵⁶ In the same column, the editors wrote, 'The red rag which protects traitors in this country...Is the blood-soaked bandage of the Anzac.'⁵⁷

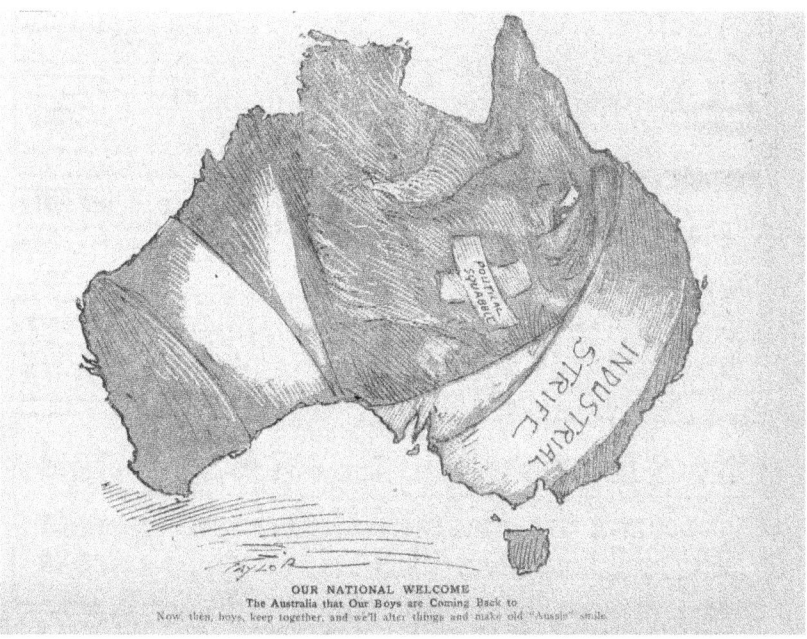

'Our national welcome', from *The Soldier at Home and Abroad*, 22 November 1918. National Library of Australia.

The police response to the 16 June Domain riot seemed to embolden local returned soldiers. At Corrimal, then a coastal mining town south of Sydney, members of the Free Speech Committee held a meeting on 10 August 1918. This committee had been set up by Labor and socialist organisations in response to the Sydney Domain riot and the subsequent threat by Premier Holman to disfranchise those convicted under the *War Precautions Act*. It was also designed to assist in collecting funds to pay for the legal defence for Ernest Judd, who was charged with three offences under the *War Precautions Act* for statements he was alleged to have made at Domain meetings in May and June 1918.[58] William Jeffery, who had been arrested on 16 June for riotous behaviour, was secretary of the Free Speech Committee. He reported a complaint to the Defence Department about 'an assault made by soldiers and others' on one of the speakers, McPherson, at a committee meeting in Corrimal on 10 August.[59] The Department of Defence told him to take his complaint to the State Government.

Jeffery did this and the police investigated. The Inspector-General of Police decided that the 'assault, if any, was of a trifling nature', and that it was 'brought about by the man McPherson himself using language which he would not dared to use if the police had been in attendance'.[60] Jeffery wrote that the soldiers and their civilian supporters who attacked the committee speaker were 'in a state of intoxication' and knocked him off the platform. Jeffery condemned the lack of action by the police and warned of the threats to liberty when 'acts of brute force by members of the military are to be winked at'.[61]

∞

Queensland was the only state at this time in the war to have a Labor government. But this did not translate into any less scrutiny of unionists, socialists and anti-war activists by the network of Military Intelligence officers who recorded public speeches and censors who opened people's mail. One of those who came to the attention of Military Intelligence was Gunner George Taylour, whose given names on his war record were listed as 'Thomas Gilbert'. As his nickname implied, Taylour was a returned soldier and had served first in the Australian Naval and Military Expeditionary Force, also known as the Tropical Force, then as a private in the AIF. He had enlisted soon after the start of the war in 1914, and transferred to the AIF in France in 1915 when his original company was disbanded. Taylour served in the 8th Machine Gun Company, with periods in field hospitals, suffering malaria. At the end of 1916, Taylour was invalided to hospital in England with a diagnosis of 'neurasthenia', which was a name used at the time for shell shock. He returned to Australia in December 1917, and was discharged medically unfit in January 1918.[62]

Taylour ended up in Brisbane, where he became a popular speaker at Labor and union rallies. With a charismatic style and good debating skills, Taylour was known as 'the Diggers' fighting orator'. In August 1918, he established an organisation called Comrades of the War League (COWL) as an alternative to the overtly right-wing and anti-Labor RSSILA in Queensland. Taylour offered membership to returned soldiers of 'private and non-commissioned rank', the soldiers he called 'dinkum diggers'. Taylour's aim to challenge the 'reactionary politics' of the RSSILA was supported by the Labor government of T. J. (Tom) Ryan, who donated £50 so the organisation could rent premises. But Taylour's promise of a large membership of Labor returned soldiers in Queensland did not eventuate, and there is no further mention of COWL after they were granted a further £500 by the State Government in October 1919.[63]

Like many of the returned soldiers who appear in this history of riots, Taylour rejected the anti-union rhetoric of the RSSILA. He called himself a 'selective socialist', and in a lecture he gave in July 1918, his description of this idea was as a kind of agrarian cooperative, where they could 'leave the cities to the capitalists'.[64] Taylour's left-wing politics were not radical, and in the Queensland state elections in March 1918 he campaigned on behalf of the Labor Party, which retained power with Ryan as Premier.[65] In Brisbane in late June 1918, Gunner Taylour participated in a debate at the Exhibition Hall over the issue of peace by negotiation. Taylour argued his case for peace talks to be held in conjunction with recruiting and reinforcement of forces at the front.[66]

Around this time, Taylour had been appointed to lecture to schoolchildren on behalf of the Red Cross Society. He had been recommended by Captain Dash, based on Taylour's speaking abilities and the fact that he had served at the front. But a complaint to the Red Cross by one of the students' parents warned them of Gunner Taylour's support for a negotiated peace. Then, a visit to the Red Cross Society from Captain Wood of Military Intelligence 'scared them considerably', and the Assistant Censor reported that the Society 'will be more careful in future' about their appointment of speakers.[67] The Military Intelligence archival file on Gunner Taylour indicated that he lost his role at the Red Cross because of Wood's intervention.

Conflicts in the Brisbane Domain were similar to those in the Sydney Domain. On 23 June 1918, there was a 'record crowd' in the Brisbane Domain, and a recruiting meeting was underway next to a peace demonstration. Returned soldiers moved to break up the peace meeting, so police formed a barrier around the peace speaker's platform and advised them to close the meeting. At the recruiting meeting nearby, the military band played 'God Save the King', during which those in the peace demonstration kept their hats on. A woman knocked the hat off one of the men with her umbrella and the 'crowd cheered vociferously'.[68] In a letter opened and copied by the censors, Jennie Scott Griffiths described a similar event on 21 July in the Brisbane Domain, when a middle-aged man who refused to take his hat off for the singing of the national anthem had it knocked off his head by a young soldier in uniform. The middle-aged man then knocked the soldier to the ground and 'police prevented the trouble spreading'.[69]

Scott Griffiths was a journalist and feminist who, while caring for children (she and her husband had six sons and four daughters), was active during the war in the anti-conscription campaigns, the Social Democratic League, the Women's Peace Army and the Children's Peace Army. Scott Griffiths was also editor of *The Australian Women's Weekly*, but was sacked in 1916 because of her opposition to conscription.[70] The family moved to Brisbane in 1917, and Griffiths wrote in July 1918 about the Brisbane Industrial Council meetings:

> The Domain meetings continue to be subjected to interruptions in the form of attempts by returned soldiers to break up the meetings by rushing the platforms and it must make all observers marvel at the patience of the crowd…Every Sunday, Recruiting Committee pitch their platform as near as possible to that of the Industrial Council and the recruiting supporters give a free exhibition of bad manners and accompanied by a chorus of abusive language.[71]

On Sunday 28 July 1918, Gunner Taylour was one of the speakers at the Brisbane Industrial Council meeting in the Domain, addressing the crowd on the topic of freedom of speech. There were about 1,500 people in the Domain that afternoon, according to police. Scott Griffiths wrote that people from the recruiting meeting rushed Taylour's speaking platform (which was actually a chair) and attempted to assault him, but Taylour 'stood his ground' and 'with the help of police got order restored'.[72] Taylour told the 'mob element amongst the young and excitable soldiers' that they should not use force at these meetings. He said that 'it was hardly a display of intelligence, courage, or fair play, whilst women were in the audience'.[73]

The violence did not last long. When Taylour was speaking, a group of returned soldiers tried to 'count out' Taylour, then they attacked the meeting and knocked Taylour off the chair. Police intervened and formed a guard between the two groups, but the returned soldiers continued to heckle Taylour by shouting, 'Are we in favour of peace by negotiation? No!'[74] They also shouted about Taylour, 'Is he a comrade of ours? No!' At one stage Taylour defended one of the returned soldiers, a man called William Lord. Someone in the crowd had shouted that Lord had never been to the front, which angered Lord, and he took his discharge papers to show Taylour, who told the crowd that 'the lad' had been misjudged. Taylour said they had been in the same battalion. Despite Taylour's attempts to diffuse the conflict, Lord and other returned soldiers continued to try and stop the meeting.[75] The soldiers sang 'God Save the King', 'Rule Britannia' and 'Australia Will Be There', and gave three cheers for 'the boys at the Front', which were countered by cheers for freedom of speech from those at Taylour's meeting.[76]

The returned soldiers who tried to stop Taylour from speaking would have known about the Domain riots in Sydney a month earlier, since they were reported nationwide. But though they may have considered they were part of the same national campaign to silence anti-war speakers, the returned soldiers in Brisbane felt they confronted police bias. Lord was reported to have said

> If this was in Sydney they'd be chucked out long ago. There's not enough of us. The "Johns" [police] are behind him. They won't lock him up.[77]

There was a major difference compared to the riot in Sydney on 16 June; those arrested in the Brisbane Domain on 28 July 1918 were all returned soldiers. William Lord, who was a member of the RSSILA, was arrested for creating a disturbance, and at his trial he was defended by solicitor P. Macgregor, while the Police Prosecutor was Sub-Inspector Brosnan. In the context of questioning whether Taylour's Domain meeting was an IWW meeting, Macgregor asked Sub-Inspector Brosnan, 'Are you an IWW man yourself?' The Sub-Inspector responded that such a question was an insult, but defence counsel persisted.[78] The implication was that if the police arrested riotous returned soldiers instead of the socialist and anti-war speakers they were attacking, then the police were suspect themselves. At

Lord's trial, Sub-Inspector Brosnan said there had been 'unwarranted innuendo right through the case' that police had 'acted aggressively towards the returned soldiers', which Brosnan rejected.[79]

Whoever was paying for Lord's defence had considerable resources, since the trial continued for twenty-three days, at the end of which Lord was convicted. There was no prison sentence imposed.[80] RSSILA Queensland Branch Secretary William Fisher was also charged with creating a disturbance on 28 July, along with Charles Peiniger, a member of the Returned Soldiers, Sailors and Citizens Loyalty League. Both were defended by the same law firm that defended Lord, and both Fisher and Peiniger pleaded guilty. Peiniger was fined 19 shillings, plus three shillings and sixpence court costs, and Fisher was released on his own recognisance. Their lawyer had argued for a nominal fine, but the magistrate said that a small fine would 'belittle the offence'. Sub-Inspector Brosnan told the court that the object in bringing the prosecutions 'was to teach returned soldiers and others that they must comply with the law.'[81]

∞

This did not stop returned soldiers in Queensland being involved in further riots and vigilante violence. Hughenden is a northwest regional pastoral centre about 500 kilometres inland from the coast, on Yirandali country. In October 1918, most publicans in Hughenden were not paying the award that had been determined in December 1917 for domestic servants and bar attendants, so the women stopped work. Their fellow unionists, particularly local shearers, supported them with a boycott of hotels that refused to pay the award. The strikers and their supporters, along with AWU organisers W. Huxley and George Bellamy, established a 'Temperance Committee' to help coordinate the hotel boycott.[82]

They had planned a street meeting for 16 October 1918 outside the Hughenden Hotel, which was one of only two hotels in town paying the proper award to barmaids. When AWU organiser Bellamy was addressing the crowd, brothers James and Tom Penny, whose father was one of the early pastoralists to occupy Yirandali country, led an attack. Bellamy was pulled from the speaking platform and there were fights among the crowd. Bellamy and a fellow organiser, R. Campbell, were 'roughly handled' as the police watched, but eventually the attackers were overpowered by union supporters in the crowd and the meeting resumed.[83]

In eyewitness accounts of the violence, the police moved in to break up the fights and 'escorted' the Penny brothers away, even though people in the crowd demanded that police arrest Tom Penny for his attack on AWU organiser Bellamy. Local alderman James Minogue Green, who was also a speaker at the 16 October meeting, said that there were reports beforehand 'that an organised party was to break up the meeting'.[84] Campbell – one of the men attacked on 16 October – wrote that

> rumours were afloat that the hotel proprietors had hired thugs to pull the speakers off the platform and deal with them. They picked a time when there were very few militants in town. The meeting was not long in progress before such interjections as, 'Get down you mongrels' were hurled at the speaker George Bellamy. But these did not satisfy the 'Black' [a reference to the boycotted hotels] beer drinking tools of capitalism… others caught Bellamy by the legs and pulled him off kicking hitting and biting was the order for the next ten minutes…[85]

The same union leaders who were involved in the Townsville union meetings addressed in Chapter 1 – Michael Kelly and Archie Eastcrabb – travelled to Hughenden to support the strikers. There was another Temperance Committee meeting planned for Friday night, 18 October, and a crowd of between 200 and 300 people gathered outside the Hughenden Hotel. This time the Penny brothers and other local pastoralists came into town with carloads of men, in what the Brisbane *Daily Standard* called 'an organised body of ruffians'.[86]

Returned soldiers also converged on Hughenden. In the archives of Military Intelligence, there are copies of two undated telegrams, both from Andrews in Hughenden to Lieutenant Byrne at the Returned Soldiers Association, Charters Towers branch. Andrews first telegrammed, 'Can you possibly get here Friday night if not send good leaders.' Then the next telegram, presumably sent on the Friday, 18 October, was, 'Most urgent you be here tonight and stay til Saturday.'[87]

On 18 October, Lieutenant Byrne travelled to Hughenden by car, along with recruiting officer Major General Furay. Both men were met at nearby Torrens Creek by solicitor Frank Hamilton and station owner Coxton. Byrne claimed he was responding to reports that returned soldiers had been 'roughly handled' in Hughenden and that their returned soldier badges had been trampled on.[88] In several newspaper reports, it had been alleged that women in Hughenden — derided as 'five women consorts of the I.W.W. agitators' — had attacked a returned soldier and one had spat on his badge.[89] This was refuted in a report by Captain Willis of Military Intelligence, who wrote that there was 'no evidence at all' that such a thing had occurred. Willis added that some returned soldiers were injured at the meeting on 16 October, but that it was 'only to be expected if they mix themselves up in these melees'.[90]

Lieutenant Byrne of the RSSILA seemed to believe the badge trampling story, and wrote

> I thought it my duty to proceed to Hughenden to help maintain law and order and to protect as far as lay in my power the men who had fought and bled in the cause of freedom, from attacks from emissaries of the Hun, in other words the IWW.[91]

When Byrne arrived at 7.20 pm on 18 October, the meeting was already rowdy, with returned soldiers and others shouting at the Temperance Committee speakers. Again, Bellamy was attacked and dragged off the speaking platform, and there were fights among the crowd, with the police apparently helpless to stop the violence. Lieutenant Byrne and Sergeant Major Furay mounted the lorry and spoke, and according to several newspaper accounts, Furay 'turned the meeting into a patriotic gathering', at the end of which cheers were given for the King.[92] In his speech, Furay referred to 'the great union of the AIF' — he named the RSSILA — and how they would 'clean up Australia and pass out the parasites'.[93] Lieutenant Byrne credited himself with placating the crowd, but it was not enough to stop the fighting, which continued until around eleven o'clock. The streets were not cleared until midnight. Byrne wrote that before he took over the speaking platform, 'it would take a war correspondent to describe the subsequent happenings, as it was one big melee'.[94]

Union organiser R. Campbell, who was there, wrote that about seventy to eighty returned soldiers had come to Hughenden, along with 'hired thugs' from surrounding pastoral stations. On Friday, 18 October, there were about an extra 150 men in town, and Campbell described these men as 'blood hounds half-drunk with grog supplied by the squatters and publicans'. Word was sent to the nearby shearing sheds and about fifty unionists came to support the Temperance Committee meeting, but they seemed to be outnumbered on the night of 18 October.[95] Campbell described the scene:

> Men were mobbed, knocked down and kicked long after consciousness had left them; they were then kicked into the gutter and left for dead; some of these unfortunate men will never be the same again; there is doubt about one man Paddy McSherry ever recovering.[96]

In his report on the incident, Military Intelligence officer Captain Willis considered that the riot on 18 October had been deliberately planned to break the beer boycott and barmaids' strike:

> The Pastoralists, Hotel Proprietors, Professional and Commercial men of the town and others appear to have organised with a view to smashing up the meeting. This they were successful in doing…I am of the opinion that the organised crowd of Pastoralists, Commercial and Professional men and others introduced the 'returned soldier incidents' with a view of inciting the public and thus getting their sympathy with the intention of breaking the 'Beer strike'. This I regret to say they have been unsuccessful in, as at present…there are good grounds for believing that T'ville [Townsville], as an outcome of the H'den [Hughenden] incident, will be plunged into a general strike within the next few days unless the Hotel proprietors (who are backed by the Pastoralists) give way.[97]

Willis' assessment of collusion and incitement to riot made sense in the context. Hughenden employers and local pastoral station owners were surrounded by what appeared to be effective worker solidarity. The beer strike was still going, and by this stage there were moves by shearers at the sheds at Hughenden, Redcliffe and Ballindalloch pastoral stations to extend the boycott to local wool stores.[98] Captain Willis also criticised the actions of Lieutenant Byrne and Sergeant Major Furay of the RSSILA, though did not go so far as to accuse them of being part of the collusion with employers and pastoralists. He thought that Byrne and Furay were 'ill-advised' in travelling to Hughenden in their soldiers' uniforms 'on a matter which in no way concerned the Defence Department'.[99] This gave the mistaken impression that 'the Military had intervened', when they had not. Willis nevertheless credited Byrne and Furay for their actions 'when the crowd were getting out of hand', even though the violence escalated after the riot of 18 October.[100]

The attacks on individual union organisers continued, and Saturday 19 October was the worst day of violence. There was further fighting in the streets, and some of the women who had gone on strike were injured, including Mrs Cooley, who was a cook at the Hughenden Hotel. She was knocked over in the street by an unnamed 'loyalist' and kicked as she lay on the ground.[101] A self-appointed group of 'loyal citizens' went to the Sub-Inspector of Police and demanded that several union organisers and their supporters leave town. These included Alderman Minogue Green, AWU officials W. Huxley and Jack Durkin, Bartholomew, who was the local secretary of the ALP, and Archie Eastcrabb of the Queensland Railway Union. Also on the list were hotel waitress Mrs Salatina, the hotel cook, Mrs Cooley, and Jack Murray, who was a shearer staying at the Hughenden Hotel with his wife.[102] A returned soldier was also reported to be among those unionists 'ordered' to leave town.[103]

AWU organiser George Bellamy was also told to leave Hughenden, and he escaped by car to nearby Winton. Three other union leaders – Michael Kelly, Durkin and Campbell – went into hiding after they were hunted out of their hotel rooms and escaped by the back door.[104] There were brawls in the streets, and in the afternoon Archie Eastcrabb was beaten up in the main street of Hughenden. He described his ordeal:

> I was attacked by a dozen men…knocked down kicked about the head and body. This was witnessed by the military authority who was in company with the mob and did not try to stop such brutal treatment. I am in hiding today, several men have suffered similar treatment; must have a two day rest…[105]

During the struggle, Eastcrabb's watch was stolen, but police recovered it.[106] He nevertheless had to leave town without his luggage, which was 'taken charge of by police' (presumably they took it from his room at the hotel) and forwarded to his fellow QRU organiser, George Rymer, in Townsville.[107] Badly injured after being attacked, Eastcrabb escaped to the railway canteen, but later the crowd followed him there and demanded his immediate departure from Hughenden. There were further fights as railway workers tried to defend Eastcrabb, and one worker was hospitalised as a result. The police escorted Eastcrabb to hospital.[108] He then went into hiding.[109]

On Sunday morning, a crowd invaded the house of railway employee Gibson, dragged him out of bed and assaulted him. Later that day, AWU organiser Huxley was threatened with being tarred and feathered if he did not leave town. James Minogue Green, the local alderman who supported the strikers and had presided over the temperance meeting on 18 October, was warned he would have his house burned down and his car destroyed if he did not also leave. By the evening, two other union supporters had left by the mail train.[110] Throughout two days of vigilante attacks and threats of violence, the police made few arrests. After 19 October, about thirty extra police were sent to the town.[111] A Hughenden resident described how 'police came from everywhere and word went around that they were going to use their firearms as soon as trouble started'.[112]

The riots and vigilante violence in Hughenden were condemned in the Labor newspapers, but lauded as loyalist action by the conservative press. In *The Northern Miner*, a Charters Towers paper, the sub-headline was 'Cleaning up the Town'.[113] In *The Townsville Daily Bulletin*, the story was headlined 'Cleaning up Hughenden'.[114] The *Daily Mail* in Brisbane described events as 'IWW banned, Hughenden's determination'.[115] The success of the returned soldiers and supporters of the publicans in driving union organisers from Hughenden captured wide attention. In a rare episode of press freedom in 1918, the censor in Brisbane was instructed *not* to scrutinise newspaper copy on the 'civil disturbances' in Hughenden.[116] The event instantly became a template for loyalist collective violence.

A 'meeting of loyalists' on Monday 21 October in the local Shire Hall repeated the demand for particular individuals to leave Hughenden, and resolved that they were 'determined to exterminate the hotbed of IWWism from our midst and to allow this town to return to more peaceful times'.[117] The meeting was presided over by the mayor, P. C. O'Neill, who was also owner of The Grand Hotel, which was being boycotted because O'Neill would not pay award wages to his female employees.[118] Mayor O'Neill addressed the meeting and said 'the IWW were a menace to the country'. Solicitor Frank Hamilton, who had met RSSILA members Byrne and Furay on 18 October, told the audience that the IWW were 'mongrels' and 'parasites'. Pastoralists' son James Penny also spoke at the meeting, which ended with resolutions demanding that certain individuals 'quietly leave this town' and that the beer strike was over.[119]

But the beer strike and the hotel boycott continued. Unionists in Townsville refused to cart any sort of liquor to Hughenden, and they were supported by railway workers, who refused to load cases of beer.[120] By early November, there were strikes in Townsville as well. The next beer strike meeting in Hughenden, on 23 October, was attended by a force of mounted police. Speakers included AWU organiser Jack Durkin and Minogue Green, and Durkin condemned the 'demonstration of hooliganism by the elite of the town'.[121] But despite the increased police presence, Mayor O'Neill and other prominent citizens who had delivered the threats were not arrested. Most newspaper reports downplayed the lawlessness of the previous few days in Hughenden. Archie Eastcrabb was referred to as a 'deported man', suggesting Eastcrabb was the criminal and his forced departure was legitimate.[122] In his account, Lieutenant Byrne questioned the use of the word 'deportation', arguing that 'those men who left for their own protection and also in the interests of public peace were not deported'. Byrne claimed it was akin to the 'peace by negotiation' advocated by the IWW.[123] A few weeks later, Alderman Minogue Green had his home raided by Captain Willis and Munro from Military Intelligence, who confiscated old copies of the worker magazine *Solidarity* along with correspondence from the recent shearers' strike. Minogue Green burned the rest of his papers in case Captain Willis came back.[124]

∽

The riots in Hughenden became a model for anti-union violence. When Sergeant Roy Inwood, introduced in Chapter 1, threatened to shoot Broken Hill socialists and unionists with a machine gun, he told his audience that he would 'drive the mongrels out and make them dance some as they went'. Inwood continued, 'We want to do the same with them as they did in Queensland. We should drive them from town to town.'[125] And someone in the crowd shouted in agreement, 'We will give them what they got at Hughenden.'[126]

The riots in Sydney, Broken Hill, Townsville and Hughenden were all linked with the centrality of soldiers' sacrifice and the way in which perceived insults to that sacrifice justified, even demanded, a violent response. In Hughenden, it was clear that the allegation that returned soldiers had been abused was invented by self-styled 'loyal' publicans and station owners as an excuse for violent attacks on unionists in order to break the beer boycott. Captain Willis of Military Intelligence, Labor newspaper editors and the union leaders involved all came to that conclusion.

But despite the invented basis for the riotous attacks in Hughenden, events there produced motifs that would be repeated across the country. A returned soldier correspondent to *The Brisbane Courier* wrote that news from Hughenden

> somewhat lightened the bitterness felt by men who, returning from the Front, have experienced the rotten sentiment all too prevalent in Queensland. Indifference and disloyalty seem to be on all sides, chiefly disseminated by scum of the earth…This abuse, however, does not fall on barren soil. It germinates in the hearts of maimed and crippled men who see how their sacrifices have been made a mockery of, apparently with impunity, by parasites and rotters…it has remained for Hughenden to take the first step towards purifying the atmosphere. Thus all honour to that town for commencing the grand work. By the memory of those lads who sleep by palm and desert and plains and by the sufferings of those who have returned broken in mind and body, Queensland must be purged clean of all skunks and curs. It is an outrage to all loyalists…that IWWism and disloyalty should be allowed to lift its head…[127]

3

'Dulce et Decorum Est': Remembering Soldiers' Sacrifice

Brothers Oliver and Joseph Cumberland, from Scone, New South Wales, enlisted in the AIF in October 1914. Oliver did not want his younger brother Joe to go on his own. Both brothers were at the landing at Gallipoli in April 2015, but they were separated when Oliver was wounded and taken to hospital.[1] From Cairo in May 1915, Oliver wrote to his sister Una.

> Dear Una,
> I suppose you received my last letter in which I told you I was slightly wounded. I am quite well now and expect to go back to the front any time, but Una, prepare yourself for the worst…poor Joe is gone…I did not know until yesterday, I went to headquarters offices in Cairo and saw the list of killed and wounded. I had been very anxious wondering where he was, and when I saw the list I did not know what to do. I wandered around the streets nearly mad, I felt so lonely…He died for his Country Una, I know how you will feel sister – God help you all to bear it…Your affectionate Brother, Oliver.[2]

Oliver's letter to Una evoked devastation, confusion and loneliness at the death of their brother. Twenty-one-year-old Joe had died from wounds received at the landing. By asserting that 'He died for his Country', Oliver made the story coherent. Dying for one's country translated the violent death of a young man into a meaningful loss.

Oliver was killed in the attack on Lone Pine in August 1915. Initially he was reported missing, and his family did not receive confirmation of his death until nearly a year later.³ His body was eventually found buried in a trench.⁴ Military authorities wrote to Una that her brother's body had been exhumed and reburied in the Brown's Dip Cemetery at Gallipoli 'with the utmost care and reverence in the presence of a Chaplain'.⁵

Families like the Cumberlands were left devastated by the human toll of the war. It was the first time that non-Indigenous Australians had experienced the mass grief and trauma caused by so many young men killed. First Nations communities across Australia had endured mass mourning since 1788, but for non-Indigenous Australians it was unprecedented. In 1918, bereavement was commonplace and the returned wounded were visible everywhere. The challenge of translating suffering into meaningful loss was one of magnitude as well as definition.

The Latin phrase 'dulce et decorum est pro patria mori' would have been familiar to many of Oliver Cumberland's contemporaries. From the Roman lyric poet Horace, writing over 2,000 years ago, it roughly translates as 'it is sweet and proper to die for one's country'. Even those who did not know the Latin phrase understood the concept of a noble death in the service of one's country. Oliver Cumberland wrote about the idea as a way for him and his family to bear the pain of the violent and sudden loss of younger brother Joe. The notion that Australian fatalities on the battlefront were purposeful and honourable deaths because they were for King and Country was ubiquitous. Before they knew about Oliver's fate, the Cumberland family erected a memorial stone for Joe in a Scone churchyard with the inscription 'Our brave hero brother, Private J. H. Cumberland'.⁶ In June 1916, when the family received the news of Oliver's death nearly a year after he went missing, his name was added to the memorial stone. Oliver's siblings (their parents had passed away before the war started) published three tributes in the local newspaper, all referring to Oliver as a hero. His sisters Una and Doris wrote that he 'died the noblest death a man can die, fighting for God and right and liberty'.⁷

Today, another recognisable context for 'dulce et decorum est pro patria mori' is where it is used with angry satire by poet Wilfred Owen. One of the English 'trench poets', along with writers such as Siegfried Sassoon, Robert Graves, Ivor Gurney and Rupert Brooke, Owen presented death at the front as dehumanising, grotesque and futile. These poets fought in the war. Wilfred Owen and Isaac Rosenberg were killed in France in 1918, and Rupert Brooke died of blood poisoning on a hospital ship in 1915. Poet and composer Ivor Gurney spent much of the remainder of his life in hospitals suffering mental illness because of his wartime experiences.[8]

In Owen's poem 'Dulce et decorum est', traditional meanings of death at the battlefront are rejected as a lie. Here is an excerpt:

> If in some smothering dream you too could pace
> Behind the wagon that we flung him in…
> If you could hear, at every jolt, the blood
> Come gurgling from froth-corrupted lungs
> …you would not tell with such high zest
> To children ardent for some desperate glory
> The old Lie: Dulce et decorum est
> Pro patria mori.[9]

For Owen and his fellow soldier poets, sacrifice was meaningless. This writing introduced into the Western imagination a new lexicon of words and images to portray war. Words such as 'horror' and 'futility' and graphic descriptions of mangled butchered bodies were not part of any literary canon at the time. In this new context, odes to soldiers' bravery and noble death were obscenely dishonest, and traditional notions of a glorious death for one's country had no place. Words were the instruments for this new imagery, since photographic images of the warfront were censored in the British and Australian press. What are today the ubiquitous visual representations of the Western Front – lunar landscapes showing corpses of men and horses, mud and devastation – were not available to most civilians back home during World War I, unless they knew a soldier with a camera.

European novels such as Erich Maria Remarque's *All Quiet on the Western Front* and Jaroslav Hašek's *The Good Soldier Švek* made the same disruptive challenge as their British counterparts, and helped established satire and rejection of traditional meanings of heroism as the literary response to the war. A central theme of these works was anger at the incompetence of the generals – the old men – who sent so many young men to pointless deaths. There was also anger at home-front patriots, who they perceived as having helped to drive the continuation of a terrible war. One of Siegfreid Sassoon's poems includes the lines:

> I'd like to see a Tank come down the stalls
> Lurching to rag-time tunes, or 'Home sweet Home'
> And there'd be no more jokes in Music halls
> To mock the riddled corpses round Bapaume.[10]

In this new language, soldier-writers expressed their complete alienation from the civilian world, their bitter estrangement from the 'business as usual' approach of the home front. The division was not between warring nations, but between the community of soldiers who lived the horror and those who stayed at home.[11] Eric Leed, in his analysis of memoirs and accounts from German, French, British and American soldiers, also identified an enduring resentment by soldiers of the civilian society for whom they had gone to war. Leed argued that the response of many soldiers to their return to civilian society was violence. Riots and soldier mutinies occurred across the United Kingdom in 1919. The 'Khaki riots', involving both British and Canadian troops, started at demobilisation camps in England in January and reached a peak in June and July. The Victory Day riots on 19 July 1919 in Lutton, Lincolnshire, resulted in hundreds of casualties as returned soldiers set fire to the town hall, burning it down. For twelve hours they battled police and fireman sent to quell the outbreak.[12]

The works of the British poets of the Great War remain standard texts in English-speaking school and university curriculums, and writers Siegfried Sassoon, Robert Graves and Edmund Blunden have been in print for over a century. In 1985, a memorial was erected in Westminster Abbey to commemorate sixteen of the 'soldier poets'. Max Egremont, Sassoon's biographer, wrote that 'the poets were made by the war and then made a lasting vision of it'.[13]

The impact of the literary response to the Great War is central to the way it has been analysed in history. This impact is reflected in Anglo-American histories of World War I, such as those by World War II veterans and academics Paul Fussell and Samuel Hynes. They explored how the slaughter of nine million soldiers was remembered and imagined in art, literature and popular culture. Hynes characterised the war as 'the great imaginative event' of modern times.[14] Fussell and Hynes both argued that the war was a fundamental discontinuity, an irretrievable break in history, in culture and in the way the societies of the combatant nations perceived their world. The industrialised butchery of men in the trenches was explained by concepts such as waste, void, and the end of history and civilisation. A specifically modern discourse had to be invented to express this kind of war.[15]

Other scholars have drawn different conclusions about the cultural remembrance of the war. Jay Winter has argued that most bereaved civilians and soldiers turned to 'older motifs' to construct a meaning for their loss. They embraced and refashioned, rather than rejected, classical and religious forms of remembrance and mourning. Far from being a symbol of disjunction between the traditional and the modern, Winter argued that World War I did not disrupt continuities with older, established ways of imagining war. Winter acknowledged that many survivors developed cultural forms of remembering which understood loss in terms of estrangement and empty despair. But he pointed out that while this language could express anger, 'it could not heal'.[16]

People sought ways of sharing and mediating their grief through communal mourning and the 'fictive kinships' of the bereaved.[17] Some practices revived and adapted secular spiritualist themes, such as communicating with the spirits of the dead, as well as older commemorative rituals.[18] With all these ways of grieving and remembering, at the core was a reverence for the dead soldier and for the grief of those left behind. He was someone's son, brother, husband and, just as importantly, a fellow soldier. The idea of meaningful loss was also the basis for the commemoration of the war in George Mosse's study of what he called the 'myth of the war experience'. Mosse argued that returned volunteer soldiers contributed to sanctifying and legitimising the confrontation with mass death.[19]

For families in Australia like the Cumberlands, whose brothers Joe and Oliver were killed at Gallipoli, the public expression of their grief drew on traditional ways of remembering. The Cumberland siblings memorialised their brothers as heroes whose deaths were for a noble cause. Analyses of the Australian experience of remembering the war dead show that traditional motifs were the only kind of cultural representation there was. Charles E. W. Bean was a war correspondent who was also Australia's official war historian, and his immediate and energetic production of the Anzac identity as the birth of a nation left no room for alternative interpretations of the meaning of loss. While Bean shared the privations and dangers of the soldiers at the front line at Gallipoli and chaffed against censorship in his reporting on the war, he was energetic in his denial of other accounts of the war experience which could undermine the vision of brave and heroic Australian soldiers. For instance, in his editing of the immensely popular *Anzac Book*, published in 1916, Bean deleted soldiers' contributions which suggested that they did not want to fight, that they thought their comrades' deaths were futile and that the 'unequal comforts or sacrifices' between officers and men showed a continuation of class privilege within the AIF.[20]

C. E. W. Bean's original formula of the Anzac legend has remained mostly unchanged for over a century. The central tenet is that the Anzacs exposed, under duress, the fine masculine qualities of the white Australian persona. While there was some effort at the end of the war to include nurses as 'Anzacettes' or 'Diggeresses', the Anzac legend was exclusively masculine. The Anzac was also white, even though approximately 1,000 Aboriginal soldiers enlisted in the First AIF and fought in defence of Australia.[21] The Anzac was without class identity, since class allegiances had been obliterated by the comradeship of the battlefield. His tendency to disobedience was not a symptom of lack of discipline but a characteristic of free white men accustomed to democracy, which in turn made them better soldiers.

The intrinsic worth of Australian soldiers, proven through their willingness to make the ultimate sacrifice, had secured Australia's nationhood. C. E. W. Bean wrote in 1919:

> Australia [has become] a new nation. Five years ago the world barely knew her. Today, the men who went to fight for her have placed her high in the world's regard.[22]

The celebratory legend which developed around the Anzac experience was one in which soldiers' sacrifice was made meaningful because it was in the service of the nation, Empire and freedom; all the things that citizen-soldiers defended. Within this legend, Anzacs could return to being civilians secure in their society's endorsement of the worth and legitimacy of their sacrifice and that of their comrades who gave their lives. The cost of sacrifice was resolved, with a smooth transition from willing fighters (there were no conscripts in the First AIF) to proud heroes.

The literary response in Australia overwhelmingly endorsed the notion of heroic warfare and portrayed the Anzac as 'the bushman reincarnate', consciously anti-modern and anti-urban.[23] The nostalgic bushman construction was despite the fact that by 1911, the majority of non-Indigenous Australians were urban dwellers, living in cities or towns. By 1916, 41 per cent of people counted in the census lived across seven capital cities (Canberra was not yet populated).[24] This highlighted another injustice towards Aboriginal soldiers who fought in defence of their country and yet were excluded from the Anzac legend. Many Aboriginal soldiers in the AIF were skilled stockmen from pastoral stations or missions, and they matched the bushman persona much better than their non-Indigenous city-dwelling counterparts.

Stephen Garton has addressed the almost exclusive emphasis on traditional ways of remembering war in Australian art and literature after World War I. He discussed the 'contradictory fertility of Anzac', the legend's function as both inspiring cultural production and inhibiting modernist expressions of the memory of the war.[25] Robin Gerster has characterised postwar literary reminiscences of Australian soldiers as 'big-noting', which was in stark contrast to the European response of 'debunking' the heroic martial figure. Gerster suggested that while the war represented collapse for the Old World, for Australia, as a young nation, it was a triumphant beginning. So when Anzacs represented themselves as heroic warriors, this was enthusiastically embraced by the Australian public.[26] Clare Rhoden has also identified Australian war literature as uniformly traditional.[27] This literary output far outnumbered and overshadowed anti-war prose that portrayed soldiers in a negative way, such as workers killing workers at the behest of their capitalist masters.

The message of heroic sacrifice was eagerly expanded by an Australian public waiting for proof of their nation's worth on the world stage, and books about soldiers' daring deeds were hugely popular.

Poet Vance Palmer referred to a terrible war, 'a quaking bog', mud and 'stark snapped trees', but most published poems avoided imagery of an ugly battlefield.[28] Compared to the works of their published English counterparts, Australian poets seemed to be writing about a different war. Here are some examples, the first from Edward Harrington of the Light Horse Regiment, and the second from Arthur Adams, a civilian poet whose work was widely published in the *Bulletin*, as well as in magazines for NSW school children:

> Anzac! Magnificent and deathless name!
> Where met the Crescent and the Cross divine,
> A solemn splendour evermore is thine…
> The dauntless sons of fair Australia came…
> And, cheering, charged hot-foot to death and fame.[29]

And:

> Coo-ee! Ye stalwart sons; Coo-ee!
> …Go! Seek the warland track!
> …On! On Ye gallant sons. On! On!
> To vict'ry grand and great;
> Go, dare and dash where bay'nets clash,
> Go, do not tarry late!
> They're calling from the trenches, boys!
> They're fighting for their King![30]

Australian soldiers' literary production during and at the end of the war did not always follow classical themes. *The Port Hacking Cough* was published on board troopship D 34, the *S. S. Port Hacking*, returning from Europe in late 1918, carrying 700 soldiers. There were seven weekly issues, from 14 December 1918 to 25 January 1919, and the editorial team was headed by G. P. J. (Jack) Sherringham of the 5th Australian Field Artillery Battery. His sub-editor was Sergeant L. V. Worle, also of the 5th Australian Field Artillery Battery, one of many examples of wartime comraderies between soldiers continuing after the war. In their first issue, the editors said that the paper was to 'amuse and entertain the diggers of the 1914 leave draft', indicating that the men on board had been away for four years.³¹ The paper combined information about entertainment and sporting events on board the ship, such as musical reviews and boxing matches, with poetry and spoof commentary. Each edition also included at least one serious piece on contemporary topics such as repatriation policy.

The format of *The Port Hacking Cough* was loosely based on that of *The Wipers Times* (Wipers was a corruption of Ypres, a battlefield town in Belgium), published by British troops on the Western Front. *The Wipers Times* parodied the war as music hall performance – '"Mined": a most uplifting performance…Best ventilated hall in the town' – or countryside excursion. Like this entry from December 1916: 'Stay at the Hotel Des Ramparts, Ypres…wonderful cuisine…climate healthy…good shooting'.³² The editors lampooned the strength of the Allies and the army high command, as well as the war correspondents of what they called the 'yellow press'. While print runs were limited (it was published on a printing press the editors found in a bombed building at Ypres), the newspaper was popular among the troops, and collected editions were reprinted back in London in 1918 and 1930. The editors of *The Wipers Times* were subject to censorship, of course, and made fun of that in their first edition in February 1916:

> There is much that we would like to say in it, but the shadow of censorship enveloping us causes us to refer to the war, which we hear is taking place in Europe, in a cautious manner.³³

The Australian editors of *The Port Hacking Cough* followed the same themes in satirising the competence of military high command and the pro-war press. For instance, an article by 'Loop Hole' described a naval battle set in the mud of the trenches with the sub-headline 'Speed our greatest factor'. One British ship collided with a duckboard (the wooden planks placed over the mud so soldiers could walk on them) and 'the main German fleet was forced to retire fully eighteen inches… it was soon in a very critical position.'³⁴

In *The Port Hacking Cough*, the 'Special War Correspondent' was dubbed 'Pillip Fibbs', a play on the London *Daily Mail*'s correspondent Philip Gibbs, who as one of the official war correspondents submitted all his articles to government censorship. In a piece called 'Tireless

Duckboards at Zonnebeke, with a German concrete dugout in the background, Belgium, October 1917. Australian War Memorial photograph, E01213.

tidings: The Great War', 'Fibbs' wrote about a new army mobilising all men between the ages of eighty-five and 103. As a prize in a competition run by the newspaper, the editors offered medical exemption certificates 'if the war breaks out again'. A stray line was 'Any fool can get in the Army, but it takes a genius to get out of it'.[35]

Like their counterparts in *The Wipers Times*, the editors of *The Port Hacking Cough* devised mock advertisements. In one for a pub, the attractions were that an undertaker 'calls every morning…for orders' and that the Pioneer Battalion would act as gravediggers.[36] Pioneer battalions had been created in 1916 within each AIF division, and they worked with engineers and other constructional troops in digging and repairing communications trenches, often under heavy artillery bombardment. A poem in the form of a children's rhyme concluded with 'Z is for Zero which we used to dread, Thank God it's all over.'[37]

The search for forgetting was also a theme and the editors included prose and poems about acquiring alcohol in any way possible, about drinking and the regular wish to be inebriated. A cartoon captioned 'Our artist's dream Christmas: getting tanked' had a digger's head sticking out of an armoured tank being bombarded with champagne and beer bottles and trailing a cartload of empties.[38] Another poem was titled 'To an empty friend' and was about a 'dead marine' (an empty bottle of beer).[39]

Other cartoons showed a darker humour. One was captioned 'That Ouderdom feeling: Digger disguising himself as a daisy'. One translation of the Dutch word *ouderdom* (very similar to Flemish spoken in Belgium) is 'the later part of one's life'. The cartoon, set at night, showed a denuded tree trunk, searchlights illuminating an aeroplane and explosions in the sky, and a soldier in the forefront lying on the ground holding something in his hand. A daisy in this landscape was incongruous.[40]

Port Hacking Cough, Vol 1, No 1, 14 December 1918. National Library of Australia.

Port Hacking Cough, Vol 1, No 2, 21 December 1918. National Library of Australia.

The literary sketches in *The Port Hacking Cough* reflected a general weariness regarding the war and sometimes grim satire. But these examples were outnumbered by copy which endorsed traditional ways of interpreting the war experience. Most of the jokes celebrated the nonchalance of the Aussie digger at the expense of English officers, officers in general, and women. The humour never challenged the image of soldiers as heroes, however insouciant they may appear. People of colour were always derided, and a spoof musical troupe was called the 'Kolombo Koons' (Colombo is the capital of what was then called Ceylon, where the ship docked in late December 1918). The first meeting of the debating society on board the ship addressed the topic of 'whether a white Australia policy should be maintained'.[41] In an article on 'postwar problems', Sergeant Worle wrote of the need to populate Australia with 'the desirable white immigrant…and so stop the chances of the Yellow Peril ever getting a hold in our fair land.'[42]

The message that Australian soldiers had sacrificed willingly to defend their country and therefore deserved appropriate reward was articulated clearly throughout the pages of *The Port Hacking Cough*. Articles on repatriation and the soldiers' new place in the nation were reprinted in all seven issues of the journal. An article by 'A. Digger' stated that soldiers did not ask for charity, but that they 'have the RIGHT to ask' that they not suffer financially after 'defending the country's freedom and honour' (their emphasis).[43] The author was specific about the form which repatriation should take. This included a uniform Commonwealth scheme with provisions for the granting of land to returned soldiers and funding for small businesses. The writer's advice to soldiers was 'show them at home that we will not accept charity but will have our rights as men.'[44]

It seemed that for the Australian soldiers returning home on troopship D 34, their enthusiasm for remembering their war through traditional structures increased as they got closer to Australian shores and a heroes' welcome. Australian soldiers had not witnessed the 'business as usual' demeanour of the home-front society from the same perspective as their British and European counterparts, even though many would have spent some time in 'Blighty' (England) on leave or in hospital. These Australian soldiers returned convinced of the coherence and worth of their sacrifice, and glad to be home:

> Everybody happy, smiling faces everywhere, for it is the first sight of the homeland and the realisation of our dreams of four long, weary years.[45]

When the troopship was boarded at Portsea in Victoria, and quarantined by civilian medical authorities, *The Port Hacking Cough* editors expressed anger. They understood the necessity of quarantine against the Spanish influenza epidemic, but queried why health officials had not acted sooner, instead waiting until the soldiers were ready to disembark. The editors argued that 'they had been risking their lives on and off for four and a half years…we deserve a little more considerate treatment'.[46] A cartoon showed a digger, muscular and square-jawed, looking on while a thin man in pinstriped trousers and wearing a mask walked past.[47]

On the arrival of the Port Hacking (a clean ship carrying 700 Anzacs) the Health Officers and their assistants came aboard wearing Masks.

UNHEALHTY ? (which) ?

Port Hacking Cough, Vol 1, No 7, 25 January 1918. National Library of Australia.

The themes of what soldiers deserved for their sacrifice, and how their war experience had set them apart from civilian society, were repeated on the pages of returned soldiers' magazines. Editors of the NSW RSSILA journal, *The Soldier*, articulated the extent and nature of the debt they held over civilian society, and what returned soldiers' place should be in the new nation. Returned Anzacs were to be the undisputed leaders of national rejuvenation because they had special access to national membership, and a distinctly Christian membership, in a way that civilians did not:

'Once the MAN OF WAR abroad, now the MAN OF PEACE at home;
The big job of the returned soldier', from *The Soldier at Home and Abroad*,
15 November 1918. National Library of Australia.

We have helped build a new world and in our hearts, thank God we were the instruments of His new creation...we are not unmindful of the part we played...We did this job for them [men of military age who did not enlist] and – they're going to pay us for it.

The war has taught us what comradeship means, and we are going to stand together to battle in another great war – a war to build our beloved Australia...[48]

These assertions from Anzac heroes, and the glorification of their wartime achievements, were for the most part devoid of any reference to damaged men. In the issue published just after the Armistice in 1918, the editors of *The Soldier* referred to the 240,000 soldiers 'sick or wounded', but most of the editorials were about the nation-building job ahead for those returned soldiers who were not sick or wounded.[49] There were numerous mentions in soldiers' writing to comrades who had 'gone West', a euphemism for being killed; those who 'lie buried in foreign soil'.[50] And the rioting returned soldiers, whose actions were endorsed by the editors of the NSW RSSILA journal, nearly always, at some stage of the violence, sought to justify their actions as being a way of honouring and protecting the memory of dead mates. But the injured survivors were rarely mentioned in the cultural representations that sanctified the memory of soldiers' sacrifice.

A look at some contemporary titles published about Australia and World War I reveals a connecting theme of brokenness. Bill Gammage's seminal work *The Broken Years* was first published in 1974, with subsequent editions continuing until 2010. Joan Beaumont's *Broken Nation* was published in 2013, and *Shattered Anzac* by Marina Larsson in 2009. As Beaumont wrote, 'the dominant mode of understanding in the memory of the war today is catastrophe and trauma'.[51] But, without exception Australian returned soldiers at the end of World War I chose not to present or memorialise their experience that way, at least not publicly. Alistair Thomson has written about the dynamic between soldiers' private and often painful and disturbing memories of war and the public legend which celebrated, and still celebrates, the war as the birth of the Australian nation. He based his work on oral histories he collected from World War I veterans in the 1980s. Thomson spoke with soldiers about how their personal memories of war were composed over time, and rarely shared. His work addresses the complex interaction between individual identities and public legends in that process.[52]

When soldiers were depicted in cartoons on the pages of daily newspapers or soldiers' magazines at the end of the war, they were nearly always tall, muscular and standing up, their masculine strength proudly on display. Sometimes cartoons in the Victorian RSSILA newspaper, *The Bayonet*, showed men with missing limbs on crutches or men with the sleeve of their jacket folded in where their arm once was.

But the images did not suggest these men were broken; they remained returned heroes to whom the nation owed a debt. Words in poetry and prose completed this image. While not a soldier himself, C. J. Dennis wrote a hugely popular poem, 'Digger Smith', first published in 1918. This epitomised the wounded hero. The Digger did labouring work on the farm of the elderly Mar and Dad Flood, even though he had lost a leg in the war. In Dennis's invented Aussie larrikin patois, Digger Smith was shy about marrying, since he considered himself 'only 'arf a man'. The narrator responded, 'the things 'e's done Out There makes 'im one man an' some to spare.'[53]

∞

Stoic wounded Anzacs were part of the celebratory legend generated at the end of and after the war, although they may not have been included in the project of postwar nation-building. But those missing from the picture entirely were the men who looked physically unharmed yet suffered debilitating mental illness because of their war experience. 'Shell shock' was a relatively new term in 1918, and was used along with 'neurasthenia' and 'war neuroses' to describe a range of conditions. George Mosse summarised it:

> Shell shock was one of the most widespread battlefield injuries during the first world war: it seemed unlike any of the other wounds contracted in the war, an injury without any bodily signs, a mass outbreak of mental disorder.[54]

Lieutenant Colonel Arthur Butler served in the AIF at both Gallipoli and the Western Front in various senior medical officer roles. He was the author of Australia's official medical history of the war. While the origins of the term 'shell shock' are unclear, Butler referred to it as 'a soldier's phrase'. He wrote that by the winter of 1916,

> The term had been in use for some time and was loosely applied to all cases of physical and mental breakdown within the battle zone without apparent wound. It had become indeed a diagnostic shibboleth and an open sesame to the base.[55]

Butler was among many senior army personnel at the time who were concerned that shell shock was not easy to diagnose, and was possibly deliberate malingering by soldiers, or simply exhaustion. But Butler and the army nevertheless took it seriously and sought to deal with shell shock 'on scientific lines'. Throughout his history of the Australian Army Medical Services, Butler always included shell shock as a war injury; it was treated as a wound even though there was 'no visible trauma', according to the definition.[56] Butler's Canadian counterpart, Sir Andrew McPhail, on the other hand, considered shell shock 'a manifestation of childishness and femininity' for which there was no remedy. McPhail wrote that the term shell shock was used to 'describe a variety of conditions ranging from cowardice to maniacal insanity'.[57]

The symptoms of shell shock as treated in the AIF included a range of 'nervous' conditions: anxiety, stupor and confusion. The official classification of shell shock patients who were to be evacuated from the field were those with 'acute and reversible psychic or psycho-physical dysfunction'.[58] Soldiers presenting with shell shock symptoms were a huge practical problem for the armies, both at Gallipoli and in France. Psychology and psychiatry were still relatively new disciplines, and regimental medical officers (RMOs) at aid posts and field ambulance stations had to treat soldiers with bullet wounds, shrapnel injuries and those suffering the effects of chlorine gassing, along with shell shock. Plus, it was the job of the medics to get the soldier functioning and back on the battlefield as quickly as possible. While individual medical officers may have been sympathetic to physically uninjured soldiers who were buried alive in the trenches, not once but repeatedly, or their bodies thrown by exploding shells, the army needed them back on the frontline.[59]

The circumstances under which shell shock cases were diagnosed were often themselves terrifying. During the trench warfare around Pozières in France in the winter of 1916, RMO Captain R. C. Winn described the aid post he commanded in an old German dugout. The entrance was 'choked with wounded' and the aid post itself was continually bombed and 'rocked with concussions'. Some of the wounded were killed 'while being attended to', and others had been on the battlefield so long before being rescued that their wounds were

Wounded soldiers being treated at an AIF advanced dressing station near Ypres, September 1917. Australian War Memorial photograph E00715.

Exhausted stretcher bearers and dressers from the 9th Field Ambulance, asleep in the mud near Zonnebeke, Belgium, October 1917. Australian War Memorial photograph E00941.

'Australian infantry wounded at a First Aid Post near Zonnebeke Railway Station', image by Frank Hurley, 12 October 1917. Australian War Memorial photograph E01202A.

Australian soldiers suffering effects of gas, waiting for medical treatment at a regimental aid post, probably near Villers-Brettoneux, 27 May 1918. Australian War Memorial photograph, E04850.

covered in maggots. Winn wrote that he judged 'with sympathy those evacuated with shell shock and formed the opinion that loss of sleep was one of the main contributing factors'.[60]

Another RMO, Captain H. R. Harris of the 2nd Field Artillery Brigade, wrote,

> At Pozières there were many cases of genuine shell shock. In evacuating cases of shell shock, I do not consider it mattered much if the case was one of stark fear or genuine shell shock – the former had to be evacuated to the ambulance because of the disastrous moral effect of a badly frightened man on his comrades.[61]

Lieutenant Colonel Butler considered shell shock a 'major medical problem of the war', and added, 'as it was to be of the peace'.[62] For an Australian public eager for information about the condition, this article by 'An Officer' was syndicated in several newspapers in July 1918. It represented theories that were also popular among medical professionals at the time:

> ...the popular name, 'shell shock', unlike many popular names, is an accurate name. It describes the principal cause of neurasthenia among soldiers. Most of the neurasthenic cases in the British army are suffering from the actual concussion of high explosive shells. Many of them have been buried alive. There are often contributory causes. Want of sleep, the general strain of war, the very suppression of emotions which a soldier cultivates – these things may contribute to shell shock; they may of themselves set up the same nervous condition; but for the most part cases of shell shock are the direct result of the explosion of shells...The usual physical symptoms of shell shock are some form of temporary paralysis, the loss of power in a limb, loss of hearing or speech. The mental and emotional symptoms are weariness, fear of closed and open spaces, loss of confidence, loss of the power to concentrate the thoughts, and in the more acute stages actual confusion of thought.[63]

While mentally broken returned soldiers were nowhere to be seen in the homecoming speeches about Anzac heroes, the reality of shell-shocked soldiers was evident everywhere. In Western Australia, at the Kalgoorlie railway sheds in 1919, union members stopped the practice of blowing whistles 'unnecessarily...on account of upsetting returned men suffering from shell shock'.[64] Returned soldier George Reidy had been a champion boxer before the war. At a pigeon shooting competition at Condobilin, New South Wales, he started physically shaking and collapsed because of the noise of the guns. Reidy had to be taken home and he was 'not normal for several days'.[65]

In 1917 and 1918, the Sydney *Sun* ran a regular, sometimes daily, column for work wanted for returned soldiers. Their injuries, including shell shock and gunshot wounds (GSW), were listed along with their skills, and many of the men seeking work were recorded as suffering from shell shock.[66] Advertisements for drugs claiming to treat shell shock filled the newspaper advertising columns. Clements Tonic was recommended for 'brain fog' as well as 'loss of sleep, poor blood and shell shock'. Aspro tablets were advertised as treatments for shell shock, sleeplessness and depression, among other ailments, and these advertisements appeared in the NSW RSSILA newspaper as well as the broadsheet dailies.[67] Lambert's Invalid Port, available from hotels, was 'highly recommended' for 'broken nerves or shell shock'.[68]

While they may not have appeared injured, shell-shocked soldiers still being treated by a hospital were made visible because of their blue armbands. In June 1918, a regulation was introduced under the *War Precautions Act* requiring soldiers who were patients still under the care of a hospital, and still 'suffering wounds or sickness', to wear blue armbands. The regulation also specified that no one, whether a hotel keeper or member of the public, was allowed to supply these soldiers with liquor. Defence Minister George Pearce announced that the consumption of alcohol was 'retarding the recovery of soldiers in hospital', which was why they introduced the armband rule.[69] The Commonwealth Government had already increased its control over the sale of liquor through the War Precautions regulations, introducing powers for military authorities to be able to shut down hotels and pubs in towns and regions.[70]

According to the editors of the NSW RSSILA journal *The Soldier*, the armband rule was a good idea since it was, 'cruelty...giving liquor to a man whose nervous system has been shattered by wounds or shock'.[71] Church of England Reverend Hammond called the armband rule 'an insult' to soldiers, and argued that the closure of hotels would be a more effective solution.⁷² For members of the Liberty League, the armband regulation was an example of 'undue interference of puritanical extremists'.⁷³ The Liberty League was an organisation based in Victoria in 1918 and early 1919, led by returned soldier Captain George Burkett, who was also on the executive committee of the Victorian branch of the RSSILA. He campaigned against any restrictions on sporting matches and alcohol consumption and condemned the 'wowsers' and 'bigots' who were a threat to the freedom of returned heroes.⁷⁴ Burkett was interviewed in 1917, in his role as a recruiting officer, and his opinion on soldiers and drinking was this:

> The man who goes to the dogs at the front, would do the same at home. At the front he hasn't time to think of liquor. He imbibes patriotism at every step.⁷⁵

Some men were prosecuted for failure to comply with the blue armband rule, or for supplying armband wearers with alcohol, though it seemed to attract the attention of police only if there was violence involved. For instance, in Sydney in November 1918, returned soldier Hugh McGuire, wearing a blue armband, was convicted of assaulting a woman at Central Station. The victim did not know her assailant, who was under the influence of alcohol. He followed her from one platform to another, finally grabbing her around the neck, nearly choking her and trying to push her in front of the train. McGuire said at his court hearing that he had no memory of the event and was sorry for his actions. Like so many returned soldiers who came before the courts for violent offences, McGuire was treated leniently; he was given a fine of £5 and returned to Randwick Hospital.⁷⁶

The links between drinking and violent behaviour among returned soldiers was another aspect of wartime and postwar society that has been erased from today's celebration of the legend of Anzac. But it was considered a big problem at the time, and in January 1918 a Senate Select Committee was appointed to investigate the issue of soldiers and excessive alcohol consumption. Hearings were held in capital cities across Australia, and the chairman of the committee was Nationalist Senator for Victoria Lieutenant Colonel William Bolton. He was also, at the time, national president of the RSSILA. Bolton and his fellow committee members focused their questioning on prohibition measures and ways to restrict the sale and consumption of alcohol, but they elicited a variety of responses from the mostly male and mostly military witnesses.[77]

Brigadier General Robert Williams told the inquiry that venereal disease was a 'much wider and bigger issue than the drink question', since it incapacitated about four per cent of the soldiers of the AIF at the time.[78] Sergeant McKenzie of the Victorian RSSILA said that when soldiers came back from overseas it was 'only natural' that they 'will have a spree'. McKenzie considered that for the shell-shocked soldier, beer 'seldom harms them', but that cheap spirits were the 'fire water' that 'drives them almost mad'.[79] Dr Frederic Bird had served as a medic at Gallipoli and in Egypt, and he also testified to the terrible effects of cheap or illegal liquor. He considered that young Australian soldiers were 'temperate' drinkers compared to their older comrades who had been born overseas. Dr Bird did not advocate prohibition, but regarded the three main poisons – in order – as 'syphilis, alcohol and tobacco'.[80]

The criminalising of returned soldiers' public drunkenness was discussed by several witnesses at the Senate Select Committee inquiry. Matron Robinson from Tasmania talked about the practice of 'shouting' drinks for soldiers, and how this got many soldiers drunk when they otherwise would have had only one or two drinks. But she was hesitant to 'parade them before a doctor', she said, since then it would be a criminal offence recorded for the soldiers, some of whom had been away for three years. Matron Robinson's evidence showed concern for the men in her care, and she talked sympathetically of the shame some men felt when they 'made a great exhibition' of themselves. She also told the committee about the wives and sweethearts who called the hospital anxious about men who had not come home, when the Matron knew that the men had stayed at the pub.[81]

Senior Constable John Hallett of Melbourne considered that most soldiers were moderate drinkers, and that those 'rolling about the streets' drunk were a small percentage.[82] Mrs Seager (her first name was not supplied) of the Adelaide Cheer Up Hut for returned soldiers said the same thing, and that it was the 'sorry spectacles' who give 'the public the wrong idea about our soldiers'. She felt sorry for the 'poor wretches' who were chronic alcoholics 'quite silly with drink', and said that the other men at the Cheer Up Hut were sympathetic to them as well.[83] Rather than drinking being the main problem, Senior Constable Hallett said that there was 'a feeling of restlessness among nearly all the returned men'. Hallett told the committee that the police tended to deal leniently with drunken soldiers, and that the policy was to 'get them off the streets and out of the way'.[84]

While the Senate Select Committee did not find evidence of widespread alcoholism among soldiers, prohibition measures like the blue armband were introduced anyway. A significant context for the committee's investigation was that it was in early 1918, when the war in Europe was raging and most serving soldiers were still overseas. Most soldiers who survived the war were repatriated in 1919. While the NSW RSSILA cited a figure of 240,000 'sick or wounded', the official figure now quoted by the Australian War Memorial is just over 155,000 men 'wounded in action', including gassing and shell shock. There were a further 431,448 instances of sickness and non-battle injuries, though within this statistic there may have been more than one episode of illness experienced by individual soldiers.[85]

∞

Off the streets and into homes with their families was where most invalided soldiers ended up. While the newly established Repatriation Department provided pensions for veterans, as well as medical treatment and hospitals, the burden of caring for the returned wounded fell on families. Marina Larsson has shown how the 'caregiving labours' of families 'underpinned the Australian repatriation system'.[86] For many it was full-time nursing, usually by the soldiers' mother or wife. For instance, Mrs Hogan hand-fed her son with liquid meals, since his lower jaw had been shot away and he could not use his right arm.[87] The unpaid labour of caregivers was primarily women's work, and children, particularly eldest daughters, shared the workload along with family in extended kinship networks. Charities, volunteer groups and returned soldier organisations provided some welfare support in the absence of official recognition of the economic cost of caregiving for families of invalid soldiers.[88]

The history of family caregiving is yet another part of the returned soldiers' experience that is 'largely absent from...the Anzac legend'.[89] Larsson's research highlights the selflessness, love and resilience of families who cared for wounded men, and in return the soldiers' gratitude for this familial care. But some families could not withstand the strain of caring for invalids, or 'mental diggers' as some were called; marriages broke down, families separated and men were taken into institutional care.[90]

Also absent from the memorialisation of soldiers' sacrifice is the history of the increased incidence of men's violence towards women. In the last 30 years, there has been substantial published research about the social cost of World War I, its impact on the family and on people's personal lives. Back in 1990, Judith Allen analysed the links between the return of soldiers and the rise in divorce rates, and returned soldiers' assaults on and murder of women and girls. Allen's groundbreaking research remains the only comprehensive analysis of gendered violence by returned soldiers in the inter-war years. It covers the period from 1920 to 1939 in New South Wales, but Allen noted that surviving archival court records and transcripts from this period were 'uneven and incomplete'. Some of Allen's key findings, though, were that returned soldiers, who comprised a significant proportion of the adult male population, were 'overrepresented among interwar defendants charged with killing women'.[91]

Most of the single young men who returned from the war were married during the 1920s, and it was in the private sphere of the family and married life that signs of mental illness became apparent. As Allen wrote,

> The interpersonal brunt both of the First World War and of the inadequacies of public provision for this population of disturbed young men fell disproportionately on Australian women. Women's bodies and minds absorbed much of the shock, pain and craziness unleashed by the war experience.[92]

The story told through the divorce and criminal courts was that police were less likely to charge men with crimes against the person, such as assault or sex offences. Killing of wives by estranged husbands 'became typical, indeed the norm' over the course of the 1920s, and Allen found in her analysis of court records that 'ex-servicemen also used murder instead of divorce'.[93] There was a rise in violence against women by returned soldiers who were not intimate partners, and the defence of shell shock as a mitigating factor in the perpetration of a serious crime such as murder usually meant that death sentences for these convicted men were commuted. And this change in judicial behaviour towards returned soldiers expanded into a general leniency shown by the courts towards all men charged with killing women. In the meantime, rates for maintenance orders sought by deserted wives increased, and more women were willing to leave abusive husbands. While the rate of divorce was extremely low, partly because it was difficult for women to prove all the requirements for divorce and because it was an expensive exercise, women comprised the majority of petitioners for divorce.

In terms of the sexual assault of women in the years after the war, the same trends in relation to the police responses to the killing of women were apparent. There was a steep decline in the rate of charges brought by the police for rape and indecent assault, and a decline in conviction rates. What increased over this time were higher court trials for sexual assaults of girls between the ages of eleven and fifteen, offences that came under the categories of 'carnal knowledge' (rape) and 'indecent assault'. Most defendants were men in their thirties.[94] Allen warned that patterns of court prosecutions were 'unlikely to reflect "real" trends in sex offences taking place'.[95] Instead, they reflected policing practices, which in turn were shaped by judicial decisions and public debates. It seemed from many of the case studies analysed by Allen that regardless of the evidence of men terrorising and assaulting women, juries believed defence arguments about immoral women and unfaithful wives.

The changes in relationships between men and women in Australia in the period after the war is a story beyond the scope of this book. Allen wrote that despite the 'grim picture' presented in crime statistics, there was 'significant renegotiation' of gender roles in the interwar period, driven in part by women's agency and refusal to be mistreated.[96] But the crime statistics about offences against women illustrated trends in judicial and community responses to returned soldiers' violence generally. Violence by returned soldiers in the form of riots is the topic at the centre of this book, and in the story so far – to November 1918 – very few soldiers who engaged in riotous behaviour and assault were arrested. As Senior Constable Hallett testified in 1918, police treated publicly drunk soldiers leniently, and this policing practice appeared to extend to other types of offending.

Leniency in the courts was also a feature of the response to violence by returned soldiers, and not just violence towards women. In Sydney in March 1920, returned soldiers William Blackburn and George Cook were charged with murder, accused of using a gun and razors to kill their adult male victim. Both returned soldiers were drunk at the time of the attack, and the prosecution argued that the victim had not provoked the soldiers in any way. Nevertheless, the juries reduced the charges to manslaughter before finding both men guilty. Blackburn was sentenced to seven years in jail and Cook to twelve years. In summing up, Justice Wade warned the returned men that if they had been civilians they would have received the maximum penalty.[97] For murder, which in 1920 was a 'capital' crime, the punishment was execution. But His Honour said,

> I recognise fully than your war service produced a certain condition of mind which possibly calls for sympathy and lenient treatment. You went away and risked your lives at the front. Your duty was to kill, and amid the horrors of war you may have become hardened, with a callousness and indifference to the value of human life by daily association with death. In a sense, your crimes may be described as war products. When our soldiers return to us they must make an effort to conform to the rules and conditions of civil life…

And he concluded,

> If this reckless use of firearms and other deadly weapons is allowed to continue we shall sink into a condition, if not of civil war, at all events of savagery…I cannot close my eyes to the fact that during the present sittings of this Court there have been three capital charges against returned soldiers all presenting the same feature of a deadly weapon being used with little or no provocation.[98]

The judge's words expressed what many people would have experienced as the unsettling disjuncture between accepted ideas about war and soldierly action, and the reality of a postwar world in which returned soldier violence was sometimes savage and murderous. There appeared to be consensus over the peacetime implications of the words 'He died for his Country', and soldiers' sacrifice was recognised as noble and something for which the civilian society was grateful.

But broken-down defenders of the nation had no place in the dominant structure of the celebration of soldiers' sacrifice. Angry and damaged returned soldiers could be frightening and dangerous. The triumphant commemoration of loss and of the birth of the nation was a powerful combination which worked against any acknowledgement that maybe the sacrifice was too great and that its only meaning was a generation of damaged men. Beneath the surface of celebration, there were rumblings of resentment and rage from the soldiers who came home. The riots involving returned soldiers got bigger and more threatening when all the soldiers returned in 1919.

4

When The Boys Came Home: Riots in Fremantle and Melbourne, 1919

Nearly forty per cent of the Australian male population between the ages of eighteen and forty-four enlisted in the First AIF, and over 330,000 men served overseas. The Australian Army Nursing Service was only open to single women, and 2,229 nurses served overseas between 1915 and 1919. Close to 60,000 soldiers lost their lives at the warfront and more than 155,000 were wounded in action. Invalided soldiers had been returning to Australia from 1915, and by the end of 1918, approximately 100,600 had returned to Australia. When the war ended in November 1918, there were 167,000 soldiers and 1,000 nurses still overseas. Homeward migration reached its peak in mid-1919 and nearly all the surviving soldiers of the AIF had come home by December 1919.[1] These soldiers and nurses returned to a very different country to the one they had left.

In Eric Leed's economy of sacrifice, the citizen-soldier temporarily replaced self-interest with the communal interest of the nation. This exchange of roles was 'understood within the language of sacrifice'. Soldiers who returned held a blood debt over the society for which they fought and suffered, and for which their comrades had died. The way this debt was paid by civilian society was through recompense to ex-soldiers, giving them heroic status and financial rewards for their sacrifice.[2] The ideal functioning of this economy was the process by which citizen-soldiers, whose exchange of roles meant removal from society into a world of fear, violence and death, were able to return to being civilians in a peaceful world.

Recompense for returned soldiers was a consistent theme in the pages of the NSW RSSILA magazine *The Soldier*. These soldier spokesmen were impatient for practical repayment for their sacrifice, and did not hesitate to use images from the celebratory pantheon of the Anzac to attack perceived hypocrisy on the part of stay-at-home civilians. An RSSILA editor claimed that soldier's pensions were 'earned by a returned soldier who spilt his blood for it', and warned 'ye patriots that waved flags…but wait!'[3] Soldiers were entirely justified in '*demanding* and *securing* [their emphasis]…the redemption of all the promises made to them'.[4]

The Returned Sailors' and Soldiers' Labor League (RSSLL) in Queensland expressed the same demands. Soldiers had been promised 'undying gratitude', and could rightly expect that gratitude would be expressed in better wages and conditions when they returned from the war, but it was not.[5] The message from returned soldiers' groups was that the consequences of the economy of sacrifice were being ignored, in both material and moral terms, by the civilians who stayed at home.

Prices had risen dramatically during the war, nearly doubling for essential goods like food and clothing, and wages had not kept pace, so wage earners suffered. Public anger over business owners 'profiteering' – making high profits from lucrative wartime government contracts or wartime shortages of goods – was widespread.[6] Soldiers returned to a labour market where the national unemployment rate was estimated at 6.6 per cent in 1919.[7] Employment preference for returned soldiers was promoted by the RSSILA as a central platform of repatriation policy. While the Nationalist government was able to implement this within the Commonwealth public service, preference for soldiers was not a feature of the system of arbitrated awards governing the employment of most workers. Federal legislation stated that an employer could not penalise an employee for enlisting in the armed forces – by, for instance, giving their job to someone else and not re-employing the soldier after the war – but this was difficult to enforce.[8]

A lot of soldiers returned to membership of their unions and did not support any overturning of hard-won employment preference for unionists. Labor returned soldier groups such as the Returned Sailors' and Soldiers' Labor League (RSSLL) in Queensland argued that soldiers' interests lay with the union movement. They stated the returned soldier should realise that, when he takes off his uniform and falls back into the ranks of the workers, his only hope...is in becoming an active member of his union and striving for the establishment of a new economic system.[9]

The year 1919 was one of widespread industrial unrest in Australia, with a total of 6.3 million strike days and nearly £4 million in wages foregone because of industrial action.[10] These figures have not been matched since, even during the industrial unrest of the 1970s.[11] The biggest strike in 1919 was by the Seamen's Union, which shut down wharves across the country from May through to August.[12] They were supported by the Waterside Workers' Federation, the union for the dockworkers who loaded and unloaded the cargo and who were known at the time as 'lumpers'. These strikes affected every coastal capital city, holding up essential supplies such as food and coal.

∞

Before the Seamen's Union strike began on 9 May, the ship the *Dimboola* arrived at the port at Fremantle in Western Australia in April 1919. It was quarantined because there had been an outbreak of influenza among the passengers. The dockworkers, members of the Lumpers' Union, refused to unload its cargo until the quarantine period was finished. Men who had been used as strike breakers in the Great Strike of 1917 (also called the General Strike) had registered themselves as the National Waterside Workers Union. During the 1917 General Strike, these strike breakers were known either as 'loyalist' workers or 'scabs', depending on who was talking. In April 1919, they sought to unload the *Dimboola*'s cargo in defiance of the quarantine ban. Because the members of the Lumpers' Union refused to unload the *Dimboola*, they were then denied all other work on the wharves and were effectively locked out of employment by the wharf managers and ship owners. The employers used the labour of the Nationalist or 'loyalist' lumpers instead.

There were demonstrations and rallies at the wharves in Fremantle throughout April 1919. The unionists had public support as well, and on 14 April a large meeting of citizens at Fremantle Town Hall passed a resolution expressing their 'gratitude' to the dockworkers for refusing to unload the *Dimboola*.[13] A week later, on 23 April, an even larger Town Hall meeting passed a resolution that

> Fremantle citizens commend the action of the Fremantle Lumpers' Union in refusing to unload the plague-infected ship *Dimboola* and deprecates the action of the Government and ship owners in refusing to allow these men to handle any cargo on the wharf.[14]

Without income for several weeks, the union lumpers and their families were facing hardship, and families were going without food. At a demonstration in support of the lumpers, on 25 April, local businesses either promised or handed out donations of food to the union leaders for distribution to the women and children who were 'suffering considerably' on account of the dispute.[15] Meanwhile, the Western Australian Government of Hal Colebatch had brought all available police from regional areas to Fremantle.[16]

In late April 1919, the marches and demonstrations at Fremantle became bigger, involving thousands of unionists and their supporters. Returned soldiers in the marches were always mentioned in the press reports, and union leader Alex McCallum said the Lumpers' Union had more returned soldier members than the entire membership of the Nationalist Waterside Workers' Union. The ship owners accused returned soldier unionists of taking a 'leading part in driving the Nationalists off the wharf'.[17] The *Dimboola* remained quarantined, despite efforts to get Nationalist workers to unload the ship.

On the morning of Sunday 4 May, there were rumours that the ship owners were bringing strike breakers or 'blacklegs' from Perth down the Swan River by vessel to unload the *Dimboola*. The passengers on the launch were in fact the Premier and a group of employers and 'volunteers', others of whom had come to Fremantle in motor cars. When the launch passed under the North Fremantle bridge, it was pelted with rocks by unionists on the bridge. Police were sent to keep the next bridge downstream, the Railway Bridge, clear of protesters, but the small force of police armed with bayonets was overwhelmed by the crowd. The launch was again pelted with rocks.

The crowd moved on to the wharves and was met by cordons of armed police. Carloads of employers had been allowed through the police blockade, but a union deputation headed by the president of the Lumpers' Union, Bill Renton, was stopped. Hundreds of men confronted armed police at the wharves. They could see employers and other volunteers erecting barricades near 'C' shed, which was on the western end of the wharf. Eyewitness accounts showed that the first injuries occurred when the police bayoneted a dockworker named Edward Brown. Renton, at the front of the crowd, called out to police to let them pass to retrieve the injured man, but the police armed with rifles and bayonets refused. The crowd started hurling rocks at the police. The men retreated when they ran out of stones to throw, and then the police started throwing the stones back into the crowd.[18]

A report circulated that the man bayoneted by police was a returned soldier, and this had the effect of enraging the many returned soldier unionists in a crowd that was already 'terribly inflamed', according to the union account. Another rumour was that the returned soldier had been killed. By this time the crowd included a lot of women, who were hurling rocks at the police. One woman shouted at police that she had 'children at home who were starving because her husband could not get work'.[19]

The Police Commissioner told the Premier, who was at the wharves, having come by launch down the river that morning, that the force of 150 police could not hold back the crowd. Many of the police were injured. Premier Colebatch said the Commissioner told him

> that the police could not hold the wharf much longer without firing point blank at the crowd, which must have meant considerable bloodshed. As this was the last thing the Government had any desire to occasion, I at once informed Mr. McCallum that he could tell the men that no further attempt would then be made to continue work.[20]

A local Justice of the Peace, Bryan Brook, read the *Riot Act*, and Inspector Sellinger of the Fremantle police held a meeting with union leader Alex McCallum and local Labor politician Ben Jones. McCallum argued that if the ship owners would remove the volunteers from the wharves, then he would try and ensure there was no more violence.

McCallum persuaded the crowds at the wharves and along the railway bridge to retreat, and to meet that afternoon at the Fremantle Esplanade to decide on a plan of action.[21]

In this riot, there were many casualties. In addition to the man who was bayoneted by police, most of the seriously injured unionists suffered head wounds, including union leader Bill Renton, who was surrounded by police and hit with stones and a baton. Dockworker Thomas Edwards, who came to Renton's aid, was also hit on the head by police with a baton, and he later died from his injuries. In addition to Edwards, there were six men in the unionist crowd who received either head injuries or broken bones. There were also twenty-six police who were injured, mostly with cuts to the head or face and bruises, with two constables reported as being in a 'serious' condition.[22] The police, even though they were armed, had to retreat several times under volleys of stones. The disparity in injuries between those in the unionist crowd, armed only with stones and road metal, and the police, armed with bayonets and batons, indicated that the police were outnumbered.

Amid the riot, the troopship *Khyber* sailed into Fremantle harbour, carrying about 1,500 returned soldiers. The president of the South Fremantle branch of the Returned Soldiers' Association (RSA), Mick Donnes, told the crowd that afternoon that the soldiers on board the ship had been signalled by the RSA onshore, giving them news of the day's events. Donnes said that the returned soldiers on the troopship were with the unionists. The troopers' reply from the *Khyber* was, 'When we get ashore we will be with you in this fight.'[23]

In the afternoon, at the rally organised at the Fremantle Esplanade, less than a kilometre from the wharves, the speakers included union leader Fred Baglin, who had been injured in the riot. Baglin told the crowd that the government had sought that morning to take possession of the wharves but had not succeeded. Now the unionists were going to take possession, and they were not going to 'be ruled by a few decrepit shipowners'.[24] Baglin was at the head of the procession which was led by groups of men, with uniformed returned soldiers in each group. Then followed a crowd of about 360 men, not in uniform, and eighty women. When they arrived at the O'Connor Memorial at the eastern end of the wharves, Baglin addressed the crowd: 'Returned soldiers and returned soldiers only, pick up the barricades and throw them into the sea – let no one else interfere.'[25] According to one newspaper report,

> The returned soldiers, followed by a number of others, left the ranks, and ran to the barricades. They picked them up, carried them to the wharf edge and threw them into the river. As each one went over a cheer was given.[26]

With the barricades gone, the men then attacked the pick-up bureau, the building where lumpers went each day to be assigned work on the wharves. They destroyed this building, then dispersed from the wharves, though a large meeting of returned soldiers gathered around the O'Connor Memorial. They were addressed by South Fremantle RSA president Mick Donnes, along with returned soldier A. H. (Frank) Panton, who was president of the Australian Labor Federation in Perth and chairman of the wharf disputes committee. Donnes addressed the crowd first, and said that civilians were welcome to listen but that the vote on the resolution would be taken by soldiers only. Here is a report of Donnes' speech:

> That morning Prussian militarism had broken out in their own country. (Hoots) One of their comrades had been bayoneted while pushing his way through to get bread and butter for his starving family. Returning home from the war and coming to the wharf to work, he was locked out by the 'Win-the-war' Government. As vice-president of the RSA executive, and president of the South Fremantle branch he drew attention to the fact that one of their comrades had been bayoneted…They had seen a mob of men come to barricade the wharf for the employers. Were the returned soldiers prepared to stick together and fight this matter out? (Cheers and shouts of 'Yes')…The names of policemen had been given to him as those who had bayoneted their comrade and they were going to carry the matter to the bitter end…He was sure the people would stand by the returned soldier in this fight and he wanted it realised that, this was not their fight alone but the fight of every unionist in the State.[27]

Frank Panton was the next speaker and told the crowd that it was 'probably the first time that returned soldiers had seen a little bloodshed since making the world safe for democracy'. Panton urged an end to violence, but repeated Donnes' claims that as returned soldiers and unionists, they were 'fighting the same vested interest' they had fought against before the war. He told the crowd to 'leave the police out of it' and that they were only doing what 'the master class told them to do'. Panton's comments on the police drew hoots and cries of 'dirty dogs' from the returned soldiers in the crowd.[28] Panton also challenged the executive of the RSA:

> The RSA was in the position that it had to avenge the blood of one of its members. If the RSA with its reactionary officers in the executive, was not prepared to do it then the rest of them would come out and do it themselves…The returned soldiers were the men with practical experience, and a bullet or a bayonet would not stop them.[29]

Then a resolution was voted on and carried unanimously: 'We, as returned soldiers, are prepared to defend the rights of the people against the tyranny of the present Government and to avenge the blood of a wounded comrade.'[30]

The disputes committee, with Frank Panton seated in the middle next to an injured Bill Renton, from *The Fremantle Wharf Crisis of 1919*. National Library of Australia.

At a meeting later that day in Perth city, nearly 20 kilometres from Fremantle, Panton told the crowd of about 2,000 people that two returned soldiers had been bayoneted by police that morning, and he reiterated the threat that

> returned soldiers have made up their minds that if the Government is going to fight with loaded rifles and bayonets they will do the same. And I send this challenge to the RSA. If it is organised for the benefit of returned soldiers, now is its time. If it does not meet tomorrow night and carry a resolution in favour of sticking to the working class returned soldiers, we will form another soldiers' organisation. Today I helped to bind up the wounds of a man who fought alongside me in France, and I am going through with this fight, now it has started.[31]

At another meeting in Fremantle on the Sunday evening, returned soldier and Federal MHR Edwin Corboy told the crowd he would rather have been wounded on the wharf fighting for his fellow workers than have received wounds in France (Corboy was wounded twice in the trenches before being discharged in 1917).[32] Returned soldiers,

A portrait of Edwin Corboy from when he was an MP in the Western Australian Parliament from 1921 to 1933. Photo courtesy of the Legislative Assembly of Western Australia.

estimated to number between 300 and 400 men, gathered again at a meeting at the Fremantle Trades Hall on Monday morning and passed a resolution expressing their 'alarm and disgust' at the government's use of armed force on the wharves, and pledged to resist such action.[33]

By Monday 5 May 1919, the union leaders were declaring victory, since the Nationalist lumpers decided to leave the wharves entirely. The Lumpers' Union had the support of fellow unionists. Secretary of the Social Democratic League in Western Australia, Percy Trainer, reported that typographers in Perth threatened to strike if the newspapers did not print a 'fair report' of what was being called Fremantle's 'Bloody Sunday'.[34] But hostilities continued, and on Monday afternoon it was reported that a crowd of about 400 men, mostly returned soldiers, had done the rounds of the barber shops, hotels and restaurants in Fremantle, asking that proprietors refuse to serve the police. The proprietors complied.[35] Waitresses at several restaurants in Fremantle refused to serve police customers.[36]

On late Monday afternoon, police were attacked just off High Street in Fremantle. Returned soldiers prevented some of the police from sitting down for a meal at a café, and this sparked the violence.[37] The situation quickly escalated, and police were forced by the crowd to retreat to a churchyard. Police reinforcements arrived and shots were fired as the crowd attacked the police with pieces of iron railing ripped from the church fence. The police drew their revolvers and further shots were fired, injuring one young man. But as with the riots on the wharves the day before, even armed police were no match for so many angry men. Six constables were hurt with cuts and abrasions, and as they retreated to the relative safety of the police station, another shot was fired from the crowd.[38] The incident prompted union leader Bill Renton to appeal to 'returned soldiers particularly to leave the police alone.'[39]

Over the course of a few days, it became known that the lumper who was bayoneted by police on the day of the riots, Edward Brown, was not a returned soldier. Thomas Edwards, whose skull had been fractured by a blow from a policeman's baton, was not a returned soldier either. Edwards died from his wounds on 7 May, three days after the riots, leaving behind a wife and three children. There was a large rally at a theatre in Fremantle on 8 May, where a citizens' resolution declared that 'Tom Edwards...was done to death on the Fremantle wharf while fighting for the liberty of his comrades'.[40] As a mark of respect on the day of Edwards' funeral on 9 May, members of the Railway and Tramways Union stopped work for three minutes from 3 pm, and this happened in Perth, Fremantle and Kalgoorlie. Unionists across metropolitan Perth also stopped work for three minutes. Edwards' funeral procession attracted a crowd of over 5,000 people, and his casket was led by Bill Renton and other unionists of the disputes committee. The Fremantle Band played a funeral march, and all shops and businesses along the route to the cemetery were closed.[41]

On Sunday 11 May, a week after the wharf riots, there was a 'monster meeting' at the Fremantle Esplanade to celebrate the union victory, and speakers including the leader of the Labor opposition, Philip Collier. He commended Edwards as the 'comrade who had laid down his life' and would serve as an inspiration 'for generations'.[42] On 12 May, the Nationalist lumpers told Premier Colebatch that 'in the public interest' and for the sake of industrial peace they would leave the wharves entirely. Work resumed on the wharves and the quarantine period for the *Dimboola* had expired, so union dockworkers started unloading the cargo.[43] Mick Sawtell, then a One Big Union organiser based in Western Australia, declared that 'the revolution has

The beginning of Tom Edwards' funeral procession, from *The Fremantle Wharf Crisis of 1919*. National Library of Australia.

started in Australia, strange that it should be in conservative Fremantle.' Sawtell suggested that the workers were so fired up that if Fremantle was declared 'a Soviet of the Australian Socialist Republic, the workers would stand behind them.'[44]

For returned soldiers in Perth and Fremantle, the conflict intensified after the riots, and at a large meeting on the night of Monday 6 May, at a theatre in the city, the press reported that 'pandemonium reigned'. There were two opposing groups at the Returned Soldiers' Association meeting, and initially they had planned to gather at two different venues. There were about 400 men already seated in the Palais de Danse theatre, and then another group of about 600 returned soldiers (another report was that it was 700), led by a pipers' band, came into the theatre. Before a chairman for the meeting had been elected, there were fist fights among the men in the crowd. Colonel Pope was elected chairman and J. Butler tried to put a motion calling for 'law and order'. There were interjections and disorder throughout the hour-long meeting, and the 'law and order' resolution was never passed. Butler tried to put another resolution in support of employment preference for returned soldiers, but that was never passed either.

There was a lot of shouting, and RSA members Panton, Corboy and Donnes sought to calm the crowd and 'appealed for some semblance of order'. Member of the House of Representatives Corboy put the motion that 'this meeting of returned soldiers strongly supports the action of returned soldier lumpers at Fremantle'.[45] This was followed by a 'tumult of applause'. When RSA executive committee member Heppingstone tried to talk about being faced with a choice between 'law and order or Bolshevism', he was booed at and counted out. Then groups of men, Colonel Pope, Heppingstone and most of the members of the RSA executive left the hall. Mick Donnes was elected the new chairman of the meeting. Although the departing RSA members turned the lights out and left the hall in semi-darkness, the meeting continued and the motion in support of the lumpers was passed. It ended with cheers for the Fremantle lumpers and 'groans for the Nationalists'.[46]

RSA branch president Donnes later said that 'the big people' in Perth had their plans upset because of the Monday night meeting. Donnes suggested that they expected the soldiers to support the Nationalist cause, but the 700 returned soldiers he had brought with him from Fremantle all supported the unionists. He condemned an RSA executive meeting that voted for a resolution in favour of employment preference for returned soldiers. Donnes was quoted as saying:

> If they talked about preference to the 1,400 soldiers who marched in procession in Perth after Monday night's meeting, they would get their heads knocked off. He denied that the returned soldier had been 'used' in the Fremantle trouble. Instead of this, the soldiers had said on the Sunday afternoon: 'No men in Fremantle will take the lead to the wharf except us. The barriers are going into the river and only returned men will throw them in'. It was alleged that the Trades Hall was utilising the returned soldiers wrongfully. This was not so. These men were members of unions affiliated with the Trades Hall. They were unionists, fighting for liberty and freedom.[47]

The action of returned soldiers during the Fremantle wharf dispute prompted Andrew Clementson ('Clem') of the Perth Trades Hall to declare that 'the returned soldiers have come across and the RSA is now in our hands'. He added that 'from now on the soldiers could be relied upon'. Clementson wrote that former executive members of the RSA had left the organisation and 'Heppingstone gets howled down and called a sooling bastard'.[48]

But a conservative, pro-Nationalist faction remained in power at the state executive level of the RSA, and at a meeting between East Perth and Fremantle RSA members in July 1919, they criticised the 'unsound methods' of the state executive. Members including Mick Donnes wanted a reorganisation of the RSA in Western Australia 'on a more democratic basis'.[49] At a local branch level, the RSA was working with the unions. Frank Rowe, the Lumpers' Union president, was at the RSA meeting along with R. B. Wright of the Australian Labor Federation (ALF), and they were part of a committee to help distribute RSA funds for 'special cases of distress' among the community because of the ongoing seamen's strike.[50]

In May 1919, a pamphlet directed at returning soldiers on troopships was found in some mail opened by the censor's office. The mail was a personal letter between two friends discussing the recent illness of a mutual friend, but the author Arnold Holmes was targeted by the censor because of his links with the Social Democratic League in Sydney. Military authorities had heard a rumour of a circular being sent to soldiers 'asking them not to fire in event of a revolution'.[51] They found a copy of the circular or pamphlet in Holmes' personal mail. This is an excerpt:

> SOLDIERS, HALT! READ, STUDY OR BE DAMNED!
> What would you do if a labour crisis arose and disturbances took place?... Soldier Unionists! Don't allow yourselves to be used as strike-breakers... Refuse to shoot down and bayonet your mates. Remember your real enemies are those who own the means whereby you live. Soldiers! You were told that the Great War was to end militarism and you know it has not...Organise into Groups; don't waste time cheering men to jail, but organise to own the workshops.[52]

The pamphlet was probably produced by the Social Democratic League or one of similar anti-capitalist organisations active at the time. The authors called on soldiers to help 'overthrow the capitalist system, the system that breeds slums and mansions...the system that makes wars possible'.

The censor released the letter with the comment that it would 'probably alienate' returned soldiers with its expressions of 'Bolshevism... which the returned soldier has set his face against resolutely'[53] Nevertheless, military authorities started distributing 'loyalist' pamphlets on troopships in an effort to counteract the anti-capitalist message.[54] A report to the Prime Minister was that 'disloyalist' propaganda literature was being taken on board troopships when they docked at Albany, south of Perth.[55]

The authors of the 'disloyal' pamphlet were well organised, apparently managing to avoid the censor and get copies across the country from Sydney to meet the troopships when they first landed in Western Australia. Either that, or groups in Perth were producing similar pamphlets there. There is no archival evidence to suggest whether returned soldiers like Mick Donnes and Frank Panton helped to get the anti-capitalist pamphlets onto troopships at Fremantle. Regardless, they publicly said they would fight on the side of the unionists of Western

Australia, and were prepared to meet the government with 'loaded rifles and bayonets' to defend workers' rights if they had to.

∞

It was not only rank-and-file returned soldiers in Western Australia who promoted an anti-capitalist message. In July 1919, Victoria Cross winner Hugo Throssell – described as 'a scion of the Tory Throssell family' (his father George had been Premier of Western Australia) – was scheduled to deliver a speech at the Peace Day reception in his hometown of Northam, in the Western Australian wheatbelt. Throssell was a hero; he had been awarded the VC for bravery as a second lieutenant in the battle for Kaiakij Aghala (Hill 60) at Gallipoli in August 1915. He stayed on the battlefield despite being severely wounded, holding the trench with his men against Turkish bomb attacks. Throssell fought again on the frontline in Gaza and in 1917 was promoted to captain.[56]

Studio portrait of Captain Hugo Vivian Hope Throssell VC, 10th Australian Light Horse. Courtesy of the Army Museum of Western Australia

To the audience in Northam in July 1919, Captain Throssell VC declared that the war had made him a man, and that the war had also made him a socialist. Throssell said his experience

> made me think and inquire what are the causes of wars. And my thinking and reading have led me to the conclusion that we never shall be free of wars under a system of production for profit, with its consequent over production, periodic crises, unemployment and the struggle for markets. I am convinced that only the reorganisation of society on the basis of production for use and for the wellbeing of the community as a whole, can give any assurance of a permanent peace. I want to work for peace because I know and have seen the horror of war.[57]

Throssell's speech was described as a 'bombshell', and in one report, 'terror was visibly observable on the faces of the Tories and warmongers' in the audience.[58] Hugo Throssell and his wife, the award-winning writer Katharine Susannah Prichard, were supporters of the new Bolshevik government in Russia. The celebrity couple were popular speakers around Perth. At a rally opposing the Allied incursions into Russia after the Bolshevik Revolution, Throssell was such a star orator that when he rose to speak 'the enthusiasm of the audience rose to concert pitch'. He told the crowd that workers should 'have nothing to do with the sending of men, munitions, or money' to fight the new Bolshevik government.[59] Prichard, who was a founding member of the Communist Party in Australia in 1920, later said she believed it was because of her political stance that her husband Hugo lost his role on the Returned Soldiers' Land Settlement Board.[60]

In a tragic postscript, during the Depression and with mounting debts, Throssell tried to sell his VC medal, but the highest bid he got for it was ten shillings.[61] On 18 November 1933 Throssell shot himself. The note he left said that he could not sleep, and that, 'I feel my old war head. It's going phut, and that's no good for anyone concerned.'[62]

A scrapbook kept by Hugo Throssell VC is now held at the State Library of Western Australia. In among the programmes for boxing events and performances by the Northam Dramatic Society is a copy of an image by official war photographer Captain Frank Hurley.[63] One of Hurley's composite images overlaying a number of negatives, it shows

Australian infantry troops moving forward over a denuded landscape after the battle of Zonnebeke in 1917. Rather than the postcards from the time of army camps or troops posing in front of the Egyptian pyramids, it was this depiction of the battlefield that Throssell kept in his scrapbook.

F. Hurely, 'An episode after the battle of Zonnebeke, Australian infantry move forward...', *Exhibition of war photographs taken by Capt. F. Hurley, August 1917 –August 1918*. State Library of New South Wales.

While Captain Throssell VC was delivering his bombshell speech in Northam, Western Australia, on Peace Day in July 1919, on the other side of the continent in Melbourne a riot was developing. During four days of violent clashes between soldiers, civilians and police on the city streets of Melbourne, one returned soldier was shot and killed. Hundreds were injured during the violence, which culminated with returned soldier rioters invading the Premier's offices in the Treasury building, ransacking the rooms and injuring the Premier. Official war historian C. E. W. Bean dismissed these riots as 'an unworthy demonstration in Victoria by some of the inevitable riff-raff' and that they were 'quickly disclaimed' at a huge meeting of soldiers led by former generals.[64] But the 'riff-raff' were in fact at least 3,000 returned soldiers, and there was a lot more to the story than Bean's one-sentence summary.

The Melbourne riots in July 1919 occurred within the context of the nationwide seamen's strike. During the winter of 1919, Victoria had been heavily hit by the shortage of imported coal, which shut down transport and other industries. By mid-June 1919, in addition to striking seamen and wharf labourers, 32,500 workers had been stood down and power was being rationed by the government.[65] As well, there were 77,000 soldiers who had returned to Victoria in 1919, which was far more than the rate of homeward migration during the years of the war. At a committee meeting of the Victorian branch of the RSSILA in June 1919, Captain George Burkett claimed that about sixty per cent of returned soldiers were unemployed (he was referring to Melbourne). He criticised the Repatriation Department for being ineffective in their efforts to secure employment for these men. Burkett described the situation as 'acute' and proposed a mass meeting of unemployed returned soldiers.[66] A cartoon in the Victorian RSSILA branch magazine, *The Bayonet*, showed a couple cowering from the spectre of unemployment.

From *The Bayonet*, 25 July 1919. National Library of Australia.

Burkett himself was a professional soldier, having served in the South African War (1899–1902) and joining the Australian Light Horse Regiment on his return. He had been among the early enlistments in October 1914 in the 10th Light Horse Regiment in the AIF.[67] As mentioned in Chapter 3, in 1918 Captain Burkett established the Liberty League in Victoria. They described themselves as 'a loyal organisation of men and women [committed to] keeping Australia free from the shackles of extremists'. On every League pamphlet, the words 'non-sectarian' were printed in bold type, and although Protestant loyalists were never identified by name, the regular references to 'wowsers' and 'bigots' made it obvious that Protestants were the targets of the Liberty League's criticism. The Strength of Empire Movement, an unmistakably Protestant organisation of Imperial patriots which was openly anti-Catholic, was condemned by the Liberty League as a camouflage for the enemy in the 'battle of democracy' being waged to save Australia from 'legislative and social slavery'.[68] The Liberty League did not last beyond the early months of 1919, but it appeared reasonably well-funded while in operation.

'Liberty League Founder', Captain G. A. Burkett, *Richmond Guardian*, 27 July 1918. State Library of Victoria.

In Melbourne, like in Fremantle, returned soldiers were part of the wharf dispute, and the story was very similar. The pro-Nationalist factions within the senior executive of the RSSILA in Victoria opposed any alliances between returned soldiers and striking unionists. Yet some of the executive committee members, as well as many other returned soldiers who were unionists, were active in the industrial dispute. In Melbourne in May 1919, there were reports that returned soldiers had attacked 'loyalist' workers, men who in the 1917 General Strike had been strike breakers. At an RSSILA Victorian branch committee meeting on 20 May 1919, a member said he had seen a returned soldier throw a loyalist worker into the river and that other returned soldiers had assaulted loyalist workers. The soldiers were cheered and 'egged on' by the unionists watching. RSSILA branch president George Palmer said that the League would 'stand aloof' from the wharf dispute, and he had gone to the wharves to urge returned soldiers to 'steer clear of trouble'. Vice president George Roberts disagreed, and argued that 'as a considerable number of returned soldiers were unionists they had a right to help their fellow unionists'.[69] At a quarterly meeting of the Victorian RSSILA on 21 May, attended by over 150 returned soldiers, RSSILA member Fitzpatrick and Captain Burkett proposed the motion that the League 'express its sympathy with our brothers who are engaged on the wharves in their fight against broken promises and the unjust treatment that has been meted out to them.'[70] This was seconded by Roberts and the motion carried.

Roberts and Burkett had attended a meeting on the wharves on 19 May, and had joined with the unionists in protesting against employment preference for the loyalist workers. Police were there expecting conflict, and Burkett and Roberts were reported to have said that returned soldiers would 'assist in every peaceable way' to address the grievances of the striking wharf workers.[71] Roberts was censured at the next RSSILA committee meeting, and told that he could not speak at wharf meetings 'in his official capacity' as a committee member in the RSSILA. Roberts conceded but queried why he needed the RSSILA's permission to speak at demonstrations at the wharves.[72]

Meanwhile, returned soldiers employed on the wharves were taking their own action. On 21 May 1919, loyalist wharf workers were attacked and beaten up, with the secretary of the Loyalists' Association saved from serious injury by the arrival of mounted police. In one section of the wharf, all loyalists were forced to leave when returned soldiers refused to work with them unloading cargo.[73]

Two months later, in July 1919, authorities were preparing public festivities to celebrate the Treaty of Versailles. Signed at the Palace of Versailles near Paris, the treaty marked an end to the war and what was supposed to be a lasting peace between Germany and the Allied forces. In Australia, the date was set for Saturday 19 July 1919 to be a public holiday called Peace Day. In Melbourne, all sailors and soldiers were called by the state commandant, Brigadier General Brand, to march in the procession. The Victorian RSSILA magazine *The Bayonet* published details of where men from the navy and the army, and all the units, companies and brigades within them, should assemble. Nurses were not included in *The Bayonet*'s call out.[74] The procession through the streets of central Melbourne started at around 10 am and finished at the Town Hall.

On Saturday afternoon, crowds congregated in Swanston Street, where a band played from the balcony of the Town Hall and an area of the street was cleared for dancing. The government had decided to shut the hotels for the day, but nevertheless there was 'much liquor in evidence' among the crowd. Returned soldiers were reported to be insulted by the closing of the hotels, and they forced entry into some places. They tore down the bunting decorations in the theatres when they 'pushed their way in' without paying. Some theatres decided to close and barricade their doors, but at the one theatre that remained open there was a rush of returned soldiers who occupied the seats. They declared they were 'on a Kitchener show' (Field Marshal Kitchener was the face on the famous British army recruitment poster). Groups of soldiers and civilians stole motor cars and offered 'joy rides'. The windows of a gun store were smashed and about £80 worth of revolvers were stolen. Some trams were overturned.[75]

Despite damage to buildings and theft of private property, the Police Commissioner, Sir George Steward, was quoted as saying the afternoon's events were 'horseplay' and not that serious.[76] Before his appointment as Police Commissioner in Victoria in 1919, Sir George Steward (he was knighted in 1918), who was quoted in the introduction to this book, was Private Secretary to the Governor-General. In a similar pattern to the Adelaide riots of November 1918, returned soldiers who demanded free entry into theatres seemed to be doing this because they felt they had the right to do so. Civilians owed them. Returned soldiers could even steal people's cars and break into closed hotels, apparently without any penalty.

The crowds stayed in the city through to the evening, and men and women were still dancing to the military band playing on the Town Hall balcony. Police arrested two returned soldiers in uniform, and they were locked up in the police depot at the Town Hall. In the police reports, the returned soldiers were calling out 'come on Diggers we will take to the bloody bastards' as they threw stones at the police. Soldiers shouted 'this is our day we fought for the likes of you buggers'.[77] A crowd led by soldiers demanded the release of the prisoners, and they tried to break their way into the depot at the Town Hall. Someone in the crowd fired a revolver, and police and mounted troopers went into the crowd on Swanston Street with batons drawn. People fought back with stones and broken bottles, and the police 'used their batons unsparingly'. People rushed to vestibules for safety, but in the crush store windows caved in.[78]

During the fighting around Swanston Street and the Town Hall, police arrested a further eleven men. Most arrests were of young men from working-class suburbs near the city. One woman and twenty-one men, including five soldiers, were treated for injuries at the hospital, along with five policemen. The injuries of those among the crowd were mostly cuts to the head, or fractures and bruises caused by being kicked by troopers' horses. The Town Hall was converted into an emergency medical centre, and over 100 people were treated there for injuries. The violence did not end until after midnight.[79]

A returned soldier witness said that at about 10.30 pm he saw a crowd of several hundred people being chased from Swanston Street towards Bourke Street by a force of mounted troopers, with foot police hitting them with batons from the footpath as they sought to flee. Returned soldier James Joseph Fawcett, who was in uniform, said that he had tried to speak with a policeman wearing a returned soldiers' badge, who told him that he had better get out. Fawcett went to help a returned soldier who was on the ground, bleeding from a head wound, when Fawcett himself was knocked over by a troopers' horse and a policeman hit him across the back of the knees with his baton. Fawcett then fled.[80] Senior Constable John Scanlon was accused of saying to his police officers, 'Knock them Khaki bastards first then we can soon clear the others out.'[81] Another witness said he heard a mounted policeman yell at the crowd, 'Get some you bastards.'[82]

Returned soldier Albert Villinger testified that earlier in the evening, around 9 pm, he saw three young women who were trying to get out of the melee and onto the footpath. One woman was hit on the back of the neck with a baton by a mounted policeman. Villinger and several others went to the woman's aid, but Villinger was then hit by police with a baton. He sought out the policeman in charge, Senior Constable Scanlon, to report what he had just seen. Villinger said Scanlon replied, 'I do not believe you, you are like the rest of the soldiers here tonight trying to run the city, but by hell we will see that you don't.'[83] Villinger, who was in uniform, tried to persuade Scanlon to hear his complaint, but instead Scanlon grabbed Villinger by the arm and he was taken to the Town Hall. Villinger admitted that he 'lost his head' and said to Scanlon, 'I went away to fight for bloody mongrels like you, you are worse than the bloody Germans.'[84]

The Victorian branch of the RSSILA made formal complaints to the Police Commissioner about eight instances of 'harsh and unnecessarily severe action on the part of the police' that night.[85] Senior Constable Scanlon was charged with 'using offensive words…injurious to the public peace and welfare and unbecoming a member of the force.' He was investigated and later exonerated on his own evidence and that of three of his officers.[86] In the aftermath of the riots, the Victorian branch of the RSSILA argued that the violence was part of a pattern of 'harsh treatment' by police towards returned soldiers since the end of the war. The editors of *The Bayonet* said that if their complaints against the police had been acknowledged eight months before, 'there would have been no riot in the city'.[87]

We do not have the records to show what happened the morning after the Saturday night riot, and who planned the next attack. But it was not spontaneous. On Sunday night, 20 July 1919, in Melbourne, a crowd of about seventy soldiers and sailors, most of them not yet demobilised and carrying their ensigns, marched down St Kilda Road to the Victoria Barracks. According to police reports, the sailors and soldiers were trying to break through the barrack gates. When one man yelled, 'we are going to get to the armoury', he was cheered by the others. A brawl started between them and the military sentries, and mounted police were called. A sailor aimed his revolver at a sentry, and shots were fired. A returned soldier, James O'Connor, was shot in the chest and died a few hours later. Military and civilian police pursued the soldiers and sailors who had fled into the Domain to hide among the bushes. Police drove them out with batons, and mounted troopers along with military sentries with fixed bayonets surrounded the undergrowth to catch men when they were forced out. In the dark, there were fights between the soldiers and sailors and their pursuers, and men were badly injured. The police arrested ten men, mostly sailors, and handed them over to military sentries for punishment.[88]

On Monday 21 July, returned soldiers vented their anger towards police. In the morning, there was a meeting at the RSSILA rooms in Swanston Street, attended by the state commandant Brigadier General Brand. Men at the meeting described how, on Saturday night, they were hit by police troopers and they witnessed mounted police attacking women and civilians as well as soldiers. A resolution was passed demanding the government 'dismiss or otherwise remove to a safe distance' the police who they claimed were responsible for the 'indiscriminate batoning of loyal citizens'.[89] RSSILA committee member Caldwell said that soldiers were 'greatly incensed' at the death of Private O'Connor. They resolved to send a deputation to the Police Commissioner Sir George Steward.[90] They told the Commissioner that 'it would be unsafe for Senior Constable Scanlon to be on duty in the city'. The Commissioner responded by removing Scanlon from street duty and confining him to the Russell Street police station, pending an investigation.[91]

There was a much bigger meeting on Monday afternoon at the Athenaeum Hall, with the building full of returned soldiers and thousands more soldiers and civilians on the street outside. Captain Burkett said that the police who were employed to maintain law and order had been 'the first to smash it up'. RSSILA committee member George Roberts told the audience that the Police Commissioner should ban his officers from using batons against returned soldiers. He also claimed that the police singled out returned soldiers 'whenever there was a disturbance'. To loud cheers, Roberts asserted that if the government did not recognise the authority of the RSSILA, then he would 'shoulder a rifle and blow the blighters off the face of the earth – if constitutional means fail.'[92]

The crowd of returned soldiers at the Athenaeum Hall were waiting for Police Commissioner Steward to arrive, but he never did. So, led by Captain Burkett, soldiers from the RSSILA meeting then marched to the Commissioner's offices in Russell Street. In the pages of *The Bayonet*, this was described as 'orderly', but after the events of the previous two days the sight of returned soldiers en masse converging on city streets, jeering at police along the way, probably made a lot of observers nervous. Commissioner Steward tried to address the crowd from a lorry outside his offices, but he was drowned out by the yelling. Burkett tried to quiet the crowd and asked for the Commissioner to be given the chance to speak, but the Commissioner did not help matters by asking that the soldiers 'stand behind him and maintain good order'. While Steward gave an assurance that Constable Scanlon would be investigated, he said he had no authority to release those returned soldiers and others arrested on the previous days. This was a central demand by the crowd of returned soldiers on Russell Street, which some estimates put at 3,000 men.[93]

The crowd then moved on to the Premier's offices at the Treasury Building. A Cabinet meeting was underway, and at least 200 returned soldiers charged up the stairways to the Cabinet room. Captain Burkett of the RSSILA was again the spokesman, and he reiterated the returned soldiers' demands: sack Constable Scanlon, release the prisoners and remit any fines imposed on them. The men in the crowd shouted demands at Premier Harry Lawson and asked that he either answer 'yes' or 'no'. Lawson then went out onto a balcony overlooking the street and told the increasingly angry crowd that to uphold 'law and order' he could not simply let the prisoners out of jail, but would release them on bail after conferring with a deputation from the returned soldiers. Someone yelled back, 'There is no bail in the army!' Men in the crowd made signals to those on the balcony to throw the Premier over the balustrade.[94]

The situation exploded and hundreds more men swarmed through the building, smashing furniture and ransacking the desks. The

Ministers barricaded themselves in the Cabinet room. In trying to get off the balcony to the safety of the Cabinet room, the Premier was hit in the head with an inkstand, drawing blood. Then the police arrived, and with baton charges dispersed the crowd in the street outside. Again, returned soldiers fled to the gardens. There were further riots in the evening outside the Russell Street police station, where a huge crowd gathered. The estimates varied widely, from a conservative 3,000 reported in *The Argus* to between 8,000 and 10,000 reported in *The Daily Telegraph*. The police reported 'several thousands' who marched on the city watchhouse, 'making loud menaces, and stones were being thrown'.[95] Speakers – possibly Burkett and Roberts, though they were not named in the reports – told the crowd that the 'only alternative to negotiation was a challenge to the police', and that the crowd should stand their ground. Again, returned soldiers and other men fought with police, using bricks and stones as weapons. The protesters were finally dispersed by mounted troopers wielding batons.[96]

On the afternoon of Tuesday 22 July, between 500 and 700 soldiers, sailors and returned soldiers marched through the city in the funeral cortege for Private O'Connor, the returned soldier who had been shot on the night of 20 July. O'Connor's coffin was draped in the Union Jack and transported on a gun carriage. Without any official military honours (there were no senior Generals or Members of Parliament attending), O'Connor's burial was made into that of a soldier fallen on the battlefield, not simply a victim in a riot. Soldiers and sailors in uniform and waving the Union Jack headed the procession north along St Kilda Road and Swanston Street, and behind them a group of about 500 returned soldiers marched. Thousands of people lined the route and traffic was stopped in the city.[97] Some newspapers cited O'Connor's autopsy and its information that the bullet that killed him was not from a military rifle but from a revolver, suggesting O'Connor was shot by someone in the crowd. But this made no difference to the anger directed by returned soldiers towards the police and military authorities.

After the burial of O'Connor at Coburg Cemetery, several hundred returned soldiers came back into the city. As they marched along, they shouted, 'Shall we be pushed off the streets? – No!', and 'Are we downhearted? – No!' The line 'Are we downhearted? No!' was from a wartime song that was composed as part of the ongoing recruiting campaign in Britain. The returned men stopped outside the RSSILA rooms in Swanston Street, 'for dismissal' according to one report, then fights broke out with the police. Mounted troopers, who had been patrolling the streets over the previous days, arrived and as before, used batons against those in the crowd. The men responded by throwing stones and bottles. After about an hour of street fighting, the crowd dispersed when mounted troopers charged into a group in Flinders Street.[98]

At a Victorian branch committee meeting at the RSSILA rooms that night, the 'disturbances', as they were being called, were the main topic of discussion. One committee member wanted to ban all further mass meetings of returned soldiers to avoid further trouble. Captain George Burkett argued against this, and said that the police were to blame and that soldiers would not have acted the way they did if it were not for the behaviour of the police. Burkett gave more examples from that day of police charging into the crowd with their batons. Burkett had suggested to Police Commissioner Steward that he withdraw the mounted police from the city. Burkett, who seemed to be one of the main people in the RSSILA liaising with senior government and police authorities, announced that there would be a mass meeting of returned soldiers with Brigadier General Brand the following morning, Wednesday 23 July.[99]

The riots in Melbourne filled the pages of daily newspapers around Australia, and from the start, conservative newspapers such as *The Argus* tried to deny the role of returned soldiers. In the reports, they claimed that most of the men involved in the violence were 'street-loafer types', or 'cold-footed eligibles'. The reports of RSSILA meetings showed that they too were concerned to distance the diggers from the violence, and at the Tuesday night committee meeting, the chairman vice president Mullins said it was the 'hoodlum element' who were responsible for the raid on the Premier's office.[100] But the reality was impossible to ignore – returned soldiers and those still enlisted fought with police, tried to break into the armoury at the Victoria Barracks and ransacked the offices of the government.

On 23 July, the 'dinkum Digger' was expunged from the picture. At a meeting of around 4,000 returned soldiers in the Melbourne Domain, the crowd was addressed by not just one or two, but six Brigadier Generals, including the Victorian state commandant, Brigadier General Charles Brand. The returned soldiers were spoken to as if they had been led astray or were simply not there amid the violence of the previous four days. Yet it was highly likely that many of them – thousands according to the reports – had been involved at some stage in the riots. The soldiers were told by their former commanding officers to keep away from 'the hoodlums and revolutionists who were using them' to win back the good name of the AIF and the RSSILA. They were warned against the 'disloyal element within their ranks'. The crowd of men was urged by the speakers to depend on their leaders and trust that the government was doing its best to assist returned men, and furthermore that the police over the previous days had only been doing their job. Brigadier General Harold Grimwade, who in civilian life was a wealthy Toorak businessman, warned that 'a small section' of returned soldiers were 'led astray by elements in the community who were no good for this country'.[101]

There were regular outbursts of cheers for the speakers, and the returned soldier audience unanimously endorsed a resolution for them to uphold law and order. The meeting finished with cheers for the King and the generals, and the audience sang 'God Save the King'. There was no longer any doubt that 'the returned men as a body were wholeheartedly behind the authorities in the preservation of law

'Great soldiers' meeting at the domain', *The Argus*, 24 July 1919. National Library of Australia.

and order'.[102] It seemed a bizarre and delusional denial of the violent reality of previous days, a fallacy reinforced by conservative newspaper headlines such as 'Upholding the law'. But while a crowd of well-dressed men listening attentively to their former leaders might seem in diametric opposition with returned soldiers fighting with police on the streets, some themes connected the 23 July meeting and the soldiers' actions of the previous days.

Over four days of riot the returned soldier spokesmen were always confident that what they were doing was legitimate. In most cases, they were careful to present a soldierly demeanour in the preludes to violence. During the attack on Victoria Barracks, the sailors carried naval ensigns as if they were on an official parade – even though their intention was to break into the armoury. On Monday 21 July, after O'Connor was shot, returned soldiers had their meetings, resolutions and deputations at the RSSILA rooms at Swanston Street or in a hall, but always in a formal setting. They never wavered from the conviction that their complaints against the police were valid. In addition to defending their digger comrades, they were defending women and 'loyal citizens' from police brutality and unjust imprisonment.

Returned soldiers represented their march to the Police Commissioner's offices, followed by the march to the Premier's offices, as 'orderly'. No civilian institution of authority was considered too august to be made to recognise returned soldiers' grievances. The invasion of the Treasury buildings was not an accidental outcome of a riotous crowd gone crazy. Returned soldiers that afternoon had progressively worked their way up the civilian hierarchy in an attempt to have their demands addressed. They consistently asserted they had a right to do so. Spokesmen from the RSSILA condemned the Premier's injury, but it was no coincidence that the returned soldier crowd was at its largest and angriest outside the Premier's offices.

Returned soldiers' retribution for perceived victimisation by police, was in a combustible mix with a deep sense of grievance returned soldiers expressed. Whatever it was they felt entitled to – respect or jobs or free entry to the theatre – the connecting theme was that civilian society owed them. And society was not paying up. Soldiers were not going to be pushed off the streets, and the insults hurled during the violence, as well as the resolutions formally passed at RSSILA meetings, showed an assumption on the part of returned soldiers that they had a particular authority. They had a mandate to act as a group. They were, as returned soldier George Roberts told the crowd, a rifle-carrying alternative to 'constitutional means'. They could issue demands to the Police Commissioner and the Premier because of who they were and what they had sacrificed, what they had endured 'for the likes of you buggers'.

The Melbourne returned soldier riots were among the most serious riots in Australia's twentieth-century history. The clear expression of returned soldier fury and resentment through violence undermined the whole celebratory edifice of the Anzac identity, and threatened to fracture the neatly resolved equation of meaningful sacrifice. The conservative press, anti-Labor politicians and most of the ex-officer executive of the RSSILA threw their considerable resources behind the denial of the reality of returned soldier riots. Angry and purposeful soldiers were reinvented as hooligans or as men too easily duped. In the RSSILA magazine *The Bayonet*, the editors depicted the hoodlum story in a cartoon, with a dummy returned soldier made of straw.

THE CROOK'S PARADICE.

From *The Bayonet*, 15 August 1919. National Library of Australia.

The Bayonet also stuck with the script that it was not a digger who threw the inkstand that injured the Premier.

Yet in the same issue, *The Bayonet* editors could not hide the fact that returned soldiers had rioted. They referred to similar soldier riots in Canada, Great Britain and other parts of Australia, and offered their explanation. In this excerpt, the reference to the 'Band of Hope' was to a Christian organisation whose members pledged abstinence from alcohol:

> There must be at least 80,000 returned men in Melbourne. Is it at all surprising, even if it were true, that a thousand of them got slightly out of hand? One could take 80,000 members of the Band of Hope and dump them in a city during a time of wild celebration and unfortunate strikes, and it is odds on that there would be at least a thousand unruly members…the soldier has come back more or less influenced…with the idea that the world is for the man who will take it. He is, and will be for many months, the same unruly fighting devil that upset the Hun, with this difference. He is no longer living a life organised by a system, and no longer possesses recognised leaders. Unless he is really repatriated and getting a far better deal…the soldier throughout the world will be restless.[103]

In the aftermath of the riots, George Roberts was forced to resign from the RSSILA Victorian executive committee, but he was back attending meetings a couple of months later. He did not show any remorse for his statements during the riots, and insisted that he had the support of some RSSILA sub-branches. Captain Burkett stayed on the committee, despite moves to censure him as well.[104] Senior Constable Scanlon kept his job and was cleared of the charges against him. At a meeting of about 260 RSSILA members on 20 August 1919, there were several motions put for further investigation into the events of 19 to 22 July, but in the end the only motion passed was that 'the whole matter regarding the Peace riots be dropped.'[105]

Marilyn Lake has argued that conservative factions within the RSSILA used the Melbourne riots as an opportunity to reinforce their control over the organisation. Martin Crotty suggested that, in part, the League needed returned soldier violence so they could present

From *The Bayonet*, 25 July 1919. National Library of Australia.

themselves to government as the best organisation to help restrain such violence and seek further concessions for their members.[106] In his first meeting with Prime Minister Hughes in September 1919, the recently elected federal president of the RSSILA, Gilbert Dyett, argued that the League's work included 'preventing any disturbances on the part of soldiers'. Dyett reminded Hughes that the League should be granted the entitlements they were seeking, since 'we have been able to suppress those almost revolutionary tendencies which were recently displayed'.[107]

Dyett is usually lauded as a skilful negotiator who secured increases in repatriation pensions and benefits for returned soldiers. He remained federal president of the RSSILA for decades, until 1946.[108] But in claiming to be able to prevent 'disturbances', Dyett was overestimating the power and role of the League in returned soldier riots. Once the violence started, the trajectory of the riot was out of the League's control. This was apparent both in Melbourne in July 1919 and in the equally tumultuous riots in Brisbane in March 1919, addressed in the next chapter.

The spectre of returned soldiers as a menace to public order during the period of demobilisation sat uncomfortably beside the legend of the Anzac hero. When returned soldiers asserted their allegiance with striking unionists at Fremantle in May, and drew direct parallels between fighting for democracy in France and fighting for liberty against the police on the wharves, the conservative press and Nationalist-supporting RSSILA Western Australian executive declared that soldiers were being duped and 'used' by Trades Hall. When returned soldiers fought against police and military sentries in Melbourne, the same coalition of conservative commentators declared that it was not returned soldiers who rioted but 'hoodlums' and 'disloyalists', and men who were not even soldiers. This strategy of denial recalled the pronouncements of the RSSILA president Captain Blackburn in South Australia in the wake of the Adelaide riots in November 1918. He said, and his words were repeated across many newspaper reports, that 'returned soldiers never would lead riots.' But they did, and other cities and towns in Australia in 1919 continued to be rocked by returned soldiers smashing up law and order.

5

The Internal Enemy and Diggers 'Uphold the Law'

> Australia's awakening: Our manhood by their valour in the war arena opened the eyes of the World to the fact that Australia is a Nation worthy of respect, and one destined to rank with the foremost. Australia has thrown aside her swaddling clothes and made her debut – a Nation with a future – and a reputation to live up to.[1]

The style and vision of this text suggests a loyalist rally or an Anzac Day speech. In fact, the words were from a Dunlop Rubber Company advertisement, for tyres, tennis balls and plumbing supplies. Australia as a 'nation' had a range of uses, and in 1919, the idea that the war was the catalyst for Australia's awakening, and that the future was a challenge to consolidate and amplify the new national status, was ubiquitous.

Returned soldiers had a special role to play in nation building, a role that they assigned to themselves and one that was reiterated across speeches and newspaper editorials. But this nation-building role conflicted with the reality of returned soldiers rioting in the streets and destroying public and private property. Conservative RSSILA executives, politicians and newspaper editors had to do some semantic gymnastics to exonerate the 'real' digger from returned soldiers' collective violence. The returned soldiers who listened to their former commanding officers after the Melbourne riots were warned against the 'disloyal element within their ranks'. Disloyalty was always there as a menace to the nation.

This was another uneasy juxtaposition: the promise of a wonderful future for the young nation and yet the constant threat of internal enemies. For the returned soldiers who attacked those they considered 'disloyal' in the riots in 1918, the perceived internal enemy took on a variety of forms depending on the context. The expressions of disloyalty were myriad, and for loyalists during the war, anyone who promoted peace by negotiation or opposed Australia's involvement in the war was disloyal. They were also disrespectful to the memory of soldiers' sacrifice. Similarly, those who opposed conscription were disrespecting soldiers' sacrifice, even though by 1917, nearly half of the enlisted soldiers at the frontline and on troopships opposed conscription as well. This information was withheld from the public under regulations of the *War Precautions Act*. Any worker who supported union militancy, strikes for better wages and a change to the economic system was a member of the IWW or a Bolshevik, and therefore disloyal. Any man who did not remove his hat for the singing of 'God Save the King' was disloyal. Anyone who did not honour the Union Jack over the Australian flag was disloyal. According to the members of the Queensland Protestant League in July 1918, 'all loyal citizens have time for one flag and one flag only – the grand old Union Jack.'[2] All these varieties of disloyalty coalesced around the assertion that they were an insult to soldiers' sacrifice, and to the memory of dead mates.

Loyalty to the nation was welded to loyalty to the Empire, the King and the Union Jack. This was enforced through legislation which criminalised certain alleged disloyal behaviours. For the Nationalist government in power federally and in all but one state (Queensland), these disloyal actions and allegiances often aligned with the actions and allegiances of their political opponents in the Labor Party and the union movement. Under the *War Precautions Act*, regulation 27A(a) specifically prohibited encouragement of 'disloyalty or hostility to the British Empire or to the cause of the British Empire in the present war'. As shown in the Domain riots in 1918, this law was used against anti-war activists and opponents of conscription. Support for republicanism, whether Irish or Australian, was prohibited under regulation 27A(b), which made it an offence to advocate 'dismemberment' of the British Empire. Under regulation 27B, it was illegal to display the Sinn Fein flag or that of any 'association who are disaffected to the British Empire'. Regulation 27BB, introduced in September 1918, gave the minister power to prohibit the use of any flags he wanted to prohibit.[3]

The 'Red Flag' was an internationally recognised symbol of socialism. The Brisbane *Worker* described it as 'the flag of humanity in general...the emblem of Socialism...a symbol of Brotherhood and Freedom'.[4] It was also an expression of opposition to a capitalist war, and, according to the *Worker*, this 'enraged' and 'infuriated' Labor's enemies because it was 'the beginning of the end of war-mongering... the Red Flag indicates a class-consciousness and an understanding of the birth of the New Order at hand.'[5]

In the riots in Broken Hill in November 1918, loyalist returned soldiers pulled down the Red Flags flying outside a residence near the centre of town. Before then, in August 1918, Acting Prime Minister William Watt had complained about the Red Flag flying above the Melbourne Trades Hall and about proposals for the Brisbane Trades Hall to do the same. Watt argued that the flying of the Red Flag was 'a direct challenge to the patriotic sentiment of a large majority of Australian citizens'.[6]

In early August 1918, newly enlisted soldiers from a recruiting march arrived in Darra, just outside Brisbane, and were told by locals that a Red Flag had been flying over the partially built workers' hall there. The soldiers ransacked the building, found a piece of red cloth, tore it up and tried to burn it, and placed the Union Jack on a makeshift flagpole. Then they sang the national anthem 'God save the King'.[7] Around the same time, questions were asked in the Queensland Legislative Assembly about a group of returned soldiers who marched on the Brisbane Trades Hall with the intention of pulling down the Red Flag flying there. But after discussion with unionists at the Trades Hall, the soldiers were persuaded to pass a resolution commending the Trades Hall for flying the Red Flag.[8]

Under Regulation 27BB, the Defence Minister used his new powers to ban the flying of the Red Flag, and this prohibition was extensive. The minister banned the exhibition of 'any red flag on any building or on any land...or on any ship...or in any public place or in connection with any procession or demonstration'.[9] At the Brisbane Trades Hall on 1 October 1918, Military Intelligence officers ordered Trades Hall officials to remove the Red Flag. But Trades Hall secretary Thomas Finney told them that he could not find anyone in the building who would comply with the order. Finney made a point of paying some unnamed person ten shillings to remove the flag.[10]

The long reach of the *War Precautions Act* continued after the war was over, as did government censorship of personal communication and newspapers. On 30 November 1918, several weeks after the fighting had stopped on the Western Front, censors were instructed to 'scrutinise the Press carefully for indications of attempts to incite revolution, sedition, bolshevism, internal strife or advocacy of repudiation of war loans, and similar matter'.[11] Individuals' personal mail continued to be opened and examined by the censor's office through to at least September 1919. Communication generally was censored, and in addition to the many rules about what kind of public speech was prohibited, under the War Precautions regulations it was illegal to speak on the telephone in any language other than English.[12]

At the beginning of the war, legislation was enacted to enable the Commonwealth to intern Australian residents of enemy nationality. In 1914, this applied to Germans, Austrians and anyone from the Balkan regions and Central Europe then under Austro-Hungarian control. These groups included Croatians, Slovenians, Slovakians, Bosnians, Czechs, Hungarians and people from parts of what is now Poland, Ukraine and Romania. Also interned were people from what was then the Ottoman Empire in Türkiye and in the Middle East, though European internees made up by far the majority. The definition of enemy aliens was expanded to cover naturalised residents from these countries, and successive amendments to the Act allowed for their property to be confiscated and their civil rights suspended.[13] Approximately 7,000 people were interned in camps around Australia during World War I, and these internees included naturalised British subjects originally from enemy nations.[14]

The original *War Precautions Act* was only valid for the duration of the war, but the decision to extend the Act was made at a Cabinet meeting on 23 October 1918.[15] In December 1918, the Federal Government passed a law extending the *War Precautions Act* until July 1919. All the regulations under the Act remained in force, including the regulations in relation to enemy aliens despite there being no actual war and therefore no wartime enemy.[16]

The continuation of the *War Precautions Act* after the end of the war was itself a source of protest, partly because of the biased way in which the Nationalist government used the Act against their political opponents. Also, the Act effectively suspended accepted civil rights of adult white males under British common law at the time. Regulations allowed, for instance, arrest without warrant on suspicion, rather than based on any alleged offence. Speaking freely in public was potentially dangerous and risked arrest. There were Military Intelligence and Commonwealth police spies at union rallies and other political gatherings whose sole task was to record what people said in case they could be prosecuted under the regulations. In Brisbane, at a rally to celebrate International May Day in 1918, staff from the censor's office attended because there were reports that speeches would be given in Russian, French, Greek, Finnish, Hebrew, Polish and German, ostensibly to try and evade the regulations about what could be said in public. The censor had tried to get the meeting banned, as he considered it would be 'practically an IWW meeting', and he hired translators as well as agents to take notes of the speeches.[17] The Commonwealth Government extended the *War Precautions Act* again in 1919, and it was not finally repealed until December 1920.[18] It enabled the Nationalist government of Billy Hughes and Nationalist state legislatures around the country to continue to police alleged disloyal behaviour, however they wanted to define it.

Australia in 1914 was not a multicultural society, and the White Australia policy was widely endorsed by non-Indigenous Australians. Writing in 1930, then history professor and later Sir William Hancock was not flattering about Australia's convict founders. They were 'transplanted British stock...of predominantly poor quality'. But Hancock considered that since around the 1830s, white Australia was populated with 'clean and vigorous' British stock.[19] While the exclusions of the *Immigration Restriction Act* of 1901 were primarily aimed at people of colour – Hancock called them 'black men and yellow men, the servile nations of the world' – some European groups such as Italians were also considered dubious. Hancock asserted that

Australians did not want to be like the United States with 'too many foreigners and hybrids' and its experimental 'melting-pot'. Australians were glad to stay 'ninety-eight per cent British'.[20]

Within this white community, German immigrants and their descendants in 1914 comprised the largest single immigrant group after those from the British Isles. Usually skilled workers and mostly Protestant, Germans were readily accepted into colonial society and as a group developed a collective reputation as hardworking and respectable citizens.[21] The identification of enemy aliens during World War I disrupted racial hierarchies within Australia at the time, with northern European immigrants such as Germans being demonised as the brutal 'Hun' and 'Bestial Bosche'. These caricatures were not at all recognisable with the German farmers or storekeepers that people would have known in their own communities. In another undermining of existing racist stereotypes, Greeks and Italians – southern Europeans who were the face of a less desirable 'melting pot' society – were allies in the war, with Greece changing from neutral to allied in 1917.

One of the outcomes of these disruptions was that self-appointed loyal nation builders rejected all ethnic, or 'racial' difference as it was then called, as alien. White Australia was asserted as an exclusively British Empire territory. Membership of the loyal nation was limited to those of British descent, which could include Scots and Irish as well as English so long as they pledged allegiance to Empire. All others were alien intruders, and this had a generative function in the proliferation of the types of disloyalty against which loyalists fought. Loyalists kept alive the threat of the alien internal enemy long after the actual enemies in the war had surrendered.

∞

The 'Red Flag' riots in Brisbane in March 1919 showed what an incendiary focus could be created when political protest and alien identity were combined into one disloyal target for loyalist action. In Brisbane in 1919, there was a small émigré Russian community, several of whom were active in the socialist and left-wing organisations in southeast Queensland at the time. The Russian Association was based in Brisbane, and a group of Russian socialists under the editorship of young Civa Rosenberg published the newspaper *Knowledge and Unity*. Civa's father Michael Rosenberg (also spelled Mikhail Rozenberg) was described in a police report as a 'dangerous extremist'. Her husband, Alexander Zuzenko, was the head of the Union of Russian Workers and also considered a radical.[22] Peter Simonov (often spelled Simonoff) was living in Brisbane when he was appointed consul general to Australia by the Bolshevik government in February 1918, although his appointment was never officially recognised by the Nationalist government. In September 1918, the military commandant in Queensland used section 17(c) of the *Aliens Restriction Order* to prohibit Simonoff from 'addressing or taking part in any meeting at which any subject in connection with the War is discussed'. Simonoff was arrested soon after for speaking at a meeting.[23]

The Russian community of a couple of hundred people lived in suburbs close to the city, in South Brisbane and Woolloongabba. They had a hall in Merivale Street, South Brisbane, where the Brisbane Convention Centre now stands. In November 1918, George Taylor (not the same as George Taylour, the Digger's orator) wrote on behalf of the members of the Russian Association to Premier Ryan protesting Simonoff's arrest. They also claimed that as 'peaceful citizens of Queensland' they were being harassed by people 'who call themselves the Loyalty League'. The members of the Russian Association protested that League members broke up their lawful meetings and called them 'enemy aliens', and that this was tolerated 'with the benevolent permission of the military authorities'.[24]

The Loyalty League were among a group of loyalist organisations in Queensland who claimed they represented 'all loyal Britishers'. They were formed in Brisbane in August 1918, and in addition to holding meetings at the Domain, they shared the rooms of the Queensland Protestant League. Also known as the Returned Soldiers' and Citizens' Loyalty League, the Loyalty League declared as their mission to 'assist the Empire in every way possible' and to 'crush' disloyalty. The League wrote to the military commandant in Brisbane in October 1918 warning of the danger of 'certain conspicuously disloyal persons... to be at large and allowed every possible freedom'. They wanted the Defence Department to 'order the exit from Brisbane' of these people, identified by Military Intelligence as returned soldiers Percy

Macdonald and Gunner Taylour, union organiser Eastcrabb and IWW organiser William Jackson.[25] The League also had obtained from Special Intelligence Bureau (SIB) officers a list of alleged disloyalists in Brisbane, which included twenty-eight members of the IWW and several members of the Russian Association. Also on the list were nine members of the Irish National Association, including a nun from the Sisters of Mercy and another woman resident at the All Hallows Convent in Brisbane.[26]

Labor Premier T. J. Ryan was not supportive of the League's tactics and referred to them as the 'so-called Loyalty League'. He condemned them for 'openly threatening the use of force to have their own way' and for 'advocating...mob rule' at a public meeting in November 1918. The Premier warned the 'prominent public men' who were associated with the League to behave more responsibly.[27]

But groups such as the Loyalty League had the support of not only officers at the SIB in Brisbane but the Queensland Police Commissioner as well. By early 1919, the Loyalty League joined in a coalition called the United Loyalist Executive (ULE), under the leadership of prominent surgeon and former AIF medic Dr Ernest Sandford Jackson. In a meeting with Police Commissioner Frederic Urquhart in February 1919, Sandford Jackson and representatives from the ULE told Urquhart that they 'would have 60 societies joined up'. They asked Urquhart if he wanted to 'take a hand in the business'. Urquhart wrote of the ULE:

> They wish to go pretty far – not only to uphold the constitution by peaceful means but to have a formidable striking force ready if required. If our organisation was ready these people would rally to it with enthusiasm.[28]

Urquhart wanted to share with the ULE representatives the Commonwealth government's secret plans for its own paramilitary defence force, comprised of regular police and special constables, but he refrained from revealing these plans.[29]

Commissioner Urquhart was already familiar with extra-legal and state-sanctioned violence, having been a sub-inspector in the notorious Native Mounted Police in Queensland in the 1880s in northwestern Queensland. He was commander of a Native Police detachment at Cloncurry and, according to historian Arthur Laurie, 'set out upon a campaign against the Kalkadoons'. Members of this First Nations community are now the recognised native title holders of nearly 38,000 square kilometres in northwestern Queensland. Urquhart led his Native Police troopers in several raids and massacres against Aboriginal people in the northwest in the 1880s before transferring to the regular Queensland Police Service in 1889.[30]

In early 1919, preparations for a paramilitary force to fight Bolshevism were discussed and approved at the highest level of government. In January 1919, a secret conference was held at Victoria Barracks in Melbourne, with the Chief of General Staff, Major General James Gordon Legge, and the commissioners of police in New South Wales, James Mitchell, and Victoria, William Davidson (who was acting in the role as Commissioner Sainsbury was suffering from the flu). The men had been appointed by the Minister for Defence, George Pearce, to consider 'the subject of Bolshevism'. They concluded that any 'revolutionary action' would be 'under the cover of an industrial dispute' and would be best dealt with by state police forces. The senior military and police representatives recommended to the Minister that

> Arrangements should be made quietly for the rapid increase of such Police Forces by the enrolment of additional and special constables, by preparation of lists of suitable citizens in every police district, and the provision of the necessary badges and equipment...as far as possible supplies of military arms and ammunition should be kept under adequate guard without attracting public attention.[31]

Legge, Mitchell and Davidson advised that Military Commandants should be ordered to start supplying police forces with 'military materials' (i.e. guns and ammunition) as requested by Police Commissioners to use 'in the event of any emergency'.[32] When Major General Legge suggested in a follow-up memo on 20 January 1919 that the special forces could be supplemented with 'small groups of picked men with MGs [machine guns]' and 'a few aeroplanes with improvised bombs', this too was forwarded by the Defence Minister for Cabinet's consideration. Cabinet, under Acting Prime Minister Watt, baulked at the idea of planes with improvised bombs, but adopted all the other plans put forward by Legge and the police chiefs.³³ Their recommendations were approved at a Cabinet meeting on 21 January 1919.³⁴

The then new Commonwealth Police Force (created in 1917) discovered that the military was supplying ammunition to 'loyal societies' in Brisbane in early 1919 in support of their 'preparations', though these were not identified. A report by Constable Foote of the Commonwealth police in February 1919 alerted his superiors, and he was told to get in contact with Captain Woods [sic] (his name was spelled Wood) of Military Intelligence. In his conversation with Wood, both referred to the loyal societies as the 'Grand Executive'. This possibly indicated a link to the anti-Catholic and anti-Semitic Masons and their 'Grand Lodge'. Wood said that much of the information about the 'Grand Executive' was coming from returned soldiers. Wood was not interested in Foote's report, and told the constable,

> Our work is only concerned with the disloyal associations. We do not worry ourselves about what the loyal societies are doing…If they form the society [Grand Executive] all the more power to them.³⁵

Constable Foote's superior Sergeant Short told his boss, the Commonwealth Police Commissioner, on 3 March 1919, that 'there seems little doubt however that some happening was immanent.'³⁶

A demonstration was scheduled for 23 March 1919 to protest the continuation of the *War Precautions Act*. The original plan had been to carry the banned Red Flag, but the Labor government in Queensland only permitted the march on the condition that they did not display the Red Flag. The Brisbane Industrial Council had been involved in the organisation of the protest march, but withdrew at the last minute because of the proposal by the demonstrators to fly the prohibited Red Flag. The Children's Peace Army, the Union of Russian Workers, members of the One Big Union Propaganda League, socialist activists and about twelve returned soldiers made up a crowd of approximately 300 people. *The Daily Standard* reported that 'quite a large percentage' in the crowd were Russians.

The demonstrators left the Trades Hall, which was then in Turbot Street near Central Station, flying Red Flags, and the men wore red ribbons on their lapels and sang 'The Red Flag'. Monty Miller, a veteran from the Eureka Stockade, marched with a red band on his hat. The march was led by Zuzenko and fellow Russian socialist Herman Bykoff. The few police who tried to halt the march were unsuccessful, and the demonstrators went on to hold a meeting in the Domain. The police reported that because of the large number of women and young girls at the head of the procession, they were hampered in their efforts to stop it, and the waving of the Red Flags by the protesters scared the horses that the mounted troopers were riding. Bykoff wrote that the marchers were 'brandishing sticks, parasols, hats and flags' and that 'the poor animals backed away in fright'.[37] Below is a photo of what was possibly part of the march through Brisbane's streets, although the provenance of the photo only gives the generic date of 1919.

That night there was the usual Sunday meeting at North Quay run by the One Big Union movement, this time protesting continued government censorship. *The Brisbane Courier* described the gathering as 'the same polyglot type of agitators', and the presence of 'foreigners' was emphasised even though the speakers were Labor politicians Senator Myles Ferricks and Queensland MLA Edgar Free. Returned soldiers attacked the meeting and threw the speaking platform into the Brisbane River. A police constable had apparently told the crowd of soldiers that 'fifty or sixty Russians', armed with guns, were at

'Procession of workers demonstrating in Brisbane, 1919'. John Oxley Library, State Library of Queensland.

the Russian Hall in South Brisbane ready to shoot. A small group of about sixteen returned soldiers headed over Victoria Bridge. The eyewitness account was slightly different. Bykoff recalled that he and the other Russians could see there was going to be trouble, as the returned soldiers at North Quay were shouting 'Let's go and smash the Union [Russian Workers' Union]! Death to the Bolsheviks!' So about ten Russian men ran over the Victoria Bridge to South Brisbane, and once they had barricaded themselves in the Russian Hall, 'a crowd of drunken hooligans appeared round the corner'.[38]

Shots were fired from within the Russian Workers' Hall in Merivale Street as the returned soldiers approached, though in Bykoff's account no one was sure where the gunshots came from. The few police on duty there persuaded the then unarmed soldiers to turn back to the city. Bykoff found it ironic that 'the police were obliged to play the part of mediators between the Union and the hooligans', and that to persuade the returned soldiers to turn back, the police gave them an 'exaggerated picture' of the numbers of Russians defending the building. In his report of the event, Sergeant Short of the Commonwealth police warned that 'counter demonstrations are likely and serious trouble is inevitable'. The Commonwealth police continued to receive 'rumours of trouble amongst returned men and the "Bolsheviks"'.[39]

With returned soldiers and other members of loyalist organisations around Brisbane secretly armed and ready for a fight, police warnings were realised. What followed the Red Flag procession was two days of serious riot led by returned soldiers. Many were injured, including Police Commissioner Urquhart, and there was extensive property damage in South Brisbane. It started with the Red Flag protestors being raided by police. On the morning of Monday 24 March, Military Intelligence officers, along with twelve military police, raided the Russian Association rooms, as well as homes of three members, including Zyzenko. The military police took away bags of literature and materials for printing.[40]

Reports from Military Intelligence to the Police Commissioner during the day of 24 March all indicated planned attacks by returned soldiers who were armed. Commissioner Urquhart wrote that intelligence agents who had been in contact with returned soldiers reported that they were 'resolute and determined to put down

Bolshevism in Brisbane for good and all'. His words suggested that Urquhart approved of the soldiers' extra-legal methods. The police also knew that a group of about forty returned soldiers armed with rifles 'obtained from civilian sources' intended to attack the Russian Association Hall in Merivale Street. That's why Urquhart himself went to South Brisbane to command the police forces there.[41]

In the evening after a rally of several thousand returned soldiers and civilians in the city, the crowd marched over the bridge to the Russian quarter in South Brisbane. Here they attacked the Russian Hall in Merivale Street along with three shops belonging to Russian businesses.[42] Herman Bykoff, who was there, recalled that everyone in the street was nervous and that they 'might be taken for bloody Russians and have their properties ransacked too'. He called it a pogrom. Bykoff described a mob of several thousand soldiers and 'solid citizens', but said they were outnumbered by the onlookers and 'seekers of sensation' who followed to watch the show. When the armed soldiers and citizens demanded that the police turn their bayonets on the Russian Hall, the police refused. So then

> the mob started pelting us with bottles, stones and bits of fencing timber, firing revolvers, and for greater effect letting off fireworks. The revolver shots, the thunder of stones on the roof, the sound of breaking windowpanes, the shouts and the clatter of hooves were terrifying to the weaker spirits. To them it all seemed like hell on earth. The women patriots exclaimed fearfully, 'Our poor boys suffered so much at the front, and here at home these blasted Bolsheviks can kill them!' And when they heard the crash of breaking glass they promptly added, 'Yes! That's the way! Kill the lot of them!' And after another crash, somebody said, 'Serves 'em right!'[43]

At Merivale Street, the armed crowd fought against police, who were armed with rifles and fixed bayonets. There were nineteen reported police casualties, including Police Commissioner Urquhart, who suffered a bayonet wound when he was accidentally stabbed by one of his own men. Police Magistrate Hewan Archdall was also injured by a bayonet when he was pushed back by the crowd. Several of the foot police suffered bullet wounds, and returned soldiers or others in the crowd shot three police horses. The number of casualties among the crowd was not reported. One of the foot constables recalled that there must have been hundreds of men stabbed with bayonets; he knew of six that he 'prodded' himself.[44]

After destroying the Russian Hall and other premises, the crowd moved back to North Quay to continue their rally, and returned soldiers addressed the crowd with statements like this: 'We have fought for this country and we intend to keep it clean. We are not going to have it ruled by these dirty greasy Russian Bolsheviks.' Then a returned major – probably Major Bolingbroke of the RSSILA – told the crowd that they would meet with the Premier the following day. The major said,

> We are not going to ask for anything. We are going to demand it and damned well see that we get it. Returned soldiers are going to run the show after this. They are not going to be dictated to by a lot of dirty Bolsheviks.[45]

'Cartoon representation of the Red Riot on Merivale Street, South Brisbane, 1919'. John Oxley Library, State Library of Queensland.

The violence continued the following day, Tuesday 25 March. In conservative newspapers like *The Brisbane Courier*, the threat to public safety was denied in headlines such as 'Exciting scenes' and 'Great loyalist demonstration'. Because the pro-Labor newspaper *The Daily Standard* reported on the riots as riots, with headlines like 'Riotous ex-soldiers' and 'Revolt against the law', the editors of the newspaper were targeted. *The Daily Standard* charged the returned soldiers with responsibility for 'one of the maddest and most disgraceful scenes ever witnessed in any part of Australia'. The editors called the soldiers 'vandals' and 'a mob' and said they were armed with a variety of weapons: bottles, sticks, knives and guns.[46]

The day the *Standard's* edition was published, the newspaper's offices were attacked by a crowd of returned soldiers and civilians. The crowd first attended a rally in the city addressed by leading members of the RSSILA. Then they headed to the *Standard's* building, where the crowd threw rocks and smashed windows, and tried to break through the police cordon protecting the front doors. Men in the crowd demanded that the *Standard's* editors apologise to the returned men and other loyalists. They claimed that the favourable reporting of Sunday's Red Flag demonstration along with the paper's account of the attack on the Russian rooms was an insult, and warned that if the editors did not publish an apology, 'God help the [Daily] *Standard*'.[47] There were also reports that the soldiers intended to attack the police headquarters in Roma Street, and to attack more Russian homes and premises, including the Russian Church, in Wolloongabba and South Brisbane.[48]

During these days of riot, the Special Intelligence Bureau (SIB) was in contact with returned soldiers. Captain Ainsworth of the SIB met a deputation of returned soldiers on 25 March, when he told them that the Queensland Government was 'sheltering behind the Commonwealth government' on the issue. On 28 March, Ainsworth met with Lieutenant Fisher, head of the Queensland branch of the RSSILA, who had been arrested for creating a disturbance in July 1918 and who was probably involved in the riots of 24 and 25 March 1919.[49] Senior members of the RSSILA were open about their role in the riots, and in a telegram to the Acting Prime Minister on 26 March, pledged themselves and their supporters to 'unity and action' in deporting Russian Bolsheviks. The RSSILA spokesmen condemned the

Queensland Government for its 'sympathetic attitude to the traitors' and declared that 'further lack of courage by our public men will surely provoke drastic action by returned soldiers'.[50]

Morton Pimentel of the Returned Soldiers' and Citizen's Political Federation (RSCPF) wrote from Melbourne accusing Queensland Acting Premier Edward Theodore of 'passiveness' in the face of 'Russian armed resistance'. Pimentel warned that if the Premier did not act, he would be 'swept aside and returned soldiers will do your duty for you'.[51] This went beyond the 'more than the men can stand' threats of RSSILA executives in 1918, and was manifest by extreme violence and clashes with police that brought the city of Brisbane to a standstill.

Acting Premier Theodore was furious and telegrammed Acting Prime Minister Watt claiming that the returned soldiers were being 'incited to disorder by certain persons and sections of the press'. Theodore demanded that the military authorities prevent soldiers from demonstrating and said that if it were not for the soldiers the police would be 'easily able to preserve order'.[52] Police Commissioner Urquhart, who only weeks earlier had been enthusiastic about the 'striking force' that the loyalists were able to command, was no longer an ally. On 25 March, a clearly worried Urquhart reported to the Queensland Home Secretary:

> The returned soldiers, with their attendant rabble, number many thousands, and without resorting to the most extreme methods...the Police Force here is too weak in a numerical strength to cope with the situation.[53]

On Wednesday 26 March, in the evening, there was a rally of about 18,000 people in the city, and speakers included Major Bolingbroke of the RSSILA. Major Taylor urged the crowd to 'do nothing rash or riotous', but this was followed by returned soldier Buchanan, who threatened that the insult made by *The Daily Standard* editors would be 'rammed down its throat'. He warned that the returned soldiers wanted to 'keep the *Standard* and Bolsheviks in their places'.[54] Torrential rains for several hours the following night put an end to large rallies in the city, and there were no further riots or battles with police.

But the rhetoric of the Bolshevik threat continued, even though government and intelligence agents knew that they were not a threat at all. Captain Ainsworth of the Brisbane SIB assessed that

> The Russians as an entity do not threaten the disruption of Australia from any point of view...They have no money, no influence...in supposing them to be sufficiently extreme to resort to armed force their numbers and cohesion are so ridiculous that they could do nothing.[55]

Only three returned soldiers were arrested during the days of riot in Brisbane. Police Magistrate Archdall, suffering from a groin injury after being accidentally bayoneted by one of his own police officers during the riot on 24 March, handed down jail terms to the socialists who had been arrested for participating in the 'Red Flag' demonstration on 23 March. Some of these men had been beaten up by returned soldiers and their loyalist supporters in the riot afterwards at North Quay. The three returned soldiers who were charged and convicted were required to pay small fines, while fifteen men who had joined the Red Flag demonstration were convicted of offences under the *War Precautions Act* and sentenced to jail terms of between one and seven months. Eight Russians, including Zuzenko, were also charged and deported.[56]

In scenes presaging the Melbourne rallies of thousands of returned soldiers after the riots there in July 1919, returned soldiers gathered in Brisbane at the Exhibition Ground on Sunday 6 April. They were well-behaved and orderly, and more than likely included the thousands of returned soldiers who had the week before participated in destroying property in South Brisbane and fighting armed battles with police. The RSSILA executives, including Major Bolingbroke who had made threatening speeches at the rallies before the riots, addressed the crowd. They called for men to volunteer for the 'army to fight disloyalty', a standing para-military force dedicated to 'upholding law and order'. The volunteer army would 'cleanse their country free of all disloyalty'. The enrolments in this army were already 2,000 men.[57]

There were reports that the Labor Volunteer Army was also recruiting and had about 320 men. They were taking enrolments at the Trades Hall and the offices of *The Daily Standard*, according to intelligence reports. But the Premier of Queensland and Police

Commissioner Urquhart denied any knowledge of this volunteer army.[58] The RSSILA army to fight disloyalty, on the other hand, received nationwide publicity and support from RSSILA branches and loyalist groups around the country.

The Red Flag march and the subsequent riots have been analysed in several publications by Raymond Evans. He located the riots in the context of ruling-class efforts to maintain their hegemony, with loyalist returned soldier violence an expression of xenophobic, anti-left hysteria deliberately fomented by a beleaguered ruling class in Queensland. This argument is substantiated, and the evidence shows that it was the military, directed by the conservative Nationalist Commonwealth government, who was supplying guns to loyalist groups in Brisbane. Every level of the police and military intelligence services knew this was happening.

But the violence got way out of control, and formerly pro-loyalist officers like Commissioner Urquhart were soon condemning 'returned soldiers, with their attendant rabble'. Also, it was a failure if the intention was to undermine wider working-class strength. The Labor government remained in power in Queensland until 1929. They were not a radical government, but in 1922 they abolished the upper house of Parliament, the Legislative Council. *The Daily Standard* continued publishing until 1936, reporting with enthusiasm throughout 1919 on socialist gains in Russia and Europe and making fun of whatever was the latest 'Tory bogey'. The paper *Knowledge and Unity* ceased publication for a few months after the riots, but was back in print in July 1919. The hardship for the families of the Russian deportees was severe and widely known, and the Labor Party and unions in New South Wales formally protested to the Federal Government in May 1919 for its 'cruel' treatment of these people.[59]

The political landscape in Queensland did not change substantially because of the Red Flag riots. What was consolidated was the idea that returned soldiers' collective violence was permissible in the name of loyalty to the nation, of 'cleansing' the loyal community. Over two days of lawlessness and destruction of property, returned soldiers were portrayed in the conservative press as defenders of the loyal nation against internal enemies, 'dirty Bolsheviks' according to the RSSILA spokesmen. Despite the reality that it was returned soldiers leading the riots, conservative newspapers around the country reported the events as the 'Bolshevik disturbances'. Just calling them riots was enough to provoke an angry and violent response from returned soldiers, as the editors and staff of *The Daily Standard* experienced.

There were the familiar exhortations to defend against 'insult' to soldiers, and that violence was an appropriate and soldierly reaction. But this was more than returned soldiers 'taking matters into their own hands'. They claimed that they were there to 'restore order', to do the job that the Queensland Government was failing to do to stop 'traitors'. Returned soldiers asserted that they had the authority to enforce their version of a loyal community. And with the same reality flip that was a feature of most of the riots that occurred in 1918 and 1919, returned soldiers were the saviours, even though it was returned soldiers who were the instigators of widespread public disorder and property destruction. Returned soldiers were not censured for their violence and lawlessness during the riots; out of the thousands of returned soldiers who were involved, only three were arrested. Instead, they were applauded. This representation of rioting soldiers as loyal defenders against internal enemies was completed a week after the riots with the formation by the Queensland RSSILA of an 'army to fight disloyalty'.

∽

The Queensland RSSILA executives were congratulated by RSSILA branches across the country for establishing their 'army to fight disloyalty'. One such message of support came from the Tasmanian branch of the RSSILA. They passed a resolution stating that the failure of government to stop

> seditious and disloyal…actions…may necessitate measures by loyal citizens to ensure the quelling of such actions that are a menace to civil peace and support the recent action of the Queensland branch.[60]

Returned soldiers and citizens who rioted against disloyalty knew they were not acting in isolation. In Launceston, returned soldiers were quoted as saying that 'with the example of Brisbane comrades before them', they were determined that there would be 'no public expression of disloyalty'. On Sunday 6 April, a group of about 100 returned soldiers attacked a One Big Union meeting being held in Cornwall Square in the city. They toppled the speaker off the platform and ended the meeting. Local members of the RSSILA had 'openly expressed a determination to end this disloyalty'.[61]

In Launceston on 13 April 1919, socialist speaker J. R. Palamountain was to have addressed another One Big Union meeting in Cornwall Square. There was a crowd of between 2,000 and 3,000 and it included a group of returned soldiers. Palamountain was sitting on the ground next to the speaking platform, which was occupied by Labor politician and member of the Legislative Council James McDonald, and Palamountain was wearing a red tie. The riot began when a returned soldier attacked Palamountain and dragged the tie from his neck. This was followed by 'pandemonium', and a crowd of several hundred surged around Palamountain, who was taken away under police protection. The crowd of civilians and returned soldiers pursued, yelling and 'howling' according to one report, some of them waving bits of the now ripped red tie. Once Palamountain was inside the police station, the crowd lined up and sang the national anthem, then gave three cheers for the King. The local press report claimed that this action 'showed that the mob was at least loyal'. No one was arrested.[62]

Riot and assault continued to be in the news in 1919, and returned soldiers were always the central characters. The Bloody Sunday riots in Fremantle in May and the returned soldier riots in Melbourne in July matched the Brisbane Red Flag riots in severity, with the major difference being that the military, through local loyalist organisations, did not supply guns to the rioters in Fremantle and Melbourne as they had done in Brisbane. But the connecting thread was the assertion by rioting returned soldiers that what they were doing was legitimate. They were taking the law into their own hands because they had both the numbers to overpower the police and a deep sense of their own validity and authority to take such actions. A deep sense of grievance was also in the mix, and in both Fremantle and Melbourne the main targets of returned soldier rage were members of the police force. In contrast, in Brisbane returned soldiers' anger was directed at 'alien' enemies, and the injured police were collateral damage.

The returned soldier riots in Brisbane showed the strands of xenophobia that underpinned loyalty to the nation. There was already the idea of the 'disloyal' internal threat – the unionist, the socialist and the 'enemy within' – and as 1919 progressed the loyalist rioters articulated a distrust of all but 'Britishers'. In August 1919, Italians were driven out of their homes from towns in the Goldfields in Western Australia, terrified and forced to sleep in alluvial mining holes. Here the local Returned Soldiers' Association (RSA) acted like an arm of civilian government, even though it was returned soldiers who had driven the Italians into hiding. Far from being censured by the government, the RSA was enabled by local police to give 'orders' for all single Italian men to leave the district. Like the Red Flag riots in Brisbane, the riots in the Goldfields combined 'disloyalty' with 'foreign' in an explosive fusion as a target for angry loyalist returned soldiers.

In Wongi country, the Goldfields are just under 600 kilometres east of Perth. Unlike many other parts of Australia, at the outbreak of the war the Western Australian Goldfields region had an ethnically diverse non-Aboriginal population. In 1914, a high proportion of workers on the mines and the woodlines (areas where workers chopped firewood for the mine operations) were 'Slav' (Croatian, Serbian and Slovenian) and Italian immigrants, and some had brought their families with them. There was some intermarriage between Italian men and Anglo-Australian women, and Italians and Slavs joined local unions. But contrasting to this appearance of harmony between European immigrants and British immigrants, during and after the war the Goldfields was the site for two serious riots against those labelled as 'aliens'.

In December 1916 Greece was still a neutral country in the war, although Prime Minister Eleuthérios Venizélos favoured joining the Allies. Press reports from the Mediterranean condemned the Royalist troops of Greece's King Constantine, who were accused of firing on Allied soldiers in Athens. This was the alleged outrage that rioters used as a justification to attack and loot Greek businesses in Perth, as well as those in Kalgoorlie and nearby Boulder in the Goldfields. In Kalgoorlie, the crowd was led by uniformed soldiers and included a lot of civilian adults and youths. On the first night of riot on 9 December 1916, the police reported that they were 'powerless' against the crowd, who smashed and stole from Greek shops, causing damage of several thousand pounds.[63] Riots against Greek shop and café owners in 1916 drove many Greek residents away from Western Australia.[64]

The context for the anti-Italian riots in August 1919 was an industrial dispute, like so many other returned soldier riots in 1918 and 1919 across the country. Negotiations over wages and conditions in the woodline industry, which provided fuel for the goldmines, had been dragging on for several months. The issue was twofold: an increase in pay for the wood cutters, (many of whom were Italian) and a reduction in the prices charged at company-owned stores on the woodline. A Military Intelligence agent argued that the woodline strikes were being promoted by leaders in the mining section of the AWU. He wrote that the union's aim was to force the closure of mines, which could not operate without firewood, while the union renegotiated a wages contract that expired at the end of July. With such a display of union power it was suggested that mine owners would agree to anything.[65]

Another industrial issue on the Goldfields was the employment of Italians on the principal mining lease at Hampton Plains, the most recent gold discovery. Although it involved only six Italian miners, the Boulder Returned Soldiers' Association cited this as a grievance, and unfair to returned soldier miners.[66] Returned soldiers complained that 'foreigners had "their" jobs'. But while some accused Italians of undercutting other workers, many Italians were unionists and supported the strike.[67]

In addition to mining and labouring work, Italians set up hotels in Kalgoorlie and Boulder, open of course to all locals, and where the Italians socialised. A Military Intelligence report from 1919 described these venues as 'centres of Italian sentiment' where

> strange card games were played to the accompaniment of strident Italian speech…the Italians having the cover of their language could plot to their heart's content and none of the 'Britishers' would be any the wiser.[68]

Local resentment towards Italians was also based on envy of the success of some Italian businessmen. One Military Intelligence agent argued that the 'Italian has never been liked, but the prosperous Italian...was actively disliked'. The 'flashness [sic] of behaviour' of wealthy Italians was 'irritating especially to the Returned Soldier'. The argument was that Italians in Australia were 'free of the claims and depressions of the war'.[69] The Italians were on the side of the Allies during World War I, and the Australian Government cooperated with the Italian Government in their attempt to conscript Italian nationals residing overseas. Anti-conscriptionist groups in Australia supported those Italians who tried to avoid conscription.

In early 1918, the Italian consul in Australia, Cavaliere Eles, complained that supporters of T. J. Ryan's Queensland Labor government were inducing Italians in Australia to defy the conscription order. So the Hughes government used the *War Precautions Act* to introduce regulations making it an offence for an Italian 'reservist' to disregard the consul's order to present for military duty. The Nationalist government also made it an offence for any person to try and encourage a reservist not to comply with the order. Of the 4,903 Italian men of military age in Australia at the time, about 500 were sent back to Europe to fight as conscripts in the Italian army.[70]

Few of the Italians working on the West Australian Goldfields had served as soldiers. As well, Italians, as 'aliens' from an Allied nation, had not been interned like many of their 'Slav' coworkers from areas of the Balkans under Austro-Hungarian rule. An intelligence officer claimed that these factors combined in the assumption that Italians had in fact 'prospered' because of the war.[71] This supposed lack of suffering on the part of Italians was the basis for resentment towards them. Just like all the other riots involving returned soldiers, the importance of sacrifice was central to understanding the motives for violence. Competition for employment mingled with a sense of returned soldier grievance to forge a powerful target for loyalist anger.

On the night of 11 August 1919, Italian Giacomo (Jim) Gatti was walking along Hannan Street in Kalgoorlie with an Anglo-Australian woman. An eyewitness account described how returned soldiers yelled derogatory names, and when Gatti reacted angrily, the soldiers rushed him. Gatti defended himself against the group with a knife, fatally stabbing returned soldier Thomas Northwood in the fight.[72] The police reported it as 'a brawl between Italians and several footballers'.

In the police report, a group of Italian men in company with several women went into the Majestic Café in the main street of town. Some youths yelled at them, 'Dago bastards', and a fight followed. The fight spread to a nearby laneway, where Northwood was stabbed, along with another returned soldier, James Dunn. In the newspaper it was reported that Gatti and other Italian men were in a large fight with 'Britishers' after a 'fracas' at the Majestic Café. By the time Northwood was taken to the hospital, he had lost too much blood and, with a severed artery, could not be saved by the doctors. *The Sunday Times* in Perth wrote that Northwood, who had only months before returned to Australia, died 'by the murderous thrust of a foreigner's knife'. That night, a large group of returned soldiers and youths paraded the streets until 2.15 am, threatening to retaliate and 'get revolvers and seek revenge', according to the police.[73]

Northwood died in hospital on the morning of 12 August, and that afternoon there was a meeting of the RSA in Kalgoorlie. The returned soldiers resolved to demand of the government that they 'deport' single Italians from the Goldfields by Saturday 16 August. After the meeting, some returned soldiers along with a large crowd of around 2,000 men and youths, destroyed a total of six hotels run by Italians in Kalgoorlie, Boulder and nearby Fimiston.[74] Reports described a pattern of riot where the people in the crowd drank everything in the bar before destroying the interior of the hotel, then moving on to the next one. There was also a report of one licensee being forced to hand over the keys to his safe, with members of the crowd taking the money. The looting of hotels in Kalgoorlie did not finish until a policeman, using an axe to smash the barrel, spilt the wine the rioters had been drinking.[75]

Excerpts from a police report described the mayhem in Kalgoorlie on 12 August.[76] The rioters started at the Glen Devon Hotel, outnumbering the police who were trying to protect the front entrance:

> The rioters took charge of the bar and consumed or took away the small stock of drink there and after doing some damage to the windows etc were got out of the hotel by the police.[77]

Then they moved onto another hotel and the police told the Italians there to hide. Then the crowd was confronted by licensee Orsatti with a revolver. With his wife, Orsatti was forced by the crowd onto the balcony, and both were screaming. The police managed to get them into the bedroom where they guarded the door, but downstairs,

> The rioters did a good deal of damage to the glass furniture etc and looted all the drink they could before they were got out…From there they went to the Kalgoorlie Wine Saloon close by and did a smaller amount of damage. A cask of wine they were taking away was smashed by the Police and the wine ran out onto the ground…All the available police were on duty and they kept their heads and acted with great discretion…[the police] prevented the riots turning into a very serious state of affairs in which many lives may have been lost, as both the Italians and the Soldiers were well armed with firearms.[78]

The police reported that in addition to extensive property damage to hotels in Kalgoorlie, the crowd stole over £32 from the till at the All Nations Hotel, as well as £90 from Orsatti's pockets.[79] But none of these rioters and alleged thieves were arrested. Only one man, 'Jim' Gatti, was arrested and charged with an offence, which was the murder of Northwood.[80] At Boulder, police arrested William Hanson, who was among the crowd looting a hotel. But because the crowd started throwing stones at the police station with the intention of breaking in and forcing the release of the prisoner, Sergeant John Fee let him go.[81]

During the riots, there were reports of returned soldiers intervening in the violence, not to stop it but to define it in terms of disciplined soldierly action. Kalgoorlie RSA members William Schwan and Boulder RSA president Harry Axford claimed that they were 'acting for the preservation of human life and property' when they told John de Paoli, the Italian licensee of the Glen Devon Hotel, that 'it would be a judicious move on the part of the Italian occupants of the place to leave for parts unknown before four o'clock'.[82] After the crowd had looted the All Nations Hotel run by Orsatti, returned soldier Lieutenant Stahl persuaded the returned soldiers involved to march off in formation.[83]

The day after the riot, the Commissioner of Police in Perth told his senior officer in Kalgoorlie in a telegram to

> Use every lawful means compel Italians leave Kalgoorlie and Boulder at once. Question of deportation is one for Federal Government; meantime secure all evidence available of act of violence by individual Italians with view deportation. Meanwhile swear in number special constables for purpose protecting life and property Kalgoorlie and Boulder; make it clear to them that they are required for that purpose only and not to assist Italians. Do all that is possible prevent returned soldiers or special constables mixing with Bolshevik element.[84]

The government in Western Australia was not interested in protecting the life and property of Italians, and treated the returned soldiers as a quasi-official authority during the riots. On 12 August, the president of the Kalgoorlie RSA, Robert Brodribb, and the secretary of the RSA in Perth, William Ross, met with the Minister for Mines and the Attorney-General. After the meeting, the Premier, James Mitchell, assured the returned soldiers that although deportation was a federal responsibility, the State Government had ordered the police 'to notify undesirable aliens that under the circumstances it is advisable for them to leave Kalgoorlie and Boulder without delay'. The Premier acknowledge the 'indignation' of the RSA in response to the 'cowardly crime' of Northwood's death, but asked that any returned soldiers' demonstration would be 'of an orderly nature'.[85]

The RSA leaders ignored the request to be orderly. The next episode of violent intimidation was presented in terms of lawful action, but it was kidnapping. On 13 August, returned soldiers in Kalgoorlie effected a successful 'deportation' when they bundled an 'undesirable foreigner', Louis Francis, on the train to Perth. He was guarded on his trip by returned soldiers. In Perth, he was 'handed over' to detectives, who discovered he was born in Armenia and his correct name was Simon Petroff. Rather than the returned soldiers being charged with any criminal offence, Petroff was arrested under the *Aliens Registration Act*. Returned soldiers on the Goldfields alleged that Petroff was a 'Bolshevik apostle', and that they would deal similarly with anyone 'who publicly gave expression to Bolshevik sentiments'.[86] On the

Goldfields, members of the Miners' Union protested the treatment of Francis/Petroff and the 'interference…with [his] liberty'. But the unionists were told by Inspector Duncan of the Kalgoorlie police that they should contact the State Government and take up the matter with them.[87]

At a well-attended RSA meeting on 18 August in Kalgoorlie, senior RSA leaders reiterated that demand for all Italians to leave the district. RSA executives had no powers outside their own organisation to tell people to do anything, yet used words like 'deport' and 'order' to give their demands the appearance of official sanction. Kalgoorlie RSA President Brodribb reported that he had assured authorities in Perth that the 'trouble' would cease if Italians were banned from coming within a ten-mile radius of Kalgoorlie and Boulder. A motion by Boulder RSA president Harry Axford demanded that all Italians leave by that Saturday. The motion was passed, with one amendment permitting married Italians and their families to stay 'until such time as the Association [the RSA] decides otherwise'.[88]

Acting like part of civilian government, Brodribb of the RSA met with the police, the head of the firewood company and a deputation of Italians on 18 August to devise arrangements for the Italian men to leave. He claimed that the RSA was sorry to have frightened the wives and children of the Italians workers and said they could stay, but that all single Italian men had to 'get out of town'. Brodribb reached an agreement with the head of the firewood company, Porter, to supply tents and food for the Italians to go woodcutting on the more remote woodlines. The Italians said they were happy to leave, according to *The Western Argus*.[89]

The Italian men were probably glad to leave. By all accounts, Italians were terrorised during the riots and afterwards. And this hostility was directed towards all non-British residents of the Goldfields. A young Croatian immigrant from the Dalmatian coast, Anthony Splivalo, claimed that while they did not suffer from being forced out of their jobs like the Italians, he and his brother decided to leave before further violence erupted. The riots had 'poisoned the air, not only against Italians, but against all other foreigners as well.'[90]

The consular agent for Italy lodged a formal complaint with the Western Australian Premier, saying that Italians at Boulder and

Kalgoorlie lived in danger and had incurred serious loss of property. The consular agent asked for 'proper protection' for Italians. A few weeks later, after consulting the Attorney-General, who was concerned to avoid any compensation claims against the government, the Minister for Police wrote to the consular agent.[91] It was a disingenuous response, and almost nonsensical in the Minister's efforts to deflect responsibility for the government's tolerance of law breaking and property damage:

> every possible step has been taken to protect the interests of the Italian people on the Goldfields. It was found necessary under the circumstances to advise many of them that a change of locality was advisable.
>
> As you are aware the trouble arose through a cowardly attack on a returned soldier by so-called Italians, and the use of knives irritated the populace to a great extent, more especially the returned soldiers and as this weapon is not favoured in a British community as a means of settling disputes, you will see that apart from the action we have already taken, the Government could scarcely be held responsible for any untoward views that may have occurred.[92]

Returned soldiers were effective in scaring Italians off the Goldfields. Many Italians were so terrified that they and their families were camped in alluvial holes, too frightened to sleep in their homes.[93] A Western Australian Labor politician estimated that 700 Italian workers left the Goldfields because of the riots and other threats to their safety.[94] A solicitor for the Italians in Kalgoorlie later wrote to the Defence Department claiming that 'Italian people were raided by the mob', and their goods had been stolen as well as broken. Men had been hounded out of their jobs, and were both unemployed and 'terrorised by threats from a certain quarter'. Most Italians wanted to leave if they could afford it, and after the riots there was a steady departure of Italians from the Goldfields. Many Italians decided to leave Australia altogether.[95]

From Brisbane's 'army to fight disloyalty', to the Kalgoorlie and Boulder returned soldiers who gave orders for 'deportations', these returned soldiers across the country behaved as if they were part of the apparatus of civilian government. Even though only days before their transformation into upholders of law and order, the same returned soldiers had been rioting in the streets. On the Goldfields, there were the familiar denials that returned soldiers had perpetrated the violence. The assaults, theft and looting were blamed on 'larrikins', 'hoodlums' and 'young men' – all the usual suspects. But as in all the other episodes of riot, it was impossible to deny the reality that returned soldiers posed a serious threat to public order and they wantonly broke the law. In both Brisbane and the Goldfields, the lawlessness directed at disloyal 'foreigners' – anyone who was not a 'Britisher' – for a time aligned with local conservative political policies. But it soon became a problem, with not enough police to maintain order and, in the case of the Goldfields, a potentially expensive compensation claim from Italian businessmen. The supposed loyalist 'armies' of returned soldiers in a volatile peacetime were fraught with danger and unpredictability. These loyalist armies were just as likely to smash law and order as to uphold it.

6

Vigilante Violence and the Beginnings of Secret Armies

Throughout 1918 and 1919, the RSSILA was always a prominent player in the riots that convulsed towns and cities. Theirs was a strident loyalist voice – even during the chaos in Melbourne in July 1919, when the RSSILA insisted they were defending 'loyal' citizens and soldiers against police brutality – and the RSSILA claimed to speak for all returned soldiers. It was a different situation in Western Australia, where the Returned Soldiers Association (RSA) branches and their state executive did not amalgamate with the national RSSILA until August 1918.[1] Through to late 1919, the local RSAs in Western Australia were the public spokesmen for returned soldiers. They seemed to operate with relative autonomy and with widely divergent political affiliations, depending on the context. The RSA executives on the Goldfields in August 1919 were the leaders in driving Italian men from their jobs and homes on the Goldfields, proclaiming themselves as loyal defenders. In contrast, during the May 1919 Fremantle riots, local RSA executives like Mick Donnes were at the forefront of the striking unionists' demonstrations. At returned soldier rallies after the Fremantle riots, returned soldier Panton condemned the 'reactionary officers in the [state] executive', and warned that they would go and set up their own soldiers' organisation if the RSA state executive did not support the strikers and their cause. The same condemnation of an anti-unionist RSSILA executive was levelled by returned soldiers after the Adelaide Peace Day riots in 1918. But in Adelaide these rank-and-file members, as they called themselves, were denied the opportunity to speak at meetings and to effectively challenge the leaders of the RSSILA in South Australia.

Although there were attempts to establish Labor returned soldier organisations, these were relatively short lived and never substantial competition for the RSSILA or RSA branches in terms of membership and public prominence. The Returned Sailors and Soldiers Labor League (RSSLL) in Queensland was formed at a meeting in the Brisbane Trades Hall in May 1919 in the wake of the Red Flag riots. Their objects were twofold; to support the Australian Labor Party (ALP) and 'to defend the patriotic sentiment attached to returned soldiers against exploitation by political adventurers'.[2] These Queensland returned soldiers argued that the Anzac identity had been appropriated by anti-Labor forces and imbued with the idea that the national interest for which soldiers had risked their lives was inimical to notions of class. The members of the RSSLL stated that 'the capitalists…have given themselves a monopoly in loyalty'. They urged returned soldiers to return to their unions and reject attempts to attack workers' interests with the 'new bogeys' of 'Bolshevism' and 'disloyalty'.[3]

The RSSLL began in 1919 with twelve regional branches and a head office in Brisbane, and by November 1919 they had a membership of about 3,000. The Queensland Labor government assisted the RSSLL by providing liquor licenses for their club rooms and a small grant of £100. In June 1920, the Queensland branch of the RSSILA protested that the defence department was according similar recognition to the Labor returned soldiers' group as it was to the RSSILA.[4] But the Queensland RSSLL did not establish the same membership base as their RSSILA counterparts, and the organisation seemed to fade after 1920. In emphasising the need for working-class soldiers to return to the ranks of their unions, the RSSLL possibly contributed to their own demise as a separate returned soldier organisation within the labour movement. Returned soldiers who heeded the RSSLL's call to resume their union affiliation may have seen little benefit in an extra membership with a returned soldiers' organisation.

It was a similar story with the Returned Soldiers' and Sailors' Political League (RSSPL) in New South Wales, established in 1918 and led by returned soldier Corporal Cecil Murphy. He stated that every member of the RSSPL was 'a pledged Labor man', and the group affiliated with the NSW Labor Party at the party's annual conference in June 1918. The affiliation was not without its detractors at the ALP conference, who queried why there needed to be a separate organisation for returned soldiers within the labour movement. Corporal Murphy echoed other soldier organisations in arguing for the special place and particular needs of the returned soldier in postwar society, but the RSSPL always operated within the ALP structure, rather than as an autonomous group. The RSSPL claimed a membership of 2,000 in early 1919, but like the RSSLL in Queensland, their membership dwindled by 1920.[5]

The Melbourne-based Returned Sailors' and Soldiers' Australian Democratic League (RS&SADL, also referred to as the RSDL) was established in 1918. Their Sunday meetings were described by Melbourne resident George Dall as 'commanding the crowd at the Yarra'. He wrote that RSDL speakers were severely critical of the government and military authorities; 'talk about hindering recruiting – no one who hears them is ever likely to enlist'. This prompted an investigation into the RSDL by Military Intelligence, which found that RSDL public statements were not what had been reported. The League's Secretary, J. J. Collins, called on 'all returned comrades' to support the organisation which represented their 'own' returned soldiers' cause as well as that of Labor. Collins claimed that the RSDL were not 'extremists', but that their policy was to secure 'better conditions and treatment for returned soldiers'.[6]

These Labor returned soldier groups that existed at different times throughout 1918 to 1920 in Queensland, Victoria and New South Wales developed a distinctly working-class returned soldier identity. But the merging of soldier and worker identities was uneven, and in some cases viewed with suspicion by those in the labour movement. There was an uneasy parallel between worker solidarity, one for which the memory of the war was secondary to the project of worker emancipation, and the shared memory of soldiers' sacrifice, a memory ground in the experience of war. Even though many within the Labor party and wider union movement criticised the RSSILA as being anti-worker and overtly political – the RSSILA was a 'Tory organisation' and a 'branch of the Nationalist party' – the League became the only enduring returned soldier organisation. They were the precursor to today's

RSL. Their construction of a classless brotherhood of arms defined the Anzac legend for over a century.

The RSSILA claimed to speak for all returned soldiers. Estimates of the peak of RSSILA membership nationally in December 1919 range from 150,000 to 167,000, with G. L. Kristianson's estimate of 150,000 members being the one most widely cited. This was even though Kristianson warned that the RSSILA branch totals at this time were not accurate, and later research indicated that this membership figure of 150,000 was a substantial overestimate.[7] It represented roughly fifty-six per cent of all soldiers who had by December 1919 returned to Australia, which was not a large majority. With a more realistic national membership figure of 100,000 to 120,000 as suggested by Martin Crotty, the RSSILA at its peak only represented about forty-five per cent of returned soldiers.

But it is the collapse of RSSILA membership after 1919 that raises questions about the organisation's assertions that they had the authority to speak for all returned soldiers. By December 1920, RSSILA national membership had plummeted to 49,721, and in 1923 membership reached the postwar nadir of 24,482. By 1923, the decline in membership meant that the RSSILA nationally represented less than 10 per cent of returned soldiers. In just one year – 1920 – the League lost two-thirds of its financial members. Closer analysis of the figures for the mass desertions from the RSSILA in 1920, and probably starting in 1919 (membership was for a year from the date of enrolment), showed the full extent of the decline. Of the 49,721 members who remained in the RSSILA at the end of 1920, around 42 per cent of these were Victorian branch members. The membership decline in the other state branches was catastrophic. In New South Wales, membership fell by around 70 per cent between October 1919 and December 1920, and in South Australia by about 60 per cent over the same period.[8]

There are a few explanations for the inflated membership figures for the RSSILA in 1919. First, the RSSILA's involvement with demobilisation placed them in a privileged position for recruiting members. General John Monash, at the time Director-General of Demobilisation in London, complied with League requests that RSSILA pamphlets be distributed among returning soldiers in camps and on troopships. The AIF branch of the Australian YMCA also assisted by distributing RSSILA literature on the homeward bound troopships. In *The Digger*, published at the AIF base in Le Havre, the RSSILA was always referred to as 'the official body of discharged soldiers'. League representatives were given column space in *The Digger* to promote their organisation. In a defence department booklet given to all returning soldiers on demobilisation procedure, the League was described as 'recognised officially as representing the returned soldiers of the AIF'.[9]

The dramatic rise and decline in membership during the period of demobilisation supports Marilyn Lake's argument that many soldiers joined the RSSILA at the wharves when they disembarked, but did not bother to renew their membership once they realised its conservative political affiliations.[10] Also, returned soldiers straight off the troopships may have thought that the League's 'official' status meant that they had to join in order to have access to repatriation benefits, then they let their membership lapse when they realised that this was not the case. The mass desertions from the League were possibly also a response by its unionist and Labor-voting members deciding that their voices were going to be ignored within an already established anti-Labor organisation.

∞

Even though it is likely that the RSSILA never represented more than forty-five per cent of returned soldiers in 1919, its spokesmen always asserted that they represented all returned soldiers. They also often spoke as if they were commanding a military force with some authority, albeit invented, like the RSA executives on the Goldfields in August 1919 who effected the 'deportations' of Italian men. On the other side of the country in December 1919, at Charleville in south central Queensland, RSSILA executives adopted similar tactics towards local union supporters. Both the Goldfields and Charleville events showed how the RSSILA sought to take control of the mechanics of law enforcement, during and after their participation in lawless violence. But in Charleville it did not end well for the RSSILA executives and their supporters.

In 1919, Charleville was an important centre for surrounding pastoral stations. As with other pastoral areas of Queensland, many shearers belonged to the AWU. There had been a severe drought throughout Queensland in 1918 and 1919, resulting in much reduced production in agriculture, as well as substantial sheep losses. Workers in rural Queensland competed for jobs in a depressed regional economy. In December 1919, just before the shearing season started, a correspondent to *The Daily Standard* in Brisbane was concerned about 'divided camps in [shearing] sheds'.[11]

Many of the riots that occurred in 1919 happened in the context of industrial disputes, and the hostility between capital and labour was intense during this year of strikes. There was also a federal election scheduled for 13 December 1919, and it was only the second federal election in which the Nationalist Party were standing against their former Labor colleagues. Billy Hughes with his Nationalists had won against Labor's Frank Tudor in May 1917, and Hughes sought a further term in government in 1919.

Major Bolingbroke of the RSSILA, who had been a prominent loyalist spokesman during the Red Flag riots in Brisbane, was secretary of the Pastoralists and Grazing Farmers' Union in Charleville. Lieutenant Russell of the RSSILA was head salesman at H. J. Carter and Co., the local insurance agents and station owners, and another returned soldier named in reports, McGregor, was the Charleville Secretary of the Primary Producers' Union.[12] This was not a workers' union but an association of farmers and was a precursor to the National Farmers' Federation. So all three men were linked through a network of owners of land and capital in this small regional community at Charleville.

On 1 December 1919, Major Bolingbroke and Lieutenant Russell went to the police in Charleville demanding that several individuals, 'undesirables' who were not named in the press, be made to leave town. Then they started what was headlined a 'riot'. This was the way it was reported:

> returned soldiers held a meeting, which was very largely attended. It was decided that the inspector of police be waited upon and asked that he rid the town of these undesirable characters, and that a certain constable be

removed otherwise they would take action themselves to clear the town. All day small altercations occurred in the streets...The police did not remove the undesirables, so the Diggers set to work. Fights developed in the streets, and big crowds assembled. The police drew their batons, but exercised restraint...Bottles and stones were freely used. Mr Jack Murphy, a well-known bookmaker, was severely knocked about...He was badly kicked about the face and body. Another man named Burke was badly maltreated, and his condition is causing anxiety...Lieutenant Russell called out: 'Diggers, use no firearms'. He appealed to them to be calm...'Follow us, and we will clean the town of these fellows', he added.[13]

In other reports, the constable that the returned soldiers wanted 'removed' had a German name, and they argued he took an 'officious' attitude to returned soldiers. There were about 200 returned soldiers involved in the riots, and by the following morning, eight men had left town, including the badly injured returned soldier Thomas Burke. Bolingbroke and Russell were praised for their 'tactful' handling of the situation. *The Cairns Post* headlined their report 'A cleansing process, people with the diggers'.[14] Though never named, the 'rowdies' and 'undesirables', also derided as 'spielers', were probably local unionists or their supporters. By late 1919, 'cleaning up the town' was a well-known euphemism for getting rid of union organisers. Also, given that one of the men, Jack Murphy, who was severely beaten, was also a local bookmaker, there may have been some personal scores or gambling debts that returned soldiers wanted to settle.

The police closed the hotels on the evening of 1 December. Then on 2 December, the day after the riot, Bolingbroke and Russell addressed a meeting of returned soldiers and civilians and commended the soldiers for not damaging any property. Their next targets of violence were some local businesses. Returned soldiers 'marched' to two premises and tacked petitions on the doors which stated that 'they would not be responsible for the premises if opened by the present tenant'. One of the shops was a printing house run by brothers Jack and Con Murphy, and Jack had been injured in the previous day's riot. The returned soldiers reiterated their demand that a constable based in Charleville be 'removed' and gave the authorities forty-eight hours to do so. At the request of local hotel licensees, the pubs were reopened by the magistrate.¹⁵

By 3 December, the situation was described as 'quiet'. Of the three arrested during the riot, one returned soldier was fined and the others, 'two young men of respectable parents', were released on bail. Major Bolingbroke informed the local police inspector that 'all the trouble was over…as the "Diggers" had accomplished what they set out to do'. *The Cairns Post* referred to the event as a 'model coup', and Bolingbroke proudly asserted that no property was destroyed and 'not even a window broken'. Returned soldiers were 'in control' of Charleville and credited with 'restoring peace'. But despite the claims that returned soldiers had 'restored peace', police reinforcements started arriving from outback police stations.¹⁶

As with all other instances of returned soldier riots where unionists were the targets of violence, soldiers' lawlessness and intimidation were represented as purposeful and reasonable civic action. There were meetings and deputations, and orders delivered to the local police. Throughout the two days of violence and intimidation, Bolingbroke and Russell behaved and spoke like commanders of a militia empowered to impose civil order. Like the RSA executives on the Western Australian Goldfields a few months before, the returned soldiers at Charleville were the true enforcers of civil order, even being able to tell the police what to do. The RSSILA ex-officers were defenders and protectors of life and property, helping respectable citizens to rid their town of an undesirable group who were 'parasites' on the community.

Despite the opportunities for bold loyalist action, the outcome was not an enduring loyalist victory for Bolingbroke and Russell and their supporters in Charleville. At the end of December, Bolingbroke and Russell were charged with creating a disturbance and released pending trial on substantial bonds of £50 each. Extra police were sent to Charleville, and after Christmas there were so many police garrisoned in the town that the local Chamber of Commerce protested, claiming that it was resented by the residents. Police Commissioner Urquhart stated that the number of reinforcements were in fact only twelve, not forty or seventy extra police as had been reported. Urquhart also stated that the reinforcements were sent at the request of Sub-Inspector Hanlan at Charleville because threats of violence were being made against the police. There were rumours of witnesses being threatened during the trial of Bolingbroke and Russell, and warnings that police would be shot and premises burned down. One constable was threatened with being tarred and feathered. A union official was also warned that he 'would have to be careful in the future, or he would have to leave the town'.[17]

Unlike the Red Flag riots of March 1919, the riots in Charleville at the end of 1919 resulted in the arrests of the returned soldier ringleaders. There was also a marked change in the government response compared to the previous year. In the Hughenden riots in October 1918, the Queensland authorities were instructed not to censor reports of the violence, and no one was arrested. The coalition of returned soldiers, publicans and pastoral station owners in 'driving out the mongrels' – i.e. union activists – in Hughenden was celebrated in newspaper reports across the nation. But in Charleville in 1919, the government sent police reinforcements to the outback town and the returned soldier leaders of the riot were arrested. By the end of 1919, the Queensland Government was less willing to tolerate returned soldier lawlessness.

∞

In rural Victoria in December 1919, a few days after the riot in Charleville, there was another episode of returned soldier vigilante violence that seemed to reach a new pinnacle of terror. Former Labor MP John (J. K.) McDougall had retired from politics with his wife to a farm near Ararat in the Central Highlands in Victoria. As the member for Wannon in the House of Representatives, McDougall was nicknamed the 'Silent Member' because he rarely spoke in Parliament. But his published poetry was considered radical, including an anti-war poem he had written in 1900 in response to the Boer War. The poem was republished in the *Labor Call*, with considerably more verses than had appeared in the original, and this was used against McDougall by his Nationalist opponents in a by-election in 1915.[18]

The opening lines – 'Ye are the sordid killers / Who murder for a fee' – indicated the tone of the poem, and it was reprinted and circulated by the Nationalist Party Campaign Council during the 1919 federal election campaign. On the Nationalist leaflet, the poem was prefaced with 'DIGGERS! Labor asks for your votes'. The staff at the Melbourne *Argus* ensured that this example of the Labor party's alleged disparaging attitude towards soldiers received plenty of media exposure, even though it was an example written nineteen years before. There was never any doubt as to McDougall's authorship of the poem, but Terry King argued that McDougall's name was deliberately withheld by the Nationalists campaign team and *The Argus* staff to gain political mileage out of a sensationalised and bogus search for the author of the poem.[19]

Members of the RSSILA branch at Essendon in Melbourne demanded that the author apologise publicly for this 'insult to their 59,000 dead comrades'. After communication between the Essendon and Ararat RSSILA branches, a group of Essendon RSSILA members drove from Melbourne to Ararat, and were joined by some members of the Ararat branch in the attack on McDougall. The local newspaper in Ararat suggested that 'prominent Nationalists' in the town were also involved, since they had been overheard referring to 'an anticipated incident'. The editors of *The Ararat Advertiser* went as far as to accuse the Nationalist Campaign Council of a 'stupidly blundered election dodge'.[20]

On the night of 6 December, McDougall was lured out onto the road by some returned soldiers in civilian clothes on the pretext that their car had broken down. His wife offered some in the group a cup of tea while they waited. It was late, around 10 pm, and after McDougall had helped push the supposedly damaged car onto the road, he was attacked by another group of men whose faces were partly covered by handkerchiefs. The men tied up McDougall and put him on the floor of one of the cars and drove off in a convoy. McDougall had admitted to writing the anti-war poem, and when he asked his kidnappers for a chance to explain, McDougall was told to shut up as they had 'means of silencing him'. While being driven in the car, McDougall was subject to verbal abuse, being called a 'bloody mongrel' and 'worse than Fritz'. One of the returned soldiers, Richard Williams, said:

> We will show Australia what the Anzacs can do. We will tar and feather an ex-member of Parliament and the news will ring to the ends of Australia tomorrow.[21]

When the men asked if McDougall was Catholic and he responded 'No', they said that they would 'tar and feather [Archbishop] Mannix and [Premier] Ryan yet'. In an isolated part of town in Ararat, McDougall was forced to strip off his clothes, and the returned soldiers painted his chest, back, legs and face with tar and hit him in the face. Then they covered him with kapok feathers, let him put on his clothes and tied him up again. The group of returned soldiers drove to the main street of Ararat and dumped the tarred and feathered McDougall on the footpath.[22]

The soldiers were right in asserting that the news would be reported across the country. The local press described the attack as 'Tarred and feathered / Poetic chickens come home to roost', and in Sydney, editors headlined the story 'Offensive verses, author tarred and feathered, indignant soldiers'.[23] The repeated message in conservative newspapers was that McDougall was asking for trouble in his slander against soldiers. But the assault was so shocking that even usually supportive loyalist voices were muted, and there was not the same national cheering as had been the response to the Charleville riots of a few days before.

At a public meeting convened in Ararat after the incident, speakers condemned the 'dastardly act'. The meeting was reported in the local *Ararat Advertiser* – not a fan of McDougall's – as being the largest meeting on record, and participants were described as 'loyal citizens of Ararat'. Speakers also suggested that the editors of *The Argus* were involved somehow in the attack, as they had published such an accurate account as soon as it had occurred. Speakers demanded to know what the Crown law department was doing to find the writer of the *Argus* article and if the 'secret service police' were involved. There were protest meetings in nearby Casterton and Castlemaine, with federal Labor leader Frank Tudor calling the assault a 'diabolical outrage'. Prime Minister Billy Hughes, at the time campaigning in Bendigo, had to defend himself against the charge that he was responsible for the tarring and feathering of McDougall. The *Labor Call* in Melbourne called it a 'Dastardly Nationalist outrage'. They reported that McDougall's property, Maroona, was being guarded around the clock by 'neighbours with loaded rifles', and that many farmers had come to express their sympathy with McDougall.[24]

The police took the assault seriously and sent senior detectives to Ararat to investigate, and a week later McDougall had an interview with the Commissioner of Police in Melbourne.[25] Seven returned soldiers, most in their twenties, were arrested. Five of the men were from the Essendon RSSILA. Harold Barker was a former captain and had been awarded the Distinguished Conduct Medal at Gallipoli, and Richard Williams was also a former captain in the AIF. Evidence in the Police Court was that there had been telegrams exchanged before the assault between one of the accused, Cyril Eastgate, secretary of the Essendon RSSILA, and the secretary of the Ararat RSSILA branch, Rogers. Accused men Wilson Bissett and Harold Williams, a former lieutenant in the AIF, were Ararat locals and known to McDougall, which was probably why he willingly followed them to help with their supposedly broken-down car. The charge against one of the men was dropped, and it was ultimately Harold Williams, Wilson Bissett, Cyril Eastgate, Richard Williams, Harold Barker and R. Dennis who went to trial in February 1920. At an Ararat branch RSSILA annual meeting in late January 1920, a member wanted to know what part the branch secretary had taken in the assault. But the branch president, Blackman, did not allow any discussion on the matter and 'it was dropped'.[26]

If the assault of McDougall was an election stunt engineered by the Nationalist party, as several commentators claimed, it backfired. The returned soldier perpetrators of the assault were charged and convicted. But their charges were downgraded to common assault, and they all pleaded guilty. Their punishment was lenient: a fine of only £5 each. While the magistrate said the soldiers had 'done wrong by taking the law into their own hands', he did not consider them to be criminals. The judge told the court that he 'would not think of sending them to jail'. He fined each man £5 and said

> The country owed a debt of gratitude to the accused for what they had done in the Great War…[but] they would have to curb their feelings otherwise there would be chaos.[27]

Returned soldiers' appetite for street fighting, riot and vigilante violence seemed to be spent by the beginning of 1920, and there were only a couple of further instances of returned soldier riot in this postwar period. An anti-deportation rally at Moore Park in Sydney had been planned in 1920 to protest the deportation of priest Father Jerger. He was born in Germany and had emigrated to Australia as a teenager with his mother and stepfather. He was interned in late 1917 for allegedly using disloyal language in front of a congregation at Marrickville, Sydney. Father Jerger was a priest of the Passionist Order and efforts were made by Catholic authorities to release him. Three separate inquiries into the case of Father Jerger, including a Royal Commission, resulted in a decision by the Solicitor General, Sir Robert Garran, that Father Jerger should be deported. The allegations were that he had made statements against 'Britishers' and was a vocal leader among the internees in the camp at Holdsworthy, on the outskirts of Sydney, where many German and Austrian internees were imprisoned.

Under the *Aliens Restrictions Order*, the Minister for Defence proposed to deport Jerger. There were widespread protests, with accusations that Father Jerger was being denied basic principles of justice in being deported without trial.[28] When Father Jerger's final appeal against his deportation was denied in May 1920, many of the protests came from his Catholic supporters. A 'monster meeting' was planned in Sydney for 23 May at the KSC Hall in the city, which was owned by the Knights of the Southern Cross, a lay Catholic group. There was also a meeting in the Domain, and a resolution was passed by Labor MLAs Percy Brookfield and William Jackson condemning the government's 'tyrannical action' in deporting Jerger.[29]

The newly elected Labor Lord Mayor of Sydney, William Fitzgerald, wrote to both the Prime Minister and the Defence Minister, George Pearce that 'an important section of the Sydney public' wanted the government to reconsider Father Jerger's case. A further rally was planned for Sunday 30 May, organised by the Catholic Federation, and the City of Sydney Council made the venue of Moore Park, in the city's east, available to the protesters. The RSSILA counteracted by arranging their own meeting at Moore Park on Sunday in favour of the Nationalist government's deportation policies. The Lord Mayor wrote again to the Prime Minister objecting to the counter-demonstration by soldiers, arguing that it would be 'inopportune for such action to be taken...as it might lead to expressions of feelings which would be regrettable'.[30] It was the first instance where the connection between Protestantism and loyalty, and Catholicism and disloyalty, was openly spoken about in the context of preludes to a loyalist riot.

Major General Sir Charles Rosenthal, RSSILA spokesman and soon-to-be Secretary of the King and Empire Alliance, was a member of the Sydney establishment, a well-known architect and highly decorated soldier who was well liked by the soldiers under his command.[31] He wrote to *The Sydney Morning Herald* condemning the introduction of the 'question of religion' into the debate. Rosenthal made the standard warning of returned soldier loyalists pushed to the limits, ready to use force as an appropriate and necessary response to disloyalty:

> In common with thousands of other loyal Australians I have given five of the best years of my life in taking my share of protecting our Empire, and I do not feel disposed to stand idly by on my return to Australia and witness without protest such exhibitions of rank disloyalty as have lately been served up to us in Sydney...I should like to urge all loyal citizens who can possibly do so to attend at Moore Park on Sunday afternoon, support the returned soldiers meeting, and thus support the Government. Are we asleep?[32]

The riot in May 1920 showed the established pattern of threatening prelude followed by riotous attack, a pattern which by this time was so familiar that everyone knew what was coming. A crowd of at least 50,000 — some estimates were as high as 150,000 — congregated in Moore Park. According to one report, 'it was a delightful afternoon to be out of doors, and there was the prospect of lively proceedings to spice the pleasantness of the invigorating sun.'[33]

The crowd was congregated around three different speaking platforms. Two of the platforms were stages for protest meetings against deportation and were presided over by prominent State Labor politicians and aldermen. Another speaker was Father O'Reilly, rector of St John's College at the University of Sydney and a prominent anti-conscription campaigner. The third meeting was the RSSILA meeting in support of the government's deportation policy.

When the RSSILA meeting finished, returned soldiers moved through the crowd towards the other meetings. Just before Queensland Premier Ryan was due to address one of the anti-deportation meetings, the returned soldiers attacked those on the platform and pushed them off. Then 'the speeches of protest gave way to patriotic songs and cheers for the King and Empire'. Only after fights started and a table was smashed did the police intervene. Police cleared everyone off the platform and allowed a returned soldier to get up and call for a vote in support of deportation. The police were praised by the press for their quick action in ending the 'fracas', and only minor injuries were reported.[34] The newspaper headlines denied the reality of riot, using words like 'fracas', 'melee' and 'nearly a riot'. They implied that the theme of the rallies was support for deportation, when two out of three meetings were anti-deportation.

The riotous attacks at Moore Park on 30 May 1920 were planned by the RSSILA, as were several of the riotous and vigilante attacks by returned soldiers in 1918 and 1919. What made the 1920 riot in Sydney different to other returned soldier riots during this period was the involvement of a nascent secret paramilitary force. Sir Charles Rosenthal and Major Jack Scott both spoke at the anti-deportation RSSILA meeting on 30 May, and both were among the organisers of the King and Empire Alliance. The Alliance was one of several loyalist groups that existed around Australia at the time. Its particular brand of loyalty was, as the name implied, to the British Empire – the 'Great British Empire' – and the disloyal enemies they identified were the Irish, the union movement, Bolsheviks and anyone who hinted at an Australian republic. The Alliance's condemnation of Catholic priests also indicated an anti-Catholic stance.[35]

The Alliance was inaugurated at a Sydney Town Hall meeting on 19 July 1920, which was attended by Nationalist MLAs, former AIF officers, the president of the Employers' Federation, and the United States consul E. P. Norton. The Alliance claimed a membership of 10,000 by mid-1922 and published their journal the *King and Empire* until at least the end of 1922. Alliance Council members included returned officers, wealthy pastoralists and businessmen, professionals and conservative politicians, along with Lady David, the wife of Lieutenant-Colonel Sir Edgeworth David, who had been a prominent conscription campaigner during the war. Consul Norton was likely referring to the Alliance when he reported to his superiors in Washington that it was an organisation of 'leading Australians' who sought 'to overcome the influence [of] Roman Catholic, Sinn Fein and labour elements'.[36]

At a time when fascism was developing in Europe, Brigadier General G. R. Campbell of the King and Empire Alliance wrote in the Alliance journal in 1922 that their organisation was 'substantially in accord with' the ideals of the Fascisti movement in Italy. Campbell drew parallels between the fascists' support for returned soldiers against the 'revolutionaries' in Italy and the Alliance's support for loyalty in Australia. He wrote that loyalty to King and Nation and the preservation of law and order were aims that the Alliance and the Italian Fascisti had in common.[37]

The King and Empire Alliance was the respectable front for a more sinister paramilitary secret organisation, whose membership were returned soldiers and, like Rosenthal and Scott, also members of the RSSILA in New South Wales. Rosenthal was Scott's superior officer during demobilisation, and both served in leadership positions in the King and Empire Alliance; Rosenthal as secretary and Scott as treasurer. In their studies of secret armies in the 1920s and early 1930s in New South Wales and Victoria respectively, Andrew Moore and Michael Cathcart have identified Scott and Rosenthal as leaders of the paramilitary auxiliary to the King and Empire Alliance. Other secret armies were the White Army in Victoria and the 'Friends of Ellen's', a pun on the acronym LNS (League of National Security). In New South Wales in the early 1930s, there was the Old Guard, which was followed by the New Guard.[38] It was the New Guard that was made famous by Captain Francis de Groot galloping in on his horse to slash the ribbon on the new Sydney Harbour Bridge before Labor premier Jack Lang could officially do so.

All of these groups were conspiratorial, anti-Labor paramilitary organisations hostile to the processes of democratic government. Deeply male chauvinist as well, these secret armies were based on the idea that good government needed strong men to run the show. For these men, action was all that was required and political debate was like poison. At various times in New South Wales and Victoria, the training and system of divisional commanders of these secret armies were in readiness for a predicted worker or socialist uprising, which never occurred.

John Alexander first suggested in 1965 in the journal *Meanjin* that the novel *Kangaroo* by D. H. Lawrence was in fact an accurate account of a secret 'diggers' army' which operated in Sydney in the 1920s. Lawrence had travelled with his wife Frieda to Australia in 1922, and they lived for just over three months at the town of Thirroul on the coast south of Sydney. It was here that Lawrence wrote *Kangaroo*, which was published in 1923 after the Lawrences had returned to England. For a long time considered a work of fiction, the parallels between *Kangaroo* and real events and people have now been extensively researched. It is clear that the character of Ben Cooley, nicknamed Kangaroo and the charismatic leader of the secret diggers' army, was based on Sir Charles Rosenthal. In Lawrence's account, the secret army was called the Maggies, short for Magpies, and these 'private squads' had a membership of about 1,400 returned soldiers in New South Wales. Jack Calcott in *Kangaroo* was a character based on Major Jack Scott, and it is likely that Lawrence knew both men and the relationships between Richard Lovat Somers (Lawrence) and Cooley and Calcott described in the book were probably close to autobiographical.[39]

In one exchange between Somers and Calcott, Lawrence gives these words to Calcott:

> There's a good many of us chaps as has been in France, you know – and been through it all – in the army – we jolly well know you can't keep a country going on the vote-catching system…We know it can't be done… If you've got to command, you don't have to ask your men first if it's right, before you give the command.[40]

While the 1920 returned soldier riot in Moore Park in Sydney was an orchestrated event and probably involved an early iteration of a secret 'diggers army' led by Rosenthal and Scott, other episodes of returned soldier riot in 1918 and 1919 were more unstructured in origin. With most of these riots and events of vigilante violence, there is no firm evidence that they were conducted by secret paramilitary organisations, apart from the connection that returned soldiers were the main agents in both the riots and the later secret armies. Whether there was substantial overlap in personnel between the riot leaders in 1918 and 1919 and later paramilitary forces is difficult to ascertain. These secret armies were clandestine, were not investigated by the police (some of whom were members) and left almost no records.

The lead up to the Red Flag riots in Brisbane involved the secret arming of loyalist groups, but the resulting 'army to fight disloyalty' did not last. Seven months after the establishment of the army, one of its leaders, Major Bolingbroke, suffered an embarrassing defeat after the Charleville riots with his arrest and the police occupation of the town. The returned soldiers who assaulted and tarred and feathered McDougall in December 1919 certainly conspired together, and probably with local Nationalist supporters. But there appeared to be no secret organisation behind them providing support, since all the returned soldiers were promptly arrested and had to endure a public trial.

Several of the riots in this postwar period were opportune coalitions between local employers and station owners in the context of industrial disputes. Returned soldiers were sometimes part of this group, or were enticed into the violence with fighting rhetoric, and often with alcohol, as well as the central motivator of an alleged insult to soldiers' sacrifice. But with most of these events, regardless of how planned the origins may have been, the riots developed a dynamic of their own once the violence started. On some occasions, they were successful in forcing union activists out of the community, but in as many instances they were not.

When returned soldiers 'took matters into their own hands', there were clear patterns in these riots, with the intent of controlling what was said in public space. There were the threatening preludes to riot and the loyalist appropriation of the legitimacy for collective violence. Through 1918 and 1919, these riots developed a framework in which violent punishment replaced negotiation and where political difference was subsumed under the notion of insult to soldiers' sacrifice.

Riotous violence by returned soldiers, in its variety of contexts, was connected through soldiers' assertions that their actions were legitimate, their anger justified and that the nation owed them. Whether it was loyalist and armed returned soldiers smashing up Russian premises in

South Brisbane or returned soldiers storming government offices in Melbourne, all claimed they were right in their actions. And returned soldiers as national heroes were so important in this immediate postwar landscape that even when it was undeniable that returned soldiers through their collective violence posed serious threats to public order, the 'real' returned soldier was exonerated by RSSILA spokesmen and nervous civilian commentators. Not all civilians responded that way, of course; there were plenty of voices who called violent returned soldiers rioters, Tory hoodlums and 'tools of the capitalists'. But the 'real' or 'genuine' returned soldier was a hero to whom the nation owed a debt. Magistrates and judges delivered their decisions with warnings and sometimes alarm at the level of criminal violence they saw coming through the courts, but returned soldiers were always treated leniently. Soldiers' sacrifice was always a determining factor.

7

The Loyal Nation

One of the final chapters in D. H. Lawrence's book *Kangaroo* is titled 'A row in town.' It depicts Somers and Calcott (characters based on Lawrence and Major Scott) attending a Labor rally at a hall in Sydney. A group of returned soldiers at the meeting start 'counting out' the Labor speaker, and there are fights among the crowd between the returned soldiers and the Labor supporters. A Red Flag is raised and a Union Jack flag 'torn to fragments'. The fighting continues with fists, weapons and furniture, and then someone (later identified as an anarchist) throws a bomb. Police and mounted troopers arrive. Three people are killed and several injured, including the diggers' army leader, Ben Cooley (the character based on Charles Rosenthal), who later dies of bullet wounds. Jack Calcott is among the fourteen returned soldiers later arrested.

In Lawrence's dialogue between Somers and Calcott after the violence, Calcott scoffs at the police – 'Bloody Johnny Hops' – and says, 'it's our boys who've got things in hand'. Calcott boasts to Somers that he has 'settled' three at the rally, hitting two men with an iron bar and breaking the neck of a third. Calcott continues, 'there's nothing bucks you up sometimes like killing a man…you feel a perfect angel after it.'[1]

Lawrence's fictionalised account contains some parallels to real events. Even his account of the newspaper reporting of the riot reflected what had happened in real life. In Lawrence's story, the returned soldiers' former commanding officer, Cooley, was praised in the newspapers for his efforts to maintain order with his 'loyal Diggers'. Jack Calcott's lethal iron bar was called 'stick' in the press reports. No one was criminally convicted, and Jack Calcott was released on bail. No one who fired shots from their revolvers were named; 'nobody chose to know', as Lawrence wrote. Nearly all the newspapers reported it this way in Lawrence's account, except the *Sun*, which he called 'the Radical poper', i.e. supporting the Pope.[2] Lawrence's anti-Catholic, anti-Semitic and racist comments are scattered throughout the text.

In this account from *Kangaroo*, apart from the anarchist bomb thrower and the fatalities, Lawrence could have been describing a riot that occurred in the Sydney Domain in May 1921. As with most of the riots covered in the previous six chapters, the violence was in response to an alleged insult to soldiers. In Sydney on May Day (1 May), there were up to 1,500 people in the Domain listening to the speeches. By the early twentieth century, May Day had become a day to commemorate the achievements of the international labour movement, including the eight-hour day. In May 1921 in the Domain, a group of about twenty men, including returned soldiers holding a Union Jack flag, charged towards a speaking platform from where the Red Flag was flying. There were fights among the crowd, but the soldier attackers were outnumbered, and their Union Jack was torn and allegedly burned. Secretary of the Labor Council, John (Jock) Garden, defended the flying of the Red Flag as 'the symbol of the workers of the world'. He claimed that it was not any of their members who tore the Union Jack, but also derided as a 'silly idea' the effort to try and supplant the Red Flag at such a meeting.[3]

Loyalists were outraged, and 'a trio of popular officers of the AIF' (possibly including Rosenthal and Scott) visited the editors of *The Sydney Morning Herald* to explain how angry and upset the 'Diggers' were. They delivered the familiar threats:

> The Union Jack is good enough for the average Digger, who does not boast much about it; but when anyone has the temerity to haul it down, or even burn it, he must be prepared to put up with the consequences.[4]

The following Sunday, returned soldiers planned their own rally in the Domain. Rosenthal was a speaker at a Sydney Town Hall meeting on Friday night, 6 May, to protest disloyalty, and crowds spilled onto the streets, many waving small Union Jacks. Rosenthal was also at the Domain rally on Sunday 8 May 1921. As with the 1920 riot in Moore Park, the public converged on the venue to watch the fight, or to participate. The Labor-affiliated Returned Soldiers' and Sailors' Political League published their intention of holding a meeting at the Domain, as too did the RSSILA.

Estimates of the crowds on 8 May ranged from 100,000 to 150,000. Groups of returned soldiers moved among the throng, attacking any speaking platform which was not flying the Union Jack. Socialist Ernie Judd, who had been a victim of returned soldier Domain rioters in 1918, waved a revolver to ward off his attackers but was pulled from his platform and beaten up. The meeting of the Returned Soldiers' and Sailors' Political League was attacked partly because they were not flying a Union Jack. Speakers there, Digger Dunn and Corporal Murphy, were 'counted out'. Dunn shouted that the RSSILA had 'lost the respect' of most returned soldiers. The loyalist diggers were successful in overrunning most of the meetings, and there was a lot of screaming as women ran for safety. The King and Empire Alliance claimed they had 'taken the lead' and were 'proud of their achievements' on 8 May 1921. This comment was quickly retracted by Rosenthal, who said that the Domain meeting had been organised by the NSW RSSILA.[5] The photograph below showed the huge crowd before the violence started.

'Yesterday's gathering in the domain', *The Daily Telegraph*, 9 May 1921. National Library of Australia.

The May 1921 riot in the Sydney Domain was the last large-scale riot involving returned soldiers in this postwar era. The focus shifted, and returned soldiers demonstrating against unemployment dominated the headlines in the early 1920s. The huge riots that had convulsed Australian cities and regional centres in 1918 and 1919 were not repeated, apart from these two events in the Sydney Domain in 1920 and 1921, which were both linked to the involvement of the King and Empire Alliance. The Alliance's vision of something like the Italian Fascisti in suburban Australia was never realised. There was no socialist uprising in Australia, and the various iterations of diggers' secret armies in New South Wales and Victoria remained secret, with not a lot to do apart from clandestine meetings and training. They never got to fight the imagined Red Army that they were expecting.

∞

Australia at the end of the war and in the years after remained a deeply divided society. Bereavement and grief had touched many families, people were surrounded by the devastating impacts of war, and damaged and broken men were visible everywhere. Yet these shared experiences seemed to be not enough to heal the rifts. The fissures were along familiar lines – class, religion, ethnicity and ideology – but animosities between people calling themselves loyalists and those they called disloyalists were imbued with new features. Disagreement became insult, specifically an insult to soldiers' sacrifice but also more widely an insult to the collective sacrifice of the nation. In this emotionally charged landscape, debate and diversity of opinion were considered an affront. Lawlessness and violent silencing were permissible to defend some invented 'higher law', and the identification of disloyal threat could encompass a wide range of people and actions. Yet while loyalists claimed to be under attack, they had the full support of the Nationalist government, who used emergency wartime powers to arrest and jail their political opponents and censor discussion about the war.

Soldiers' disruptive violence and assault were usually reshaped as manly, soldierly action for a just cause. Allegedly disloyal statements were 'more than the men can stand'. And when returned soldiers en masse posed a serious threat to civil order and waged armed battles with police, they were not 'real' soldiers. Even though the stark reality was that soldiers led riots.

The loyalty expressed through riots was that of a limited community, intolerant of difference and fearful of internal enemies. It excluded more groups than it included, and at various times the exclusions were against union members, socialist and anti-war activists, advocates for any kind of republic, the working class generally, Catholics generally and anyone who was not a Union Jack waving 'Britisher'. Australian loyalty after Gallipoli was not appropriated by conservative white men after the fact; in its invention it was xenophobic and hostile to working-class allegiance. The violent intolerance thrown to the surface with the riots showed a society in which the loyalist conviction to build on the promise of Gallipoli was only ever expressed in terms of struggle and vigilance against internal threats and dissolution. An optimistic vision of the future that the birth of the nation at Gallipoli was supposed to deliver was not the future imagined by many Australians in 1920. The loyal nation was beleaguered, and their war continued on the home front against adversaries who were identified everywhere.

Returned soldiers played a major role in shaping these definitions through collective violence, both as loyalist defenders of the nation and as angry crowds attacking the police. This was partly because returned soldiers by 1919 constituted such a large bloc in the overall population, so they were always there. As well, returned heroes were given by the home front society a central role in nation building, and many soldiers asserted this role for themselves. The loyal nation and what we now know as the Anzac legend were formed together by the same social forces that convulsed Australia at the end of the war. Even when returned soldiers battled with police and attacked the Premier's office in Melbourne in July 1919, they said they were doing this on behalf of 'loyal citizens' who were subject to police brutality. One of the returned soldier leaders of the Melbourne riots, George Roberts, may have been expelled from the RSSILA Executive for a short while for his incendiary statements and implied threats to shoot the police, but he soon returned.

There were also many emphatic assertions from returned soldiers rioters that they were fighting with striking unionists. RSSILA Executive committee members, most of whom were former officers, called for a brotherhood above class and a rejection of class allegiances.

But these calls were not heeded by many returned soldiers across Australia, and they totally ignored RSSILA Executive exhortations to stay away from 'party politics'. While these Executive members usually did not want the rank and file to engage with politics, the leadership of the RSSILA at senior levels were closely allied with the Nationalist government. On the pages of returned soldier magazines and in their public statements, these leaders were overtly anti-Labor and anti-unionist, with particular hostility towards socialism and 'Bolshevism'. At the time the term 'Bolshevism' appeared to have a malleable definition and could be used to deride any left-leaning ideology.

Yet from Fremantle to Adelaide to Melbourne, RSSILA members and some local executive committee members stood in violent opposition to the self-styled loyalists for whom striking unionists were anathema. Private Corboy, who had been wounded twice in France, declared in Fremantle in 1919 that he would rather be wounded fighting next to fellow unionists on the wharves. There were returned soldiers across the country who worked to forge organisational ties between the returned soldier movement and the labour movement, and who marched with striking unionists and sang along with socialist anthems.

The loyal Anzac promoted by the RSSILA Executive was 'non-sectarian and non-political', though in reality closely linked to conservative politics. He was devoted to defending an Australian nation bound by unbreakable ties with the King and the British Empire. But this idea of the loyal Anzac was not endorsed by the overwhelming majority of returned soldiers. By 1923, the League membership represented less than ten percent of potential returned soldier members. The RSSILA claimed to speak for all returned men, but they did not. And throughout 1918 and 1919, returned soldiers said this publicly at meetings and demonstrated it with their actions. Like the loyal nation defined through the riots, the loyal Anzac excluded more returned soldiers than it included, so they left the RSSILA. Men went back to their jobs if they had them, and back to their unions and their communities, and had no further involvement with the RSSILA that claimed to represent all of them.

C. E. W. Bean wrote that the men of the AIF 'merged quickly and quietly into the general population', apart from the 'unworthy demonstration' by 'riff-raff' in Melbourne in July 1919.[6] But there was nothing quiet about the return of soldiers in 1918 and 1919, and nor was their reintegration into civilian society quick. Soldiers' return was characterised by riot and violence. Negotiating the significance of soldiers' sacrifice and what that meant in a postwar world exposed deep divisions within Australian society, as well as between the soldiers who left to fight in the war and the civilians who stayed at home. In some of the episodes of riot, this division between war front and home front seemed to be the only division that mattered, and soldiers were driven by a sense of grievance about what civilian society owed them. Whether it was better wages or jobs or respect, or a combination of all these things, the blood debt and how to resolve it was a pressing issue for returned soldiers. Some men were politically radicalised by their war experience, and returned determined to fight alongside their fellow unionists to change the economic system. Other soldiers returned to fight on the side of fellow loyalists to uphold a conservative and imperial worldview. Other soldiers possibly just wanted to fight, and violence was their language. They returned to a society unprepared for these conflicts which brought disorder to the streets and public meeting places, and riots that shook the nation.

NOTES

Unless otherwise stated, all the references to newspapers have been sourced from Trove online digitised newspapers.

Introduction

1. 'Angry soldiers', *The Sydney Morning Herald*, 30 October 1919, p. 7; 'Newcastle police court', *Newcastle Morning Herald and Miners' Advocate*, 31 October 1919, p. 7.
2. 'Newcastle police court', p. 7. In 1919, what was then referred to as the basic wage was £3 17/- (three pounds and seventeen shillings) per week. See H. W. Foster, *A brief history of Australia's Basic Wage*, Australian Bank Officials' Association, Melbourne, 1965, p. 11.
3. G. Souter, *Lion and Kangaroo: The Initiation of Australia 1901–1919*, Fontana, Sydney 1976, pp. 244–5.
4. Queensland State Archives, Item ID ITM19110, 'Printed copy of statistical returns of voting on the question of conscription and summaries of elections and referendums (Commonwealth) 1903–1917.'
5. Ibid.
6. Ibid.
7. Regulations 19 and 20 of the *War Precautions (Supplementary) Regulations*, 'Votes of members of forces and crews of transports', S. R. 1916 No. 273, 3 November 1916. For referendum results see Queensland State Archives, Item ID ITM19110.
8. H. W. Allen to 'Dear Latham', 21 November 1917, *Papers of Sir John Latham, 1856–1964 [manuscript]*, National Library of Australia, MS 1009/1/328.
9. Australian War Memorial, 'Enlistment statistics, First World War', https://www.awm.gov.au/articles/encyclopedia/enlistment/ww1, viewed 8 April 2025.
10. S. Macintyre, *The Oxford History of Australia. Volume 4, 1901–1942: The Succeeding Age*, Oxford University Press, Melbourne, 1993, p. 182.
11. E. Campion, *Australian Catholics*, Penguin, Ringwood, Vic., pp. 82–7, quote pp. 86–7.
12. George Steward to 'Dear Hall', 30 January 1918, correspondence marked 'secret', 'Reverend Dr D. Mannix (Anti-Conscription and Anti-British Utterances: Sinn Feiner)', National Archives of Australia (NAA), NAA: A8911, 240.
13. Ibid.

14 S. Garton, *The Cost of War*, Oxford University Press, Melbourne, 1996, p. 15; S. Macintyre, *The Succeeding Age*, pp. 187–8; National Museum of Australia, *Defining moments: Influenza pandemic*, https://www.nma.gov.au/defining-moments/resources/influenza-pandemic, viewed 8 April 2025.

15 M. Cathcart, *Defending the National Tuckshop: Australia's Secret Army Intrigue of 1931*, McPhee Gribble / Penguin Books, Melbourne, 1988, p. 88.

16 'Serious offences', *The Sydney Morning Herald*, 24 March 1920, p. 10.

17 J. Maynard, 'The First World War', in J. Beaumont and A. Cadzow (eds), *Serving Our Country: Indigenous Australians, War, Defence and Citizenship*, NewSouth Publishing, Sydney, NSW, 2018, p. 74.

18 Beaumont and Cadzow (eds), *Serving Our Country*, pp. 18–19.

19 J. Chesterman and B. Galligan, *Citizens Without Rights: Aborigines and Australian Citizenship*, Cambridge University Press, Cambridge, 1997, p. 8.

20 R. Hall, *The Black Diggers: Aborigines and Torres Strait Islanders in the Second World War*, Aboriginal Studies Press, Canberra, 1997, p. 1.

21 F. Skyring, 'Taking matters into their own hands: riots against disloyalty, 1918–1920 in Australia', PhD thesis, University of Sydney, 1997, Chapter 7, 'Mothers, wives, sisters and sweethearts', pp. 320–49.

22 Ibid., pp. 8-9 in footnote 10.

23 J. Hilvert, *Blue Pencil Warriors: Censorship and Propaganda in World War II*, University of Queensland Press, St Lucia, Qld., 1984, p. 12.

24 Entry for 'War Precautions Act', in P. Dennis et al. (eds), *The Oxford Companion to Australian Military History*, 2nd edition, Oxford University Press, South Melbourne, Vic., 2008, p. 583.

1: Riots on Peace Day, November 1918

1 'Terms of the Armistice, the full text, announced by President Wilson', *The Advertiser* (Adelaide), 13 November 1918, p. 4.

2 E. Scott, *Australia During the War, Volume XI of The Official History of Australia in the War of 1914–1918*, University of Queensland Press, St Lucia, Qld., 1989, (first published 1936), p. 740.

3 R. Evans, *The Red Flag Riots*, University of Queensland Press, St Lucia, Qld., 1988, pp. 63–4.

4 'Amazing tramway strike to celebrate peace; disgraceful scenes in the streets', *The Register* (Adelaide), 15 November 1918, p. 4.

5 'Tramway employees' wages', *The Register*, 28 September 1918, p. 7.

6 'Meeting of strikers', *The Register*, 16 November 1918, p. 10.

7 'No trams today', *The Advertiser*, 14 November 1918, p. 5.

8 Ibid.

9 Ibid.

10 'Amazing tramway strike to celebrate peace', p. 4.

11 Ibid.

12 Ibid.

13 'Amazing tramway strike, lasted six days', *The Observer* (Adelaide), 23 November 1918, p. 30.

14 *The Daily Herald*, 16 November 1918, p. 6.

15 'Soldiers interfere', *The Daily Herald*, 15 November 1918, p. 4.

NOTES

16 'The tramway trouble, disturbances in the city', *The Advertiser*, 15 November 1918, p. 5.
17 'We don't want scabs', *The Daily Herald*, 15 November 1918, p. 4.
18 Ibid.
19 'Soldiers interfere', *The Daily Herald*, 15 November 1918, p. 4.
20 'Blacklegs mobbed by returned soldiers', *The Daily Herald*, 15 November 1918, p. 4.
21 'Amazing tramways strike', *The Register*, 15 November 1918, p. 4.
22 Superintendent Edward Priest to Commissioner of Police, 15 November 1918, State Records of South Australia, GRG24/6 Correspondence files Chief Secretary's Office ('CSO' files), file number 1303 of 1918, 'Disturbance in city on Thursday 14th November 1918 – Requesting a report re'.
23 Superintendent Priest to Police Commissioner, 15 November 1918, 'General report of proceedings in Adelaide 14/11/1918', GRG24/6.
24 'Amusements shut down', *The Advertiser*, 15 November 1918, p. 4.
25 'Mob rule on top', *The Register*, 15 November 1918, p. 7.
26 *The Advertiser*, 15 November 1918, p. 4.
27 Ibid.
28 'The usual libel, those dreadful returned men!', *Returned Soldier*, 28 November 1918, p. 28. The editors of the *Returned Soldier* weekly magazine were not identified in the publication (though it was likely a faction within the South Australian RSSILA),.
29 *The Advertiser*, 15 November 1918, p. 4.
30 Superintendent Priest to Police Commissioner, 15 November 1918, 'General report of proceedings in Adelaide 14/11/1918', GRG24/6.
31 'Serious police crisis, more than 100 Resignations', *The Register*, 16 September 1918, p. 7, and 'The police trouble, final demands to government', *The Register*, 19 September 1918, p. 5.
32 G. L. Kristianson, *The Politics of Patriotism*, Australian National University Press, Canberra, 1966, p. 7.
33 Cheer-up Society (SA) & Returned Sailors' and Soldiers' Imperial League of Australia, South Australian Branch, *RSA magazine*, Vol. 3, No. 12 (December 1918), p. 7.
34 Ibid., p. 8.
35 Ibid., p. 8.
36 'Not scabs, returned heroes support tramway men', *The Daily Herald*, 19 November 1918, p. 2.
37 Ibid. See also 'A big meeting of the RSA', *Returned Soldier*, 28 November 1918, p. 29
38 'Trams and soldiers, a lively meeting', *The Advertiser*, 19 November 1918, p. 5.
39 'Not scabs, returned heroes support tramway men', *The Daily Herald*, 19 November 1918, p. 2; 'A big meeting of the RSA', *Returned Soldier,* 28 November 1918, p. 29.
40 'Trams and soldiers, a lively meeting', p. 5; 'A big meeting of the RSA', *Returned Soldier*, 28 November 1918, p. 29.
41 'Trams and soldiers, a lively meeting', *The Advertiser*, 19 November 1918, p. 5.
42 Ibid.
43 Ibid.
44 Kristianson, *The Politics of Patriotism*, p. 12.
45 'Trams and soldiers, a lively meeting', *The Advertiser*, 19 November 1918, p. 5.
46 'Mass meeting of men', *The Register*, 18 November 1918, p. 4.
47 Ibid.

48 'Trams and soldiers, a lively meeting', p. 5.
49 'A city on foot', *The Advertiser*, 16 November 1918, p. 9.
50 'Tramway trouble ended', *The Advertiser*, 20 November 1918, p. 7.
51 'Tramways trouble, some personal explanations', *The Daily Herald*, 22 November 1918, p. 4.
52 Ibid.
53 *The Observer*, 23 November 1918, p. 31; *The Register*, 19 November 1918, p. 5; *The Advertiser*, 19 November 1918, p. 5.
54 *The Observer*, 7 December 1918, p. 27.
55 *The Worker* in Brisbane (5 December 1918, p. 17) and the *Barrier Daily Truth* (29 January 1918, p. 2) both referred to Broken Hill as 'that Gibraltar of Unionism', as did *The Evening Echo* in Ballarat (7 December 1918, p. 2). See also B. Kennedy, *Silver, Sin and Sixpenny Ale: A Social History of Broken Hill 1883–1921*, Melbourne University Press, Carlton, 1978, pp. 120, 136–42.
56 Copy of LVA pledge, in report by Detective-Sergeant Gibson, 29 November 1918, forwarded to Military Intelligence by the Inspector General of Police in Sydney, 'Labour Volunteer Army – Workers Defence Army or Workers Defence Corps', NAA: A6122, 109.
57 Report by Detective-Sergeant Gibson, 29 November 1918, forwarded to Military Intelligence by the Inspector General of Police in Sydney, NAA: A6122, 109.
58 Ibid.
59 'A.S.P...Barrier Branch', *The International Socialist*, 23 November 1918, p. 4.
60 Ibid.
61 J. Connell, 'The Red Flag, the International Hymn of Labor', Socialist Party of Victoria, Melbourne, undated c. 1919.
62 'In Broken Hill, news borne stoically', *Barrier Daily Truth*, 12 November 1918, p. 1. The *Barrier Daily Truth* is held at the National Library of Australia.
63 'The news in Broken Hill', *The Barrier Miner*, 12 November 1918, p. 2.
64 'In Broken Hill, news borne stoically', *Barrier Daily Truth*, 12 November 1918, p. 1.
65 Ibid.
66 'In Broken Hill, an open air demonstration', *The Barrier Miner*, 13 November 1918, p. 2; *Barrier Daily Truth*, 13 November 1918, p 4.
67 *Barrier Daily Truth*, 18 November 1918, p. 2.
68 'In Broken Hill, an open air demonstration', *The Barrier Miner*, 13 November 1918, p. 2.
69 'Heros honoured', *The Advertiser,* 21 October 1918, p. 6.
70 'Corporal Inwood's VC reception', *The Barrier Miner*, 21 October 1918, p. 4.
71 'Sergeant R. R. Inwood, V.C.' *The Barrier Miner,* 12 November 1918, p. 2.
72 L. Wigmore and B. Harding, *They Dared Mightily*, 2nd edition, Australian War Memorial, Canberra, 1986, p. 71.
73 Ibid.
74 'In Broken Hill, an open air demonstration', *The Barrier Miner*, 13 November 1918, p. 2.
75 'V.C.'s Views on "Mongrels"' was one example in *The Register*, 14 November 1918, p. 6. Other newspapers that ran the story included *The Young Witness* in rural NSW (15 November), *The Toowoomba Chronicle* (19 November), *The Bundaberg Mail* in Queensland (21 November) and fifteen other titles across New South Wales, Queensland, South Australia and Tasmania.

76	'Today's peace demonstration', *The Barrier Miner*, 13 November 1918, p. 4.
77	'Returned Soldiers Association, annual general meeting', *The Barrier Miner*, 14 December 1918, p. 12.
78	Editorial, 'This is not Hughenden', *Barrier Daily Truth*, 14 November 1918, pp. 2–3.
79	'Red Flags pulled down', *The Barrier Miner*, 13 November 1918, p. 2.
80	'Mishap to Mr G. C. Dempster', *The Barrier Miner*, 14 November 1918, p. 2.
81	Editorial, *Barrier Daily Truth*, 14 November 1918, p. 2.
82	*Barrier Daily Truth*, 14 November 1918, p. 4.
83	Ibid.
84	Ibid.
85	'The truth about Broken Hill', *Labor News*, 7 December 1918, p. 7.
86	Letter from 'G. D.' to Percy Brookfield, 'The truth about Broken Hill', published in *Labor News*, 7 December 1918, p. 7,
87	Ibid.
88	*Barrier Daily Truth*, 14 November 1918, p. 4.
89	Ibid., p. 2.
90	Ibid., p. 4.
91	*The Barrier Miner*, 14 November 1918, p. 3.
92	Ibid.
93	Letter from 'Jacques', Chloride Street Broken Hill to Dorrie, 21 November 1918, DMI Report 97/696, First Military District Intelligence Report (Censor's Office Report), NAA: A6286, 1/13.
94	*Barrier Daily Truth*, 15 November 1918, p. 2, *The Sydney Morning Herald*, 15 November 1918, p. 8, *Evening News*, 15 November 1918, p. 3; *The Observer*, 23 November 1918, p. 33.
95	'Riots at Broken Hill', *The Herald (Melbourne)*, 15 November 1918, p. 5.
96	'Last night's march', *Barrier Daily Truth*, 15 November 1918, p. 3; 'Riots at Broken Hill', *The Herald*, 15 November 1918, p. 5.
97	'The truth about Broken Hill', *Labor News*, 7 December 1918, p. 7.
98	Letter to the editor from 'Eyes Right', *Barrier Daily Truth*, 15 November 1918, p. 3.
99	'The sort of talk we don't want', *Australian Worker*, 21 November 1918, p. 10.
100	*Commonwealth of Australia Parliamentary Debates*, 7th Parliament, 2nd Session, 21 November 1918, pp. 8192–3.
101	J. Smeshurst, editor of *The Barrier Miner*, to Acting Prime Minister Watt, 19 November 1918, 'Unrest in Queensland – "Bolshevism", "Sinn Fein"', NAA: A456, W26/241, (note that this NAA file includes reports in relation to Broken Hill).
102	Ibid.
103	'The law's a hass', *The Soldier at Home and Abroad*, 22 November 1918, p. 5. *The Soldier* is held in hard copy at the National Library of Australia.
104	'Broken Hill and our comrades', *The Returned Soldier*, 28 November 1918, p. 53.
105	George Steward, to 'Dear Hall', 30 January 1918, correspondence marked 'secret', NAA: A8911, 240.
106	'Constable assaulted VC winner sentenced', *Maitland Daily Mercury*, 26 December 1919, p. 8.
107	J. Gibberd, 'Inwood, Reginald Roy (1890–1971)', *Australian Dictionary of Biography*, National Centre of Biography, Australian National University, adb.anu.edu.au/biography/inwood-reginald-roy-6795/text11753, published first in hardcopy 1983, viewed 18 March 2024.

108 Articles in *The Barrier Miner*: 'RSSILA', 10 May 1921, p. 4, 'RSSILA' 14 April 1921, p. 4 and 'RSSILA', 8 July 1920, p. 2.
109 'Townsville strike, cleansing the town', *Daily Mail*, 30 October 1918, p. 8.
110 'Townsville strike, a serious position, public health endangered', *Daily Mail*, 25 October 1918, pp. 5–6.
111 Ibid.
112 'Townsville strike, cleansing the town', p. 8.
113 Captain Willis, Townsville Military Intelligence, to Captain Wood, Victoria Barracks, Brisbane, 9 December 1918, 'IWW [Industrial Workers of the World] activities in Queensland', NAA: BP4/1, 66/5/115 PART 1.
114 Captain Willis, Intelligence Section General Staff to Captain Wood, Victoria Barracks, Brisbane, 30 October 1918, NAA: BP4/1, 66/5/115 PART 1.
115 Ibid., and Regulation 17 (1) of the War Precautions Regulations, Commonwealth of Australia, *Statutory rules made under Commonwealth Acts during the year 1915*, Butterworth and Co., Sydney, 1916, p. 225.
116 'Report of public meeting held at Townsville 6 December 1918', attachment to report from Captain Willis, Townsville Military Intelligence, to Captain Wood, Victoria Barracks, Brisbane, 9 December 1918, NAA: BP4/1, 66/5/115 PART 1.
117 Ibid.
118 Newsclip from the 'Townsville Bulletin', attached to report from Captain Willis, Townsville Military Intelligence, General staff, to Captain Wood, Victoria Barracks, Brisbane, 16 November 1918, NAA: BP4/1, 66/5/115 PART 1.
119 Captain Willis, Townsville Military Intelligence, General staff, to Captain Wood, Victoria Barracks, Brisbane, 16 November 1918, NAA: BP4/1, 66/5/115 PART 1.
120 Ibid.
121 'The Red Flag, raises more bovine rage, jingoes strike a snag', *The Daily Standard*, 15 November 1918, p. 5.
122 Captain Willis, Townsville Military Intelligence, to Captain Wood, Victoria Barracks, Brisbane, 16 November 1918, NAA: BP4/1, 66/5/115 PART 1; 'Diggers to the rescue', *The Brisbane Courier*, 16 November 1918, p. 4; 'Red Flag singers', *The Queenslander*, 23 November 1918, p. 12.
123 'The enemy within, Bolsheviks, red-raggers and the hateful IWW', *Farmer and Settler*, 19 November 1918, p. 3.
124 'Red Flag singers', *The Brisbane Courier*, 15 November 1918, p. 6. See also Captain Willis to Captain Wood, 16 November 1918, NAA: BP4/1, 66/5/115 PART 1.
125 Captain Willis to Captain Wood, 16 November 1918, NAA: BP4/1, 66/5/115 PART 1.
126 Ibid.
127 'Red Flag singers', *The Queenslander*, 23 November 1918, p. 12.
128 Captain Willis to Captain Wood, 16 November 1918, NAA: BP4/1, 66/5/115 PART 1.

2: Taking Matters Into Their Own Hands

1 Dr Thomas Roseby to Mr Fuller, Chief Secretary, 19 June 1918, Museums of History New South Wales (MHNSW) - State Archives Collection: Chief Secretary; NRS 905, Main series of letters received, [5/7996] 18/36119.
2 'Fight in a church, Returned soldiers object to peace talk', *The Leader*, 7 June 1918, p. 6; 'Trouble in a church', *The Sydney Morning Herald*, 8 June 1918, p. 14.

3   'Fight in a church', *The Leader*, 7 June 1918, p. 6.
4   *The Daily Telegraph* (Launceston), 7 June 1918, p. 4, *The Kalgoorlie Miner*, 7 June 1918, p. 4, *The Herald* (Melbourne), 6 June 1918, p. 1, and *The Sun* (Sydney), 6 June 1918, p. 5.
5   'Brawl in a church', *The Bathurst Times*, 7 June 1918, p. 4.
6   'Peace meeting in a church', *The Age*, 7 June 1918, p. 5.
7   *Commonwealth of Australia Parliamentary Debates*, Vol. LXXV, 1918, p. 5659.
8   'Pulled from the pulpit, Mr Roseby's explanation', *The Sun*, 8 June 1918, p. 6.
9   Ibid.
10 Ibid.
11 'Melee in church, letter to the editor', *The National Advocate*, 8 June 1918, p. 2.
12 'Offensive cartoons, big meeting of Catholics resents an affront', *Cowra Free Press*, 8 June 1918, p. 2.
13 The motion passed was: 'That this synod is so convinced that the forces of the Allies are being used of God to vindicate the rights of the weak and to maintain the moral order of the world that it gives its strong support to the principle of universal service, or the conscription of men and income'. See 'Church and conscription', *The Age*, 8 September 1916, p. 5.
14 'The Reverend T. B. Roseby, why he is agitating for peace', *The Leader*, 10 June 1918, p. 1.
15 Dr Thomas Roseby to Mr Fuller, Chief Secretary, 19 June 1918, MHNSW-StAC: NRS-905 [5/7996] 18/36119.
16 'The Reverend T. B. Roseby, why he is agitating for peace', *The Leader*, 10 June 1918, p. 1.
17 See letter from Amy, 'Redlands', Military Road Neutral Bay, to Rev. T. B. Roseby, Orange, 8 July 1918, 'DMI Report 97/668, First Military District Intelligence Report (Censor's Office Report) dated 6 February 1918, containing Censor's Office Serial Nos QF552 to QF568', NAA: A6286, 1/6.
18 Ibid.
19 Regulation 28 (b) of the *War Precautions Act 1914–1915* made it an offence to 'spread reports or make statements likely to prejudice the recruiting, training, discipline, or administration of any of His Majesty's Forces'. In *Commonwealth Statutory Rules 1915 &c., No. 130, War Precautions Act—Regulations*, p. 399. For the 1917 amendment see Regulation 28 (1) (c) *Commonwealth Statutory Rules 1917*, p. 282.
20 'Domain scenes soldiers v. socialists', *The Sydney Morning Herald*, 17 June 1918, p. 8.
21 'Member of Parliament fined', *The Sydney Morning Herald*, 10 July 1917, p. 4.
22 R. Gollan and M. Scollay, 'Brookfield, Percival Stanley (1875–1921)', *Australian Dictionary of Biography*, National Centre of Biography, Australian National University, adb.anu.edu.au/biography/brookfield-percival-stanley-5374/text9093, published first in hardcopy 1979, viewed 11 April 2024.
23 'Conscription, immense gathering in the Domain, lively scenes', *The Sydney Morning Herald*, 14 August 1916, p. 10.
24 'Disloyal utterances', *The Evening News*, 10 June 1918, p. 4.
25 NSW Parliamentary Debates, Legislative Assembly Questions and Answers, Session 1918, Vol. LXXI, 12 June, p. 26.
26 'Domain oratory, "Clear them out"', *The Sun*, 16 June 1918, p. 2.
27 Ibid.

28   Reports by James Mitchell, Inspector General of Police, 19 June 1918 and Metropolitan Superintendent Tait, 17 June 1918, MHNSW-StAC: NRS-905 [5/7996] 18/36104.
29   General Secretary P. C. Evans, NSW Labor Party to Hon. G. F. Pearce, Minister for Defence, 17 June 1918, NRS-905 [5/7996] 18/36104.
30   Report by Sergeant Robertson, 16 June 1918, NRS-905 [5/7996] 18/36104.
31   Ibid.
32   Report by Constable Tindale, 17 June 1918, NRS-905 [5/7996] 18/36104.
33   Reports by Detectives H. Jordan and N. Moore, 16 June 1918, NRS-905 [5/7996] 18/36104.
34   Ibid.
35   A. Wishart, 'Good Friday 1915', https://www.awm.gov.au/articles/blog/good-friday-1915 viewed 16 April 2025.
36   'Rioting in the Domain', *The Sun*, 17 June 1918, p. 5.
37   'Charges under War Precautions Act – Rex v. Judd et al', NAA: A456, W26/199/410.
38   'Soldiers run riot', *Australian Worker*, 20 June 1918, p. 5.
39   Report by Inspector Turbet, 16 June 1918, NRS-905 [5/7996] 18/36104.
40   Metropolitan Superintendent Tait, 17 June 1918, NRS-905 [5/7996] 18/36104.
41   General Secretary P. C. Evans, NSW Labor Party to Hon. G. F. Pearce, Minister for Defence, 17 June 1918, NRS-905 [5/7996] 18/36104.
42   Report by Inspector Bannan, 16 June 1918, NRS-905 [5/7996] 18/36104.
43   Ibid., report by Inspector Drew, 17 June 1918, and report by Metropolitan Superintendent Tait, 17 June 1918, NRS-905 [5/7996] 18/36104.
44   Report by Inspector Drew, 17 June 1918, NRS-905 [5/7996] 18/36104.
45   'Domain orators', *The Daily Telegraph*, 17 June 1918, p. 4.
46   General Secretary P. C. Evans, NSW Labor Party to Hon. G. F. Pearce, Minister for Defence, 17 June 1918, NRS-905 [5/7996] 18/36104.
47   'Soldiers run riot', *Australian Worker*, 20 June 1918, p. 5.
48   General Secretary P. C. Evans, NSW Labor Party to Hon. G. F. Pearce, Minister for Defence, 17 June 1918, NRS-905 [5/7996] 18/36104.
49   For Holman's proposal, see *NSW Parliamentary Debates*, 2nd Series, Session 1918, Vol. LXXI, 18 June, p 105. The bill was not enacted until November, and then only with substantial amendments.
50   'Splitting a citizen in two', *The Sun*, 19 June 1918, p. 4.
51   'Domain safety valve, ringed with police', *The Daily Telegraph*, 24 June 1918, p. 4.
52   'Domain scenes', *The Sydney Morning Herald*, 17 June 1918, p. 8; 'Domain orators, Hostile demonstrations', *The Daily Telegraph*, 17 June 1918, p. 4; 'Domain disturbance', *The Evening News*, 17 June 1918, p. 5.
53   'Domain orators, Hostile demonstrations', *The Daily Telegraph*, 17 June 1918., p. 4.
54   'Domain scenes', *The Sydney Morning Herald*, 17 June 1918, p. 8.
55   'Disloyalists of the Domain', *The Mirror*, 21 June 1918, p. 3.
56   *The Soldier at Home and Abroad*, 21 June 1918, p. 3.
57   Ibid.
58   'Free Speech Committee', *People*, 1 August 1918, p. 3.
59   Inspector General of Police to Under Secretary, 19 September 1918, NRS-905 [5/7996] 18/36183.
60   Ibid.
61   'Free Speech Committee', *People*, 5 September 1918, p. 4.

62. 'Particulars of Service in the AIF', Taylour Thomas Gilbert: SERN 32 13664: POB Portobello Scotland: POE Brisbane QLD: NOK D Taylour Lalage, NAA: B2455, Taylour T. G.
63. M. Cryle, "'Gunner' Taylour and the Comrades of War League', *Queensland History Journal*, Volume 24, No. 1, May 2019, pp. 39–52, pp. 39 and 45–6. Also 'State parliament', *Warwick Daily News*, 4 October 1919, p. 5.
64. 'Selective socialism', *The Daily Standard*, 15 July 1918, p. 3.
65. Cryle, "'Gunner' Taylour', pp. 43–4.
66. 'Peace debate', *Daily Mail*, 1 July 1918, p. 5.
67. 'Gunner Taylour a Red Cross lecturer', undated report c. August 1918 by F. W. S. Cumbrae Stewart, Assistant Censor, 'Regarding 'Gunner' Taylour [Taylor] – Red Cross lecturer', NAA: BP4/1, 66/4/3048.
68. 'Empire's call for men', *The Brisbane Courier*, 24 June 1918, p. 9, and 'Speakers in the Domain, lively doings yesterday', *Telegraph*, 24 June 1918, p. 5.
69. Jennie Scott Griffiths to R. S. Ross, 31 July 1918, 'Melbourne censors secret intelligence reports, July - August 1918 [suspicious actions]', NAA : MP95/1, 169/26–34.
70. T. H. Irving, 'Scott Griffiths, Jennie (1875–1951)', *Australian Dictionary of Biography*, National Centre of Biography, Australian National University, https://adb.anu.edu.au/biography/scott-griffiths-jennie-11641/text20793, published first in hardcopy 2002, viewed 12 June 2024.
71. Jennie Scott Griffiths to R. S. Ross, 31 July 1918, NAA: MP95/1, 169/26–34.
72. Ibid.
73. 'Straight talk in the Domain', *The Daily Standard*, 29 July 1918, p. 5.
74. 'Domain speeches, peace platform upset', *Daily Mail*, 29 July 1918, p. 5.
75. 'Returned soldiers prosecuted', *Daily Mail*, 8 August 1918, p. 5.
76. 'Domain speeches, peace platform upset', *Daily Mail*, 29 July 1918, p. 5.
77. 'Returned soldiers prosecuted', *Daily Mail*, 8 August 1918, p. 5.
78. Ibid.
79. 'Police and soldiers, bitter feeling alleged', *Daily Mail*, 23 October 1918, p. 5.
80. 'Disturbance in the Domain, prosecution of returned soldiers', *The Brisbane Courier*, 27 November 1918, p. 8.
81. 'The Domain Case, disturbances must be stopped', *The Daily Standard*, 26 November 1918, p. 5.
82. R. Evans, *Loyalty and Disloyalty: Social Conflict on the Queensland Homefront, 1914–18*, Allen & Unwin, Sydney, 1987, pp. 155–6.
83. 'Hughenden fight, a violent development', *The Daily Standard*, 18 October 1918, p. 5.
84. 'A Hughenden echo, remarkable inquiry', *The Brisbane Courier*, 11 July 1919, p. 7. This was evidence at the July 1919 inquiry into police conduct at Hughenden.
85. Censored letter QF2317, R. Campbell, Hughenden Hotel, to Mrs Betsy Matthias Sydney, 4 November 1918, 'DMI Report 167/54, First Military District Intelligence Report (Censor's Office Report) dated 13 November 1918', NAA: A6286, 1/78.
86. 'Ruffianism, latest profiteer move', *The Daily Standard*, 22 October 1918, p. 5.
87. Copies of telegrams from Andrews to Byrne, Returned Soldiers Association, Charters Towers, 'IWW [Industrial Workers of the World] activities in Queensland', NAA: BP4/1, 66/5/115 PART 4.
88. Lieut. Byrne to North Queensland Recruiting Committee, 23 October 1918, NAA: BP4/1, 66/5/115 PART 4.

89   'Hughenden riots', *The Queensland Times*, 21 October 1918, p. 5; 'Street fights', *Daily Mail*, 21 October 1918, p. 8; 'Riots at Hughenden', *Darling Downs Gazette*, 21 October 1918, p. 4; and 'Riots at Hughenden', *Warwick Examiner and Times*, 23 October 1918, p. 1.

90   Report 27 October 1918 from Captain Willis to Captain Wood, Intelligence Officer, 1st military District, re 'Hughenden Incident', NAA: BP4/1, 66/5/115 PART 4.

91   Lieut. Byrne to North Queensland Recruiting Committee, 23 October 1918, NAA: BP4/1, 66/5/115 PART 4.

92   'The Hughenden trouble, An exciting two days', *The Evening Telegraph*, 21 October 1918, p. 3.

93   'The Hughenden fracas', *Townsville Daily Bulletin*, 19 October 1918, p. 5.

94   Lieut. Byrne to North Queensland Recruiting Committee, 23 October 1918, NAA: BP4/1, 66/5/115 PART 4.

95   Censored letter QF2317, R. Campbell, Hughenden Hotel, to Mrs Betsy Matthias, Sydney, 4 November 1918, 'DMI Report 167/54, First Military District Intelligence Report (Censor's Office Report) dated 13 November 1918', NAA: A6286, 1/78.

96   Ibid.

97   Report from Captain Willis to Captain Wood, Intelligence Officer, 1st military District, 27 October 1918, re 'Hughenden Incident', NAA: BP4/1, 66/5/115 PART 4.

98   'The Hughenden fracas', p. 4.

99   Captain Willis to Captain Wood, Victoria Barracks, Brisbane, 15 November 1918, NAA: BP4/1, 66/5/115 PART 4.

100   Ibid.

101   'The Hughenden beer strike', *Labor News*, 16 November 1918, p. 7.

102   Ibid.

103   'Hughenden outlawry', *The Daily Standard*, 26 October 1918, p. 5.

104   'Ruffianism, latest profiteer move', *The Daily Standard*, 22 October 1918, p. 5.

105   Censored letter QF 2287, from Archie Eastcrabb, Hughenden, to General Secretary, QRU, Brisbane, 21 October 1918, 'DMI Report 167/52, First Military District Intelligence Report (Censor's Office Report) dated 6 November 1918', NAA: A6286, 1/76.

106   Ibid.

107   Censored letter, QF2306, from Paddy, Hughenden, to Archie Eastcrabb, QRU, Brisbane, 3 November 1918, 'DMI Report 167/54, First Military District Intelligence Report (Censor's Office Report) dated 13 November 1918', NAA: A6286, 1/78.

108   'Hughenden riots', *Daily Mail*, 30 October 1918, p. 7.

109   'Ruffianism, latest profiteer move', *The Daily Standard*, 22 October 1918, p. 5.

110   Ibid.

111   'Hughenden riots', *Daily Mail*, 30 October 1918, p. 7.

112   Censored letter, QF2306, from Paddy, Hughenden, to Archie Eastcrabb, QRU, Brisbane, 3 November 1918, NAA: A6286, 1/78.

113   'The Hughenden trouble, cleaning up the town', *The Northern Miner*, 21 October 1918, p. 3.

114   'Cleaning up Hughenden', *Townsville Daily Bulletin*, 21 October 1918, p. 5.

115   'IWW banned, Hughenden's determination', *Daily Mail*, 22 October 1918, p. 4.

116   Chief Censor's entry for 29 October 1918, *'Diaries of the Chief Censor'*, NAA: MP390/8, Vol. 4 (January–December 1918).

117   'Trouble at Hughenden', *The Telegraph*, 22 October 1918, p. 2.

118	'The Hughenden beer strike', *Labor News*, 16 November 1918, p. 7.
119	'The Hughenden rumpus', *The Brisbane Courier*, 22 October 1918, p. 7.
120	Censored letter, QF 2284, from Dash, Townsville to Dunstan, *The Worker* Office Brisbane, 2 November 1918, 'First Military District Intelligence Report (Censor's Office Report) dated 6 November 1918', NAA: A6286, 1/76.
121	'Meeting of the beer strikers', *The Northern Miner*, 25 October 1918, p. 2.
122	'A deported man's account', *Townsville Daily Bulletin*, 22 October 1918, p. 4.
123	Lieutenant Byrne to North Queensland Recruiting Committee, 23 October 1918, NAA: BP4/1, 66/5/115 PART 4.
124	Censored letter, QF 2542, from J. Green, Hughenden to Michael Kelly, Townsville, 1 December 1918, 'First Military District Intelligence Report (Censor's Office Report) dated 11 December 1918', NAA: A6286, 1/86.
125	'In Broken Hill, an open air demonstration', *The Barrier Miner*, 13 November 1918, p. 2.
126	Ibid.
127	'Doings in the north, to the Editor', *The Brisbane Courier*, 24 October 1918, p. 6.

3: 'Dulce et Decorum Est': Remembering Soldiers' Sacrifice

1	Oliver to 'Dear Sister', Cairo, 8 May 1915, *The Anzac Letters of Joseph and Oliver Cumberland*, compiled by Joan Crommelin, Scone and Upper Hunter Historical Society, Scone, 1986, p. 38.
2	Oliver to 'Dear Una', Cairo, 31 May 1915, pp. 39–40.
3	'The Late Private O. J. Cumberland', *The Scone Advocate*, 2 June 1916, p. 7.
4	*The Anzac Letters of Joseph and Oliver Cumberland*, pp. 5–6 and 44.
5	Ibid., p. 44.
6	Ibid., p. 45.
7	'Family notices, Roll of Honour', *The Scone Advocate*, 8 August 1916, p. 2.
8	'Nine poets of the First World War', https://www.iwm.org.uk/history/9-poets-of-the-first-world-war, viewed 16 April 2025.
9	W. Owen, 'Dulce Et Decorum Est', in J. Silkin (ed.), *The Penguin Book of First World War Poetry*, Second edition, Penguin Books, London, 1981, pp. 182–3, quote p. 183.
10	S. Sassoon, 'Blighters', https://www.poetryfoundation.org/poems/57215/blighters, viewed 16 April 2025. Bapaume was a town on the Somme that saw fierce fighting throughout the war.
11	S. Hynes, *A War Imagined: The First World War and English Culture*, The Bodley Head, London, 1990, pp. 235–41.
12	E. Leed, *No Man's Land: Combat and Identity in World War I*, Cambridge University Press, New York, 1979, Chapter 6. For details of riots see pp. 201–3.
13	M. Egremont (ed.), *Some Desperate Glory: The First World War the Poets Knew*, Picador, London, 2014, 'Preface', p. xi.
14	Hynes, *A War Imagined*, p. ix.
15	P. Fussell, *The Great War and Modern Memory*, Oxford University Press, New York, 1975. See also S. Hynes, *A War Imagined*.
16	J. Winter, *Sites of Memory, Sites of Mourning: The Great War in European Cultural history*, Cambridge University Press, Cambridge, 1995, quote p. 5.
17	Ibid., Chapter 2.
18	Ibid., Chapter 3.

19	G. L. Mosse, *Fallen Soldiers: Reshaping the Memory of the World Wars*, Oxford University Press, New York, 1990.
20	A. Thomson, *Anzac Memories: Living with the Legend*, Oxford University Press, Melbourne, 1994, pp. 58–72, quote p. 68; D. A. Kent, '*The Anzac Book* and the Anzac Legend: C. E. W. Bean as Editor and Image Maker', *Historical Studies*, Vol. 21 No 84, April 1985, pp. 376–90.
21	J. Maynard, 'The First World War', in Beaumont and Cadzow (eds), *Serving Our Country*, pp. 74–93.
22	C. E. W. Bean, 'Introduction' to *Anzac Memorial*, published by the NSW Branch of the RSSILA, Sydney, 1919.
23	J. F. Williams, *Quarantined Culture: Australian Reactions to Modernism 1913–1939*, Cambridge University Press, Melbourne, 1995, pp. 107–25, quote p. 125.
24	ABS population statistics, 'Population capital cities and rest of the country, Australia', https://www.abs.gov.au/statistics/people/population/historical-population/latest-release, viewed 17 April 2025.
25	Garton, *The Cost of War*, pp. 39–45, quote p. 43.
26	R. Gerster, *Big-Noting: The Heroic Theme in Australian War Writing*, Melbourne University Press, Carlton, Vic., 1992 edition (first published 1987), pp. ix–6, 12–20.
27	C. Rhoden, *The Purpose of Futility: Writing World War I, Australian Style*, UWA Publishing, Crawley, Western Australia, 2015, pp. 76–85.
28	V. Palmer, 'The farmer remembers the Somme', in D. Holloway (ed.), *Dark Somme Flowing: Australian Verse of the Great War, 1914–1918*, Robert Andersen and Associates, Malvern, Vic., 1987, p. 110.
29	E. P. Harrington, 'Anzac', in *Dark Somme Flowing*, p. 71.
30	Sgt. C. T. O'Neill, 'Anzacs calling from the trenches', *Soldiers Poems*, Melbourne, 1917.
31	*The Port Hacking Cough*, Vol. 1, No. 1, 14 December 1918, p. 1.
32	*B.E.F. Times*, 25 December 1916, *Kemmel Times*, 3 July 1916 and *Somme Times*, 31 July 1916. From *The Wipers Times and After: A Facsimile Reprint of the Trench Magazines*, Herbert Jenkins Ltd, London, 1918.
33	*The Wipers Times*, February 1916.
34	*The Port Hacking Cough*, Vol. 1, No. 2, 21 December 1918, pp. 23–4.
35	*The Port Hacking Cough*, Vol. 1, No. 1, 14 December 1918, pp. 10, 3 and 11.
36	Ibid., p. 8.
37	Ibid., p. 14.
38	Ibid., p. 4.
39	*The Port Hacking Cough*, Vol. 1, No. 3, 28 December 1918, p. 38.
40	*The Port Hacking Cough*, Vol. 1, No. 2, 21 December 1918, p. 23.
41	*The Port Hacking Cough*, Vol. 1, No. 3, 28 December 1918, p. 36.
42	Ibid., p. 42.
43	*The Port Hacking Cough*, Vol. 1, No. 4, 4 January 1919, p. 57.
44	Ibid., pp. 56–7.
45	*The Port Hacking Cough*, Vol. 1, No. 7, 25 January 1919, p. 102.
46	Ibid., p. 113.
47	Ibid., p. 115.
48	*The Soldier*, 15 November 1918, p. 2.
49	Ibid.
50	Ibid.

51 J. Beaumont, *Broken Nation: Australians in the Great War*, Allen & Unwin, Sydney, 2013, p. xx.
52 A. Thomson, *Anzac Memories*, pp. 1–13.
53 C. J. Dennis, *Digger Smith*, Angus and Robertson, Sydney, 1920, (first edition November 1918, reprint January 1919), quotes from pp. 46 and 65.
54 G. L. Mosse, 'Shell shock as a social disease', *Journal of Contemporary History*, Vol. 35, No. 1, Special Issue: Shell-Shock (January 2000), pp. 101–8, quote p. 101.
55 A. G. Butler, *Official History 1914–1918 War: Records of A. G. Butler, Historian of Australian Army Medical Services*, Vol. II, Australian War Memorial, Canberra, 1940, p. 72.
56 Butler cited the British Expeditionary Force (BEF) definition for a 'wound stripe' in 1916, p. 270.
57 Sir A. McPhail, *Official History of the Canadian Forces in the Great War: The Medical Services*, Minister of National Defence, Ottawa, Canada, 1925, pp. 278 and 276.
58 Butler, *Official History*, Vol. II, p. 498.
59 M. Tyquin, *Madness and the Military: Australia's experience of shell shock in the great war*, Australian Scholarly Publishing, North Melbourne, 2019, Chapters 3 (pp. 28–51) and 5 (pp. 79–107).
60 Butler, *Official History*, Vol. II, p. 63.
61 Ibid., p. 59.
62 Ibid., p. 72.
63 'Shell shock, by an Officer', *The Argus*, 20 July 1918, p. 8.
64 'Special Constable's action', *The Western Argus*, 25 November 1919, p. 11.
65 'Shell shock', *Dubbo Dispatch and Wellington Independent*, 21 June 1918, p. 1.
66 'For soldiers work wanted', *The Sun*, 24 April 1918, p. 6.
67 Advertisements, *The Sun*, 12 May 1917, p. 6; 15 December 1917, p. 4; 5 April 1918, p. 7; 19 April 1918, p. 3; 20 April 1918, p. 4.
68 Advertisement, *Daily Mail*, 15 May 1918, p. 7. The same ad was repeated almost daily throughout May, June and July 1918 in the advertising columns.
69 'Liquor forbidden to sick soldiers', *The Herald*, 5 June 1918, p. 6.
70 Regulation 12A of the *War Precautions Act 1914–1916* allowed for the closure of hotels by military order and, in an amendment in 1917, Regulation 12B allowed for prohibition of the supplying of liquor to members of the armed forces and navy by anyone other than 'Licensed Victuallers'. In *Commonwealth Statutory Rules &c. 1916*, p. 481 and *Commonwealth Statutory Rules 1917*, p. 269.
71 *The Soldier*, 14 June 1918, p. 6.
72 'The blue armband', *The Advertiser*, 12 July 1918, p. 8.
73 Advertisement for 'Liberty League, non-political, non-sectarian', *Papers of Herbert and Ivy Brookes, 1869–1970 [manuscript]*, National Library of Australia (NLA), MS1924/21/759.
74 Newspaper advertisements for the Liberty League, also G. A. Burkett, Organising Secretary, 'The Liberty League of Victoria: Objects', October 1918, NLA MS1924/21/ items 753-761.
75 'A chat with Lieutenant Burkett', *Western Women*, 1 April 1917, p. 6.
76 'Returned man's lapse', *The Newcastle Sun*, 27 November 1918, p. 2.
77 'List of witnesses', Select Committee on Intoxicating Liquor & Australia. Parliament. Senate, *Progress Report from the Select Committee on Intoxicating Liquor: Effect on Australian soldiers and Best Method of Dealing with Sale; Together with Minutes*

        of Evidence up to 27th March, 1918, http://nla.gov.au/nla.obj-2769287381, viewed April 17, 2025.
78   Ibid., p. 22.
79   Letter from McKenzie submitted as evidence, Ibid., p. 21.
80   Ibid., pp. 28–9.
81   Ibid., pp. 10–11.
82   Ibid., pp. 31–2.
83   Ibid., pp. 160–1.
84   Ibid., pp. 31–3.
85   Australian War Memorial, 'At end of war', https://www.awm.gov.au/articles/encyclopedia/enlistment/ww1#end, viewed 17 April 2025.
86   M. Larsson, 'The part we do not see', in M. Crotty and M. Larsson (eds), *Anzac Legacies: Australians and the Aftermath of War*, Australian Scholarly Publishing, North Melbourne, Vic., 2010, pp. 39–60, quote p. 41.
87   Ibid., p. 47
88   Ibid.
89   M. Larsson, *Shattered Anzacs: Living with the Scars of War*, University of NSW Press, Kensington NSW, 2009, pp. 21–22.
90   Ibid., p. 21.
91   J. Allen, *Sex and Secrets: Crimes Involving Australian Women Since 1880*, Oxford University Press, Melbourne, 1990, p. 132.
92   Ibid., p. 131.
93   Ibid., pp. 131–3, quotes pp. 132–3.
94   Ibid., p. 144.
95   Ibid., p. 146.
96   Ibid., pp. 155–6.
97   'Serious offences', *The Sydney Morning Herald*, 24 March 1920, p. 10.
98   Ibid.

4: When the Soldiers Came Home: Riots in Fremantle and Melbourne, 1919

1   My figures on return are calculated from B. Gammage, *The Broken Years: Australian Soldiers in the Great War*, Australian National University Press, Canberra, 1974, p. 283, C. E. W. Bean, *Anzac to Amiens*, Australian War Memorial, Canberra, 1983, first published 1946, p. 532 and E. Scott, *Australia During the War: The Official History of Australia in the War of 1914–1918, Volume XI*, pp. 825–7. See also Adjutant General, Department of Defence, to General Secretary, Returned Sailors' and Soldiers' Imperial League of Australia (RSSILA) 26 July 1918, in *Records of the Returned Services League of Australia, 1916–1997 [manuscript], (RSL Papers)*, National Library of Australia, MS 6609/1/273. For casualty statistics see Australian War Memorial, https://www.awm.gov.au/articles/encyclopedia/enlistment/ww1#end, viewed 17 April 2025.
2   Leed, *No Man's Land*, p. 204.
3   *The Soldier*, 7 June 1918, p. 27.
4   *The Soldier*, 22 November 1918, p. 26.
5   Returned Sailors' and Soldiers' Labor League (RSSLL), *The Returned Soldiers and the Labor Movement*, Brisbane, 1919, p. 2.
6   Macintyre, *The Succeeding Age*, p. 163; Garton, *The Cost of War*, p. 12.

7   I. Turner, *Industrial Labour and Politics: The Dynamics of the Labour Movement in Eastern Australia 1900–1921*, Hale & Iremonger, Sydney, 1979, table of unemployment rates, p. 253.
8   Garton, *The Cost of War*, pp. 89–90.
9   RSSLL, *The Returned Soldiers and the Labor Movement*, pp. 5, 17–18.
10 Turner, *Industrial Labour and Politics*, p. 194.
11 J. Stanford, *Briefing Note: Historical Data on the Decline in Australian Industrial Disputes*, The Australia Institute, 2018, p. 10, https://australiainstitute.org.au/wp-content/uploads/2020/12/Industrial_Disputes_Briefing_Note_FINAL.pdf, viewed 17 April 2025.
12 C. Rasmussen, 'Maurice Blackburn and the 1919 Seamen's Strike in Australia', in J. Lack (ed.), *1919: The Year Things Fell Apart?*, Australian Scholarly Publishing, North Melbourne, 2019, p. 70.
13 Australian Labor Federation, *The Fremantle Wharf Crisis of 1919*, The Westralian Worker, Perth, 1920, p. 9.
14 Ibid.
15 'Another big demonstration', *The Daily News (Perth)*, 25 April 1919, p. 7.
16 *The Fremantle Wharf Crisis of 1919*, and 'Fremantle fragments', *The Westralian Worker*, 18 April 1919, p. 5.
17 'At Fremantle', *The West Australian*, 3 May 1919, p. 7; 'Employers statement, rejoinder by Mr McCallum', *The West Australian*, 28 April 1919, p. 4.
18 *The Fremantle Wharf Crisis of 1919*, pp. 16–20.
19 Ibid., p. 20; 'Bloody clash at Fremantle', *The Daily News*, 5 May 1919, p. 4.
20 'Statement by Premier', *The Daily News*, 5 May 1919, p. 6.
21 *The Fremantle Wharf Crisis of 1919*, pp. 21–2; 'Bloody clash at Fremantle', *The Daily News*, 5 May 1919, p. 4.
22 *The Fremantle Wharf Crisis of 1919*, pp. 19–23; 'Wharf trouble, police and lumpers in conflict', *The West Australian*, 5 May 1919, p. 5.
23 'Returned soldiers' meeting, indignation expressed', *The West Australian*, 5 May 1919, p. 6.
24 'Yesterday's meetings, direct action decided upon', *The Daily News*, 5 May 1919, p. 6.
25 'A procession', *The Daily News*, 5 May 1919, p. 6.
26 Ibid.
27 'Returned soldiers' meeting', *The West Australian*, 5 May 1919, p. 6.
28 Ibid.
29 Ibid.
30 Ibid.
31 'Meeting in Perth', *The West Australian*, 5 May 1919, p. 6.
32 'Corboy and McCallum', *The Westralian Worker*, 9 May 1919, p. 5.
33 *The Fremantle Wharf Crisis of 1919*, p. 26.
34 Percy Trainer to R. S. Ross, 19 May 1919, 'DMI Report 169/85, Third Military District Intelligence Report (Censor's Office Report) dated 28 May 1919', NAA: A6286, 3/107.
35 'Barring the police', *Daily News*, 5 May 1919, p. 2.
36 Percy Trainer to R. S. Ross, 19 May 1919, NAA: A6286, 3/107.
37 'Still more bloodshed', *The Daily News*, 6 May 1919, p. 6.
38 Ibid.

39 'Fremantle wharf trouble', (from Perth 6 May), *The Western Argus*, 13 May 1919, p. 30.
40 *The Fremantle Wharf Crisis of 1919*, pp. 28–30.
41 Ibid, pp. 28–30.
42 Ibid., pp. 34–5.
43 'The wharf settlement, work started', *The Western Argus*, 13 May 1919, p. 14.
44 Mick Sawtell, East Perth, to Don Cameron, 'The Socialist', Melbourne, 7 May 1919, 'DMI Report 169/83, Third Military District Intelligence Report (Censor's Office Report) dated 14 May 1919', NAA: A6286, 3/105.
45 'Meeting of returned soldiers, utmost disorder prevails', *The Daily News*, 6 May 1919, p. 7.
46 'Position of returned soldiers, A disorderly meeting', *The West Australian*, 6 May 1919, p. 5.
47 '"No preference" says Mr Donnes', *The Daily News*, 9 May 1919, p. 7.
48 'Clem', Trades Hall, Perth to Don Cameron, Melbourne, 7 May 1919, 'DMI Report 169/83, Third Military District Intelligence Report (Censor's Office Report) dated 14 May 1919', NAA: A6286, 3/105.
49 'South Fremantle branch', *The Fremantle Times*, 18 July 1919, p. 7.
50 Ibid.
51 Military Commandant, Sydney to Department of Defence, Melbourne, 30 May 1919, 'Disloyal literature placed on returning troopships', NAA: MP367/1, 512/1/961.
52 Pamphlet from intelligence reports for week ending 21 May 1919, NAA: MP367/1, 512/1/961.
53 'Censor's notes from intelligence reports for week ending 21 May 1919', NAA: MP367/1, 512/1/961.
54 Secretary, Prime Minister's Department to Secretary, Department of Defence, 7 June 1919, NAA: MP367/1, 512/1/961.
55 Undated c. early June 1919, from George Lloyd, Methodist Parsonage Caufield to Prime Minister, NAA: MP367/1, 512/1/961.
56 'Captain Throssell dead', *The Argus*, 20 November 1933, p. 10; L. Wigmore (ed. et al.), *They dared mightily*, Australian War Memorial. Canberra, 1986, pp. 119–21; S. Welborn, 'Throssell, Hugo Vivian Hope (1884–1933)', *Australian Dictionary of Biography*, National Centre of Biography, Australian National University, https://adb.anu.edu.au/biography/throssell-hugo-vivian-hope-8806/text15445 viewed 17 April 2025.
57 'Captain Hugo Throssell, V.C. Declares Himself a Socialist', *The Westralian Worker*, 25 July 1919, p. 4.
58 'Throssell VC, Nonplusses Northam', *Truth* (Perth), 26 July 1919, p. 3.
59 'The Russian Commemoration', *The Fremantle Herald*, 14 November 1919, p. 5.
60 Welborn, 'Throssell, Hugo Vivian Hope (1884–1933)'.
61 'A VC for Peace', *The Sunday Telegraph*, 30 September 1984, pp. 18–19.
62 'Captain Throssell dead', *The Argus*, 20 November 1933, p. 10.
63 H. Throssell, *Scrapbook kept by H. V. H. Throssell, 1903–1912*, State Library of Western Australia.
64 Bean, *Anzac to Amiens*, p. 529.
65 Rasmussen, 'Maurice Blackburn and the 1919 Seamen's Strike in Australia', pp. 77–8.
66 Minutes of Committee meeting, Sunday, 29 June 1919, *RSSILA Victorian Branch Archives*, Anzac House, Melbourne (no index numbers).

NOTES

67 Lieutenant Burkett, in *Echuca and Moama Advertiser and Farmers' Gazette*, 8 July 1915, p. 4.
68 Liberty League pamphlets and newspaper advertisements, undated, but probably late 1918, *Papers of Herbert and Ivy Brookes, 1869-1970 [manuscript]*, National Library of Australia, MS1924/ 21/ items 753–761.
69 'Attitude of Soldiers' League', *The Age*, 21 May 1919, p. 10.
70 Ibid.
71 'Unionists v. loyalists', *The Age*, 20 May 1919, p. 7.
72 'Attitude of Soldiers' League', *The Age*, 21 May 1919, p. 10.
73 'Conflicts on wharves', *The Telegraph*, 22 May 1919, p. 5.
74 'Peace celebrations', *The Bayonet*, 18 July 1919, p. 1.
75 'Soldiers riot in Melbourne', *The Sunday Times*, 20 July 1919, p. 3; 'Street riots', *The Daily Telegraph*, 21 July 1919, p. 12.
76 Ibid.
77 Report from Senior Constable Scanlon, 20 July 1919, Public Records Office of Victoria (PROV), VA 724, Victoria Police (Including Office of the Chief Commissioner of Police), VPRS 807/P0000, Unit 0000703.
78 'Peace Day riots, police v. soldiers', *The Daily Standard*, 21 July 1919, p. 5.
79 'Disorder in city', *The Argus*, 21 July 1919, p. 6; 'Street riots', *The Daily Telegraph*, 21 July 1919, p. 12.
80 Statement by James Joseph Fawcett, 24 July 1919, VPRS 807/P0000, Unit 0000703.
81 Statutory declaration by James Joseph Fawcett, 21 July 1919, VPRS 807/P0000, Unit 0000703.
82 Statement by Taylor, 18 August 1919, VPRS 807/P0000, Unit 0000703.
83 Copy of complaint by Albert Villinger, 22nd Battalion, undated, VPRS 807/P0000, Unit 0000703.
84 Statement by Albert Villinger 31 July 1919, also statement of Constable Pierce Fennessy 6–8 August 1919, VPRS 807/P0000, Unit 0000703.
85 22 July 1919 memo from Chief Commissioner GS (George Steward) to Superintendent Davidson, VPRS 807/P0000, Unit 0000703.
86 Charge sheet – report of misconduct against Senior Constable Scanlon, also statement in VPRS 807/P0000, Unit 0000703.
87 Editorial, *The Bayonet*, 1 August 1919, p. 2. *The Bayonet* is held in hard copy at the National Library of Australia.
88 'Peace Day riots, Police v. soldiers', *The Daily Standard*, 21 July 1919, p. 5; 'Disorder in city', *The Argus*, 21 July 1919, p. 6; see also report from Constable Whitlock, VPRS 807/P0000, Unit 0000703.
89 *The Bayonet*, 25 July 1919, p. 1.
90 Report of Monday 21 July events to RSSILA Victorian Committee meeting, 20 August 1919, *RSSILA Victorian Branch Archives*, Anzac House, Melbourne.
91 Memo from Chief Commissioner to Inspector Superintendent Davidson, Melbourne VPRS 807/P0000, Unit 0000703.
92 'Meeting at Athenaeum', *The Bayonet*, 25 July 1919, p. 1; 'Big disturbance in Melbourne', *The Daily Standard*, 22 July 1919, p. 5.
93 Ibid.; 'An angry outburst, Denunciation of police', *The Argus*, 22 July 1919, p. 5.
94 Ibid.
95 Both newspaper reports 22 July 1919, also report by Sub Inspector Wardley, 22 July 1919, VPRS 807/P0000, Unit 0000703.

NOTES

96 'Big disturbance in Melbourne', *The Daily Standard*, 22 July 1919, p. 5; 'An angry outburst, denunciation of police', *The Argus*, 22 July 1919, p. 5.
97 'Funeral of O'Connor thousands stand in city in silence and bareheaded', *The Herald*, 22 July 1919, p. 10; 'Military funeral', *The Argus*, 23 July 1919, p. 9.
98 'More riots police and soldiers collide', *The Daily Telegraph*, 23 July 1919, p. 9.
99 'The committee meets', *The Bayonet*, 25 July 1919, p. 4.
100 Ibid.
101 'Upholding the law', *The Argus*, 24 July 1919, p. 7; 'Loyal soldiers', *The Sydney Morning Herald*, 24 July 1919, p. 7; 'The Melbourne riots', *The Brisbane Courier*, 24 July 1919, p. 7; 'The Melbourne riots', *The Advertiser*, 24 July 1919, p. 7; 'In defence of the AIF', *The Age*, 24 July 1919, p. 8; see also M. Cathcart, *Defending the national tuckshop*, p. 92.
102 Ibid.
103 'Editorial', *The Bayonet*, 1 August 1919, p. 2.
104 Minutes of RSSILA Victorian Branch Committee meeting, 5 August 1919, and minutes for 16 September 1919, *RSSILA Victorian Branch Archives*, Anzac House, Melbourne. See also M. Crotty, 'Returned soldier violence in Australia', R. Mason (ed.), *Legacies of Violence: Rendering the Unspeakable Past in Modern Australia*, Berghahn, New York, 2017, p. 193.
105 Minutes of meeting at meeting at Athenaeum Hall, 20 August 1919, *RSSILA Victorian Branch Archives*, Anzac House, Melbourne.
106 M. Lake, 'The power of Anzac', in M. McKernan and M. Browne (eds), *Australia: Two Centuries of War and Peace*, Australian War Memorial, Canberra, 1988, p. 210; M. Crotty 'Returned soldier violence in Australia', in R. Mason (ed.), *Legacies of Violence*, p. 194.
107 RSSILA, The Official Report of the Conference of League Delegates with Rt Hon. Hughes, 11 September 1919, reprinted from *The Soldier*, Sydney, p. 3.
108 M. Crotty, 'The veteran's voice' in A. Ekins (ed.), *1918 Year of Victory: The End of the Great War and the Shaping of History*, Exisle Publishing, Auckland., 2010, pp. 239–41; Kristianson, *The Politics of Patriotism*, p. 241.

5: The Internal Enemy and Diggers 'Uphold the Law'

1 *The Bulletin*, 5 June 1919.
2 'Protestant League', *The Brisbane Courier*, 31 July 1918, p. 7.
3 *Statutory Rules 1918*, No. 86, Regs 27A(a–b), 27B, p. 219; see also *Commonwealth of Australia Gazette*, 12 September 1918, No. 145, p. 1823 for notification of Regulation 27BB.
4 'Red Flag in "Random Reapings"', *The Worker (Brisbane)*, 22 August 1918, p. 7.
5 'All about the Red Flag', *The Worker*, 8 August 1918, p. 9.
6 'The Red Flag', *The Brisbane Courier*, 10 August 1918, p. 4.
7 Evans, *Loyalty and Disloyalty*, pp. 122–23; 'The Red Flag', *The Brisbane Courier*, 9 August 1918, p. 6.
8 'The Red Flag, appeal to reason', *The Daily Standard*, 8 August 1918, p. 5.
9 *Commonwealth of Australia Gazette*, 21 September 21, 1918, p. 1861.
10 Brigadier-General Irving, Commandant 1st Military District, to Secretary, Department of Defence, 2 October 1918, 'The Red Flag', NAA: BP4/1, 66/4/2165.
11 30 November 1918, *'Diaries of the Chief Censor'*, NAA: MP390/8, 1918.

12 For the regulation about telephone communication see War Precautions Regulation 21A in *Statutory Rules 1916*, p. 478.
13 Amendments to the *War Precautions Act* in 1916 allowed for search of premises and confiscation of books and documents, and for regulating alien-owned businesses, property and 'their civil rights and obligations'. The amendments also conferred power for 'requisitioning of any goods, articles or things of any kind'. See *Commonwealth Acts 1916*, Sections 5 (1) (f & j) and 4 (1A) (a-c) pp. 136–7.
14 National Archives of Australia Fact Sheet 'Wartime internment camps in Australia', https://www.naa.gov.au/explore-collection/immigration-and-citizenship/wartime-internment-camps-australia#ww1, viewed 12 April 2025.
15 Acting Prime Minister Watt to Acting Attorney-General Groom, 24 October 1918, 'War. War Precautions Act', NAA: A461, A420/1.
16 *An Act to Extend the Duration of the War Precautions Act 1914–1916 and for Other Purposes*, Commonwealth of Australia, December 1918.
17 Censor's Office, Brisbane to Intelligence Officer, Military Headquarters, Brisbane, 2 May 1918; telegram 29 April 1918 from Luscombe to Secretary Dept of Defence, Melbourne; 27 April 1918 from Sgt. Munro, Commonwealth Police, Brisbane to Commissioner, Commonwealth Police, Sydney. All correspondence in 'Peace demonstrations at Brisbane', NAA: BP4/1, 66/4/2360.
18 *War Precautions Act Repeal Act 1920–1934*, assented to 2 December 1920.
19 W. K. Hancock, *Australia*, The Jacaranda Press, Brisbane, 1961, first published 1930, p. 24.
20 Ibid., pp. 59–60 (quote p. 60) and p. 218.
21 B. Kingston, *The Oxford History of Australia, Volume 3: Glad Confident Morning*, Oxford University Press, Melbourne, 1988, pp. 128–30.
22 Constable William O'Rourke, South Brisbane to Inspector Ferguson, 19 January 1919, in 'Gall Estrays', 14404 of 1920 (A/ 7137), Queensland State Archives, Item ID ITM339188.
23 Order signed by Brigadier General G. G. Irving, Military Commandant, 24 September 1918, 'Re Peter Simonoff', NAA: MP16/1, 1918/2146.
24 George Taylor to Premier Ryan, 13 November 1918, attaching resolution dated 10 November 1918, Queensland State Archives, Item ID ITM862667.
25 T. J. Mills, Secretary, Queensland Loyalty League to Military Commandant, 1st Military District, 24 October 1918, 'Regarding disloyalists in Brisbane [Papers relating to the Queensland Loyalty League]', NAA: BP4/1, 66/4/3035.
26 Undated, c. October 1918, 'list of disloyalists in Brisbane', NAA: BP4/1, 66/4/3035.
27 Newsclip, *The Brisbane Courier*, 11 November 1918, NAA: BP4/1, 66/4/3035.
28 Commissioner Urquhart to Herbert Brookes, 23 February 1919, quoted in T. Botham, 'The Red Flag riots [manuscript]: conservative reactions', Honours thesis, Australian National University, 1975, National Library of Australia, p. 38.
29 Ibid.
30 A. Laurie, 'The Black War in Queensland', *Journal of the Royal Historical Society of Queensland*, Vol. 6, No. 1, 1959, pp. 155–73, p. 171. See also J. Richards, *The Secret War*, University of Queensland Press, St Lucia, Qld, 2008, p. 265.
31 Report of conference in Melbourne, 18 January 1919, 'Bolshevism, Sedition and Disloyalty', NAA: A3932, SC294.
32 Ibid.

NOTES

33 Minutes of Cabinet decisions, 21 January 1919, '[Hughes Ministry Cabinet Decisions] January to October 1919', NAA: A2717, Volume 1 Folder 3.
34 Ibid.
35 Constable H. Foote to Sergeant Short, Commonwealth Police Force, Brisbane, 3 March 1919, 'Miscellaneous Papers of Commonwealth Police Force', NAA: BP230/4/1.
36 Sergeant Short to the Commissioner, 3 March 1919, handwritten note on memo, NAA: BP230/4, 1.
37 R. Evans, *The Red Flag Riots*, pp. 111–17; 'The Red Flag carried through the streets', *The Daily Standard*, 24 March 1919, p. 5. Also report by Constable Driscoll, Roma Street Station, Brisbane, 23 March 1919 Queensland State Archives, Item ID ITM339188 and report marked 'secret', 26 March 1919, probably from SIB Captain Ainsworth, in NAA: A456, W26/241. See also translation of 'Nabat' (*The Tocsin*), in K. Windle, '"A crude orgy of drunken violence": A Russian account of the Brisbane "Red Flag Riots" of 1919', *Labour History*, No. 99 (November 2010), p. 172.
38 'Sensational sequel', *The Brisbane Courier*, 24 March 1919, p. 6; 'Who inspired it, Russian Rooms attacked', *The Daily Standard*, 24 March 1919, p. 5; Windle, '"A crude orgy of drunken violence"', p. 173.
39 Ibid. (all sources), and report from Sergeant Short, Commonwealth Police Force, Brisbane, 24 March 1919, NAA: A456, W26/241.
40 Report from Lieutenant Wearne, Military Intelligence, 25 March 1919, 'File on Russians, Russian Association, Soviet of Souse in Brisbane; relating to meetings, demonstrations, deportations, prosecutions', NAA: BP4/1, 66/4/3660. Also telegram from Anderson to Solicitor General, Melbourne, 27 March 1919, NAA: A456, W26/241.
41 Report by Sergeant Short, Commonwealth Police, 25 March 1919 and report from secret agent 'Subsided' (Captain G. Ainsworth), 25 March 1919, NAA: A456, W26/241. Also report by Inspector Carroll, 25 March 1919, Queensland State Archives, Item ID ITM339188.
42 Report from Lieutenant Wearne, Military Intelligence, 25 March 1919, NAA: BP4/1, 66/4/3660. Also telegram from Anderson to Solicitor General, Melbourne 27 March 1919, NAA: A456, W26/241.
43 K. Windle, 'A crude orgy of drunken violence', pp. 174–5.
44 Report by Sergeant Short, Commonwealth Police, 25 March 1919 and report from secret agent 'Subsided' (Captain G. Ainsworth) dated 25 March 1919, NAA: A456, W26/241. Also Inspector Carroll to Commissioner of Police, 25 March 1919 and Police Commissioner Urquhart to Home Secretary, 25 March 1919, Queensland State Archives, Item ID ITM339188. And R. Evans, 'Some furious outbursts of riot', *War and Society*, Vol. 3 No. 2, 1985, pp. 75–98, p. 89.
45 Report by Sergeant Short, Commonwealth Police, 25 March 1919, NAA: A456, W26/241.
46 'Riotous ex-soldiers', *The Daily Standard*, 25 March 1919, p. 5.
47 'Exciting scenes', *The Brisbane Courier*, 26 March 1919, p. 7; 'Newspaper office attacked', *The Daily Telegraph*, 26 March 1919, p. 9.
48 Police Commissioner Urquhart to Home Secretary, 25 March 1919, Queensland State Archives, Item ID ITM339188.

49. 'Diary of G.F. Ainsworth', NAA: BP230/3, 3. Also report marked 'secret', 26 March 1919, probably from Captain Ainsworth, code name 'subsided', SIB, NAA: A456, W26/241.
50. Copy of telegram, 26 March 1919, RSSILA resolution to Acting Prime Minister, Melbourne, NAA: A456, W26/241.
51. Ibid. and Pimentel to Acting Premier, 25 March 1919, NAA: A456, W26/241.
52. Telegram 25 March 1919, NAA: A456, W26/241.
53. Police Commissioner Urquhart to Home Secretary, 25 March 1919, Queensland State Archives, Item ID ITM339188.
54. Sergeant Short, Commonwealth Police to Commissioner, 27 March 1919, NAA: A456, W26/241.
55. Report marked 'secret', probably from Captain Ainsworth, code name 'subsided', SIB, 26 March 1919, NAA: A456, W26/241.
56. *The Daily Mail*, 8 August 1918. See also R. Evans, *The Red Flag Riots*, pp. 163–6. For lists of seven Russians deported on 19 September 1919, not including Zuzenko, who was deported separately, see memo from the Chief of General Staff, Melbourne to the Commandant, 1st Military District, Qld, 17 October 1919, 'File on Russians, Russian Association, Soviet of Souse in Brisbane; relating to meetings, demonstrations, deportations, prosecutions', NAA: BP4/1, 66/4/3660. For list of convictions for breaching the War Precautions Regulation prohibiting the Red Flag, see undated document, c. April 1919, correspondence between Commandant, 1st Military District, Brisbane, to the Secretary, Department of Defence, Melbourne, 'The Red Flag', NAA: BP4/1, 66/4/2165.
57. 'Fighting disloyalty', *The Sydney Morning Herald*, 7 April 1919, p. 7.
58. Decoded telegram from 'Subsided', SIB, Brisbane (Captain Ainsworth), 29 March 1919 and decoded telegrams Acting Prime Minister to and from Military Commandant, Brisbane, 31 March 1919, NAA: A456, W26/241.
59. ALP and NSW Trades and Labor Council to NSW Chief Secretary, 20 May 1919, *Premier's Department Correspondence, 1919*, MHNSW, 9/4812; B19/1434.
60. 'Returned Soldiers' and Sailors' League', *The Mercury*, 7 April 1919, p. 6.
61. 'Bolsheviks beware!', *The Examiner*, 7 April 1919, p. 5.
62. 'Rival political meetings', *The Mercury*, 14 April 1919, p. 5; 'Labor in Launceston', *The World*, 14 April 1919, p. 6.
63. See reports in 'Rioting in Kalgoorlie & Boulder: Damage to Greek Shops', State Records Office of Western Australia (SROWA), Acc. 430, 1916/6695.
64. Reports and correspondence, 'Treasury Dept. West Aust. Anti-Greek Riots', NAA: A167, WA 21/1042.
65. Report from Colonel F. Heritage, Perth to Adjutant-General, Victoria Barracks, Melbourne, 7 July 1919, 'Woodline strike – Kalgoorlie', NAA: B197, 2021/1/236.
66. By this time Western Australian Returned Soldiers' Associations were affiliated with the RSSILA nationally but RSA and RSSILA branches continued to operate autonomously. On the Boulder RSA complaint about Italian workers, see confidential report by Major H. A. Corbet, Intelligence Section, 5th Military District, 13 September 1919, forwarded to the Prime Minister's Department, 'Kalgoorlie – industrial position', NAA: B197; 2021/1/235.
67. B. Bunbury, *Timber for Gold: Life on the Goldfields Woodlines 1899–1965*, Fremantle Arts Centre Press, Fremantle, 1997, p. 34.
68. Report by Major H. A. Corbet, 13 September 1919, NAA: B197; 2021/1/235.

69   Report to Director of Military Intelligence, Victoria Barracks, Melbourne, from a Captain (handwritten initials only) Intelligence Section, 18 November 1919, 'Italian Aliens on the Goldfields', NAA: B197, 2021/1/237.
70   E. Scott, *Volume XI – Australia during the war*, p. 430. See also War Precautions Regulation 17EA, in *Commonwealth Statutory Rules 1918*, p. 216.
71   Report to Director of Military Intelligence, Victoria Barracks, Melbourne, from a Captain (handwritten initials) Intelligence Section, 18 November 1919, NAA: B197, 2021/1/237.
72   A. Splivalo, *The Home Fires*, Fremantle Arts Centre Press, Fremantle, 1982, pp. 217–18.
73   Telegram to Commissioner of Police, Perth from Duncan Inspector, 12 August 1919, and report from Sergeant Metcalfe, Kalgoorlie station, 11 August 1919, 'Racial Riots on Eastern Goldfields (Italians)', SROWA, Acc 430, 1919/3871. See also 'Serious stabbing affray', *The Kalgoorlie Miner*, 13 August 1919, p. 2; 'The knifing of Northwood', *The Sunday Times*, 17 August 1919, p. 1.
74   'Meeting of returned soldiers', *The Western Argus*, 19 August 1919, p. 7. See also report from Major H. A. Corbet, Intelligence Section, 5th Military District, 13 September 1919, NAA: B197, 2021/1/235.
75   Report from Captain, Intelligence Section, to Director of Military Intelligence, Victoria Barracks, Melbourne, 18 November 1919, NAA: B197, 2021/1/237. See also report from Major H. A. Corbet, Intelligence Section, 5th Military District, 13 September 1919, NAA: B197, 2021/1/235.
76   Report by Sergeant H. Fortescue on 'Raiding of the Italian Hotels', 13 August 1919, 'Racial Riots on Eastern Goldfields (Italians)', SROWA, Acc 430, 1919/3871.
77   Ibid.
78   Ibid.
79   Ibid.
80   'Serious stabbing affray', *The Western Argus*, 19 August 1919, p. 7.
81   Report by Sergeant John Fee, 13 August 1919, SROWA Acc 430, 1919/3871.
82   'Serious stabbing affray', *The Western Argus*, 19 August 1919, p. 7.
83   'Hotels raided', *The Western Argus*, 19 August 1919, p. 7.
84   Telegram from Commissioner of Police to Inspector Duncan, 13 August 1919, SROWA Acc 430, 1919/3871.
85   Premier James Mitchell to General Secretary, Returned Soldier's Association Perth, 13 August 1919, SROWA Acc 430, 1919/3871.
86   'Man's hurried departure', *The Western Argus*, 19 August 1919, p. 9; report from Captain, Intelligence Section, to Director, Military Intelligence, Victoria Barracks, Melbourne, 18 November 1919, NAA: B197, 2021/1/237.
87   'Alleged Bolshevik agent', *The Advertiser*, 15 August 1919, p. 9.
88   'Italians on the goldfields' and 'The Racial Trouble', *The Western Argus*, 19 August 1919, p. 9.
89   Ibid.
90   Splivalo, *The Home Fires*, pp. 218–19.
91   Minister for Police to H. W. D. Shallard, Consul for Italy, Perth, 2 September 1919; memo from Minister for Mines and Railways to Attorney-General, 30 August 1919; Italian Consul to Premier 16 August 1919, all correspondence in SROWA Acc 430, 1919/3871.

92 Minister for Police to H.W.D. Shallard, Consul for Italy, 2 September 1919, SROWA 1919/3871.
93 'Italians at Kalgoorlie', *The Advertiser*, 15 August 1919, p. 9.
94 B. Oliver, *War and Peace in Western Australia: The Social and Political Impact of the Great War, 1914–1926*, University of Western Australia Press, Nedlands, W.A., 1995, p. 158.
95 Report to Director of Military Intelligence, Victoria Barracks, Melbourne, from a Captain (handwritten initials only), Intelligence Section, 18 November 1919, 'Italian Aliens on the Goldfields', NAA: B197, 2021/ 1/ 237.

6: Vigilante Violence and the Beginnings of Secret Armies

1 Kristianson, *The Politics of Patriotism*, pp. 11–12.
2 'An appeal to returned soldiers', *The Daily Standard*, 3 May 1919, p. 4.
3 Returned Sailors' and Soldiers' Labor League, *Soldiers and the Labor Movement*, Brisbane, 1919, pp. iii, 15–18.
4 J. Popple, '"The Bolshevik element must be stamped out": Returned soldiers and Queensland politics, 1918–1925', Master's thesis, Australian National University, 1988, p. 176. See also 'State Parliament', *Warwick Daily News*, 4 October 1919, p. 5; Queensland RSSILA State Secretary Kerr to RSSILA National Secretary Henderson, 30 June 1920, *RSL Papers*, National Library of Australia, MS 6609/1/294A.
5 'Returned soldiers and politics', *Australian Worker*, 6 June 1918, p. 13; 'Soldiers for Labor, Sydney Secretary's tour', *The Daily Standard*, 6 January 1919, p. 5.
6 'Returned Sailors' and Soldiers' Democratic League', *Labor Call*, 16 May 1918, p. 11. See also Defence Department secret correspondence, 11 February and 22 March 1918, Intelligence section reports, 'Returned Soldiers' Democratic League', NAA: MP16/1, 1918/403.
7 Kristianson, *The Politics of Patriotism*, Appendix B, pp. 234–5; M. Crotty 'The RSSILA 1916–1946' in Crotty and Larsson (eds), *Anzac Legacies*, pp. 175–6.
8 Kristianson, *The Politics of Patriotism*, Appendix B, pp. 234–5.
9 RSSILA General Secretary W. Henderson to General Monash 8 April 1919, and 16 May 1919 to Monash from Henderson's successor A. P. K. Morris; H. A. Wheeler, Executive Officer of Australian YMCA with the AIF to W. Henderson, RSSILA 6 March 1919. All in *RSL Papers*, National Library of Australia, MS 6609/1/247. See also *The Digger*, 13 October and 25 December 1918, and 'Booklet for Returned Soldiers Pay Instructions', NAA: MP367/1, 418/4/27.
10 Lake, 'The power of Anzac', p 207.
11 'What next?' Is Bolingbroke dictator?', *The Daily Standard*, 31 December 1919, p. 4.
12 Ibid.
13 'Western riots, Charleville parasites', *The Daily Mail*, 3 December 1919, p. 7.
14 'Riot at Charleville', *The Age*, 3 December 1919, p. 12; 'A cleansing process', *The Cairns Post*, 4 December 1919, p. 5; 'Charleville riot', *The Sun*, 2 December 1919, p. 7.
15 'Western riots, Charleville parasites', *The Daily Mail*, 3 December 1919, p. 7.
16 'A model coup', *The Cairns Post*, 4 December 1919, p. 5; 'Western riots, soldiers in control', *The Daily Mail*, 4 December 1919, p. 7.
17 'Armed police, arrival in Charleville', *The Daily Standard*, 27 December 1919, p. 5; 'Armed police at Charleville', *The Brisbane Courier*, 31 December 1919, p. 6; 'A stupid lie, police at Charleville', *The Daily Standard*, 30 December 1919, p. 5; 'What next? Is Bolingbroke dictator?', *The Daily Standard*, 31 December 1919, p. 4; 'Charleville riots', *The Daily Mail*, 30 December 1919, p. 4.

NOTES

18   T. King, 'The tarring and feathering of J. K. McDougall: "Dirty tricks" in the 1919 federal election', *Labour History*, No. 45 (November 1983), pp. 54–67.
19   Ibid., pp. 60–2.
20   *The Ararat Advertiser*, 2 and 9 December 1919. Each edition of *The Ararat Advertiser* was only four pages, with no page numbers. The editions cited here are held as microfilm at the National Library of Australia.
21   *The Ararat Advertiser*, 23 December 1919 (includes a report of McDougall's evidence in court).
22   *The Ararat Advertiser*, 9 and 23 December 1919.
23   *The Ararat Advertiser*, 9 December 1919; *The Sydney Morning Herald*, 8 December 1919, p. 7.
24   *The Ararat Advertiser*, 9 and 11 December 1919, 'J. K. McDougall's Rough Treatment', *Labor Call*, 11 December 1919, p. 4.
25   *The Ararat Advertiser*, 9 December 1919, 'Tarred and feathered', *The Daily Herald*, 12 December 1919, p. 4.
26   *The Ararat Advertiser*, 13, 23 and 31 December 1919 and 12 February 1920.
27   *The Ararat Advertiser*, 12 February 1920.
28   Scott, *Australia During the War*, pp. 162–5.
29   'Catholic notes', *Freeman's Journal*, 20 May 1920, p. 23, 'Father Jerger', *The Daily Telegraph*, 24 May 1920, p. 5.
30   'Lord Mayor Acts', *Evening News*, 25 May 1920, p. 5; 'Father Jerger', *The Sydney Morning Herald*, 28 May 1920, p. 10.
31   A. J. Hill, 'Rosenthal, Sir Charles (1875–1954)', *Australian Dictionary of Biography*, National Centre of Biography, Australian National University, adb.anu.edu.au/biography/rosenthal-sir-charles-8268/text14483, published first in hardcopy 1988, viewed online 4 November 2024; T. Kemm, '"Rare among brass hats": Charles Rosenthal in the First World War', Australian War Memorial, https://www.awm.gov.au/sites/default/files/rosenthal.pdf, viewed 18 April 2025.
32   'Father Jerger', *The Sydney Morning Herald*, 29 May 1920, p. 13.
33   'Nearly a riot', *The Daily Telegraph*, 31 May 1920, p. 4.
34   'Deportations', *The Sydney Morning Herald*, 31 May 1920, p. 9; 'Moore Park melee, Diggers defend flag', *The Newcastle Sun*, 31 May 1920, p. 5.
35   See inaugural edition of *King and Empire, The Official Journal of the King and Empire Alliance*, Sydney, Vol. 1, No. 1, 21 January 1921.
36   Ibid. and *The Sydney Morning Herald*, 'For empire', 20 July 1920, p. 7. See also A. Moore, *The Secret Army and the Premier: Conservative Paramilitary Organisations in New South Wales 1930–1932*, New South Wales University Press, Kensington, 1989, pp. 34–9.
37   'Fascisti', *The King and Empire*, Vol. II No. 11, 25 November 1922, Sydney, pp. 7–8.
38   Cathcart, *Defending the National Tuckshop*, Chapter 1 'The White Army'; Moore, *The Secret Army and the Premier*, Chapters 2–4.
39   Ibid. and K. Inglis 'Returned soldiers in Australia', *Collected seminar papers on the Dominions between the Wars*, Institute of Commonwealth Studies, London, 1971, p. 59. See also R. Darroch, *D. H. Lawrence in Australia*, Macmillan, Melbourne, 1981; D. H. Lawrence, *Kangaroo*, Times House Publishing, Silverwater, NSW, 1984, first published 1923, p. 205.
40   Lawrence, *Kangaroo*, p. 94.

7: The Loyal Nation

1. Lawrence, *Kangaroo*, pp. 351–9.
2. Ibid. pp. 359–60.
3. 'Union Jack, torn to ribbons', *The Daily Mail*, 2 May 1921, p. 6; 'The Union Jack', *The Sun*, 2 May 1921, p. 3.
4. 'Soldiers angry, counterdemonstrations', *The Sydney Morning Herald*, 3 May 1921, p. 9.
5. 'Summary', *The Sydney Morning Herald*, 7 May 1921, p. 1; 'Huge open air meetings', *The Sydney Morning Herald*, 7 May 1921, p. 14; 'Australia first', *The Sydney Morning Herald*, 6 May 1921, p. 9; 'Labor platform attacked', *The Daily Telegraph*, 9 May 1921, p. 5; A. Moore, *The Secret Army and the Premier*, p. 40.
6. Bean, *Anzac to Amiens*, p. 529.

INDEX

Aboriginal soldiers 75
Adelaide 11–12
    café and theatre closures 18–19
    tramways strike 14, 16–19
Ainsworth, Captain, Special Intelligence
    Bureau 147, 149
Allen, Horace 4
Allen, Judith 94
AMA (Amalgamated Metalliferous
    Affiliation of the Australian Coal and
    Shale Employees' Association) 27
AMIEU (Australasian Meat Industry
    Employees Union) 39
Anti-Italian riots 153
Antill, Brigadier General John 17
Anti-Socialist League 5
Anti-war activism 55
Anzac and Anzacs 215
    Buffet 49
    Cairo riots 50
    heroes 12, 22, 31, 70, 73, 74, 75, 84, 99,
        131, 181, 187
    sacrifice 2, 12, 25, 67, 69–97, 134, 186
Anzac legend and identity
    construction and cultural significance 74,
        85, 166, 187
    contemporary celebration of 2, 6
    editorial role of C. E. W. Bean 74, 202
    formation through postwar conflict 10
Archdall, Police Magistrate Hewan 145, 149
Armistice, 11 November 1918

Australasian Meat Industry Employees Union
    see AMIEU
Australian Imperial Force (AIF) 7
    casualty statistics 4, 99
    enlistment 2, 5
    regimental medical officers (RMOs) 86
    recruitment marches and meetings 5
Australian soldiers
    alcohol use 36, 40, 42, 79, 90, 91, 92, 93,
        180
    citizen soldier 8, 12, 75, 99
    humour 79
    involvement in strikes
    medical treatment and caregiving of
        invalid soldiers 90, 93, 94
    nationhood and sacrifice 74
    repatriation 81
    unemployment 100, 114, 116, 186
    union membership 24
    violent assault by 7, 9, 13, 44, 48, 55, 91,
        94, 95, 96, 173, 174, 180, 186
    wounded 7, 18, 31, 69, 84, 85, 86, 87, 88,
        90, 93, 99, 107, 113, 188
Australian war literature 75
Australian War Memorial 191
AWU (Australian Workers' Union) 3, 60, 61,
    64, 65, 66, 154, 168
Axford, Harry 157, 159

Baglin, Fred 104
Basic wage 191
Barker, Harold 174

INDEX

Barwell, Attorney-General Henry 22, 27
Bean, Charles E. W. 74, 188
Beer strike 61, 201
Bellamy, George 60, 61, 62, 64
Beaumont, Joan 84
Bissett, Wilson 174
Blackburn, Captain 21–24, 27
'Bloody Sunday' 108, 152
Bolingbroke, Major 146, 148, 149, 168–71, 180
Bolsheviks and Bolshevism 141, 187, 211
Bolton, Senator William Kinsey 91
Brand, Brigadier General Charles 126
Brisbane Domain 57
Broken Hill 31, 194
Brodribb, Major Robert 158–9
Brosnan, Sub-Inspector 59–60
Brookfield, Percy 47
Burkett, Captain George
Butler, Lieutenant Colonel Arthur 85
Bykoff, Herman 143–5
Byrne, Lieutenant 61, 62, 64, 66

Campbell, R. 61, 63, 64
Campion, Edmund 6
Carney, Pearce 39
Catholic Australians
    bigotry towards 5, 6, 45, 117, 142, 177, 184, 187
    of Irish descent 43, 178
    protests by 175
Catholic Federation 45, 175
Censorship and censor's reports 112, 136, 192, 201
Children's Peace Army 58, 142
Church of England 44, 45, 90
Colebatch, Hal, Premier of Western Australia 102, 103, 109
Commemoration of soldiers' sacrifice 12
Commonwealth Police Force 142
Comrades of the War League (COWL) 56
Conscription
    referendum defeat 6
    impact on Australian Labor Party 4
    of Italians 155
    opposition to 5, 12, 28, 44, 46, 48, 58, 134, 155, 176
    referendum voting statistics 191
    sectarian divisions over 6

Considine, Michael MHR 36
Cooley, Mrs 64
Corboy, Edwin 107
Crotty, Martin 129, 166,
Cumberland, Joseph 69, 70, 73
Cumberland, Oliver 69, 70, 73

Deakin, Alfred 5
Defence Department 55, 64, 139, 160, 164, 167
Dempster, George 30
Dennis, C. J. 85
de Paoli, John 157
deportation / deported man 156, 175, 176, 177
Diggers – *see* Australian soldiers
Dimboola quarantine 101
Donnes, Mick 104
Duguid, Dr 22, 23, 24
Dunn, Digger 156, 185
Durkin, Jack 64, 66
Dyett, Gilbert 131

Eastcrabb, Archie 39, 61, 64, 65, 66, 140
Easter Rising (Ireland) 5, 45
Eastgate, Cyril 174
Economy of sacrifice 12, 99
Edwards, Police Commissioner (South Australia) 18
Edwards, Thomas 104, 108, 109
Eles, Cavaliere 155
Enemy Aliens 9, 136, 138
    arrest under the *Aliens Restriction Order* 139
    internment 9, 155
    regulations about 136, 137
Evans, P., NSW Labor Party 50, 51, 52
Evans, Raymond 150

Father Jerger 175
Fawcett, James Joseph 120, 121
FEDFA (Federated Engine Drivers and Firemen's Association) 28
Fisher, Lieutenant William 60, 147
First Nations communities 8, 70, 141
Fitzgerald, William 175
Foote, Constable 142
Free Speech Committee 55
Furay, Major General 62, 64
Fussell, Paul 72, 73

INDEX

Gallipoli 10, 21, 70, 73, 74, 85, 86, 92, 113, 187
Gammage, Bill 84
Garden, John (Jock) 184
Garran, Robert, Solicitor General 10, 175
Garton, Stephen 75
Gatti, Giacomo (Jim) 155, 156
Gendered violence 94
German immigrants 138
Gerster, Robin 75
'God Save the King', anthem 30, 33, 44, 45, 59, 126, 134, 135
Government surveillance 46
Great Strike (also called the General Strike) 101, 118
Grief and mourning 70, 73, 186
Grimwade, Brigadier General Harold 126

Hallett, Senior Constable John 92, 93, 96
Hamilton, Frank 62, 66
Hancock, Sir William 137
Harris, Captain H. R. 86
Hašek, Jaroslav 71
Hebbard, James 30, 33
Hill, Lionel 13, 26
Hilvert, John 9
Holman, William, NSW Premier 52, 53, 55
Homefront 72, 81, 187, 189
Hughes, Prime Minister William 4, 5, 9, 131, 137, 155, 168, 173
Hurley, Captain Frank 88, 114, 115
Huxley, W. 60, 64, 65
Hynes, Samuel 72, 73

Immigration Restriction Act of 1901 137
Industrial disputes 101, 111, 153
International Workers of the World (IWW) 38, 196
Inwood, Reginald Roy 31

Jackson, William 140, 175
Jeffery, William 55, 56
Jeffries, Vincent 50
Judd, Ernest 50, 51, 52, 55, 185
Judicial responses to returned soldiers' crimes 95

Kalgoorlie riots 155
Kelly, Michael 39, 61, 64

Kelly, Robert 1
Kerr, George 34
Khaki riots 72
Khyber troopship 104
King and Empire Alliance 176, 18
Knowledge and Unity 139, 150

Labor government in Queensland 149
Labor movement 100, 183, 194
Labor opposition 109
Labor Party 4, 55
Labor Returned Soldier Organisations 164
Lake, Marilyn 129
Larsson, Marina 84, 93
Lawrence, D. H. 179, 183, 184
Lawson, Harry, Premier of Victoria 123
Leed, Eric 72, 99
Legge, Major General James Gordon 141
LVA (Labor Volunteer Army) 27, 28
Liberty League 91, 117, 203
Lord, William 58
Loyalists 31, 41, 61
Loyal nation 183
Loyalty League 139
Lumpers' Union 101

Mannix, Archbishop Daniel 5, 6, 173
Marshall, Vance 50, 51
McCallum, Alex 101
McDougall, John K. 171, 214
McKenzie, Sergeant 92
McPhail, Sir Andrew 86
Melbourne Domain 126
Memory of war 84, 202
Military and police coordination 141
Military censorship 77
Military honours 113
Military Intelligence
    assessment of Hughenden violence 62
    report 154
    surveillance of anti-war activists and returned soldiers 56
    surveillance of union activities in Queensland 38
Minogue Green, James 61, 64, 65, 66
Monash, General John 166
Moore Park 175
Mosse, George 73

Municipal Tramways Trust/ Tramways Trust 13
Murphy, Corporal Cecil 164, 165
Murphy, Con 169
Murphy, Jack 169

Nationalist government 9, 24, 100, 134, 137, 139, 155, 186, 188
Nationalist party 5, 53, 165, 168, 171, 174
Nationalist Waterside Workers' Union 101
Northwood, Thomas 155, 156, 157

O'Connor, Private James 122
One Big Union (OBU) 38, 109, 152
O'Neill, P. C. 66
Orsatti, Mr 157
O'Reilly, Father 176
Owen, Wilfred 70, 71

Palamountain, J. R. 152
Palmer, Vance 76
Panton, A. H. (Frank) 105
Peace Day 1919 114
Pearce, George, Defence Minister 24, 52, 90, 141, 175
Peiniger, Charles 60
Penny, James 60, 61, 66
Penny, Tom 60, 61
Petroff, Simon aka Louis Frances 158, 159
Pozières 86, 89
Police
　arrests 156
　bias 58
　response to Domain riots 51
　response to returned soldiers 119
　violence 103, 121
Pope, Colonel 110
Prichard, Katharine Susannah 114
Priest, Superintendent Edward 17, 18, 19
Profiteer 34, 36, 100
Protestant Australians 45, 46, 117, 134, 138, 139

Quarantine and public health 101
Queensland Loyalty League *see* Returned Soldiers, Sailors and Citizens Loyalty League
Queensland Protestant League 134, 139

QRU (Queensland Railway Union) 39, 65

Red Cross Society 57
Red Flag 34, 37, 135, 183, 184
　anthem 29, 30, 31, 35, 36, 40, 135
　demonstration 142, 144, 149
　War Precautions Regulations re 28, 136
Red Flag Riots 138, 144, 150, 164, 168, 180
　arrests 149
　causes and police reports 208
　comparison with other returned soldier riots 152, 153, 168, 171
　legal consequences and deportations 211
　newspaper coverage by the Daily Standard 192
red-raggers 37, 51
Remarque, Erich Maria 71
Renton, Bill 103
Repatriation Department 100
Returned Sailors' and Soldiers' Australian Democratic League (RS&SADL) 165
Returned Sailors' and Soldiers' Imperial League of Australia (RSSILA)
　anti-union position and opposition to strikes 34, 57, 118, 163
　formation and development 19
　internal divisions and involvement in industrial disputes 116
　involvement in riots 145
　links with Nationalist Party
　membership statistics and decline 166
　organizational structure and political influence 211
　political affiliations 163
　recruitment during demobilisation 167
　relationship with Returned Soldiers' Association 20, 21, 49
　support for employment preference 91
Returned Sailors' and Soldiers' Labor League (RSSLL) 164
Returned soldiers
　alcohol consumption and violence 91
　family caregiving of 93, 94
　gendered violence and court leniency towards 9
　magazines 82
　nation-building role 133
　protests 122

220

role in postwar politics 185, 211
role in postwar riots 2, 11, 31, 51, 121, 131, 143, 151, 161, 183
role in postwar violence 41, 171, 163, 181, 204
role in union disputes and political activism 101, 111
Returned Soldiers' and Sailors' Political League (RSSPL) 165
Returned Soldiers, Sailors and Citizens Loyalty League / aka Queensland Loyalty League 60
Returned Soldiers' Association (RSA) 20, 21, 30, 49, 164, 167, 170, 195
   conflict over tramway strike involvement 22–27
   formation and role 19
   internal disputes 25, 104
   involvement in Fremantle riots 104–7, 110, 111
   involvement in Goldfields riots 153–7, 159
   political affiliations and class conflict 24
   variations in state branches 163
Riots,
   Adelaide 11, 12, 13, 14, 16, 17, 18, 19, 21, 24, 27, 35, 42
   Brisbane 'Red Flag' riots 43, 131, 135, 138, 146, 152, 153, 180
   Brisbane Domain 47, 57, 58, 59,
   Broken Hill 11, 12, 27, 35, 37, 38, 42, 67, 135
   Canada 129
   Charleville 168, 170, 171, 173, 180
   England (Khaki riots) 72
   Fremantle 9, 101–113, 131, 152, 163
   Hughenden 43, 60–7, 171
   'in a Church' (Orange, NSW) 43–6
   Melbourne 10, 115–31, 133, 149, 152, 163, 187
   Moore Park, Sydney 175, 176, 177, 179, 185
   Press coverage of 10, 16, 19, 20, 22, 30, 33, 35, 36, 53, 62, 65, 66, 127, 131, 133, 147, 171, 172, 177, 183
   Sydney Domain 47, 48, 49, 50, 51–5, 184, 186
   Townsville 9, 11, 12, 38–42, 65, 66, 67

Rhoden, Clare 75
Roberts, George 118, 122, 123, 128, 129, 187
Robinson, Matron 92
Rosa, Sam 51, 52
Rosenberg, Civa 139
Rosenberg, Michael 139
Roseby, Reverend Thomas 43–6
Roseby, Amy 46
Rosenthal, Sir Charles 176, 177, 178, 179, 183, 184, 185
RSSILA *see* Returned Sailors' and Soldiers' Imperial League of Australia (RSSILA)
'Rule Britannia' anthem 30, 41, 59
Russell, Lieutenant 168, 169, 170, 171
Russian Bolsheviks – *see also* Bolsheviks
Russian Community in Brisbane 139
Russian Workers' Union 143
Ryan, T. J. (Thomas) 39, 57, 139, 140, 173, 177

Salatina, Mrs 64
Sandford Jackson, Dr Ernest 140
Sassoon, Siegfried 72
Scanlon, Senior Constable John 121
Schwan, William 157
Scott, Ernest 11
Scott, Major Jack 177, 178, 179, 183, 184
Scott Griffiths, Jennie 58
Seamen's Union strike 101
Secret Armies 178
Sectarianism 6, 44
Senate Select Committee on soldiers and alcohol 91
Short, Sergeant 142, 144
Shell shock 7, 36, 56, 92, 93, 95
   definition and diagnosis 85, 86
   mitigating factor in judicial sentencing 86
   public perception of shell shock 89, 90
   symptoms of shell shock 86
Simonov/ Simonoff, Peter 139
Smeshurst, J. 36, 38
Social Democratic League 50, 58, 108, 112
Socialist Party 28
Soldier poets 71
Souter, Gavin 2
Spanish flu pandemic 7
Special Intelligence Bureau (SIB) 147

INDEX

Stahl, Lieutenant 157
Steward, Police Commissioner George (later Sir) 6, 38, 119, 122, 123, 125
Strikebreakers 14
Strikes 66, 129, 134, 154, 168
    Adelaide tramway 14, 16–19
    Beer 61, 201
    Great strike 101, 118
    RSA conflict 22–27
    Seaman's Union 101

Tait, Superintendent 50, 51
Taylour, George 56
Temperance Committee 59
The Australian Women's Weekly 58
The Barrier Daily Truth 30, 33, 34, 36
The Barrier Miner 30, 34, 35, 36
The Bayonet 84, 116, 119, 121, 123, 128, 129, 130
The Daily Herald 16, 17
The Daily Standard 142, 147, 148, 149, 150, 151, 168
The Digger 167
The Port Hacking Cough 76, 77, 78, 80, 81
The Soldier, at Home and Abroad 54, 55, 82, 83, 84, 90, 100
The Wipers Times 77, 78
Throssell, Hugo 113, 114, 115
Thomson, Alistair 84
Tories/Tory 5, 114
Townsville Industrial Council 39
Trades Hall
    Adelaide 24, 25
    Brisbane 135, 142, 149, 164
    Broken Hill 12, 28, 33, 34, 35
    Fremantle 108
    Melbourne 135
    Perth 111
    Sydney 51, 52, 53
Trainer, Percy 108
Tramway Employees' Union 13, 23
Trench poets 70
Tudor, Frank, MHR 168, 173

Unionists and union organisers 31
Union Jack 124, 134, 183, 184, 185, 187, 215
United Loyalist Executive 140
Urquhart, Frederic 140, 141

Vigilante violence 60, 65, 163–81
Villinger, Albert 121

War Precautions Act 40, 142, 155
    amendments 208
    arrests under 38, 51, 149
    extension and political use post-war 137
    government powers and censorship 9, 10, 37, 134, 136
    liquor regulations and military orders 203
    political use of 37, 46, 52, 55
    regulation re blue armband 90
    regulation 27A, re support for republics 134
    regulation 27B re prohibiting flags 28
    regulation 28 and impact on anti-war speech 47
    regulations on referendum results 192
Waterside Workers' Federation 101
Watt, Acting Prime Minister William 45, 135, 141, 148
Weir, Colonel Stanley 17
Western Front 71
White Australia policy 80, 137
Williams, Harold 174
Williams, Richard 172, 174
Williams, Brigadier General Robert 92
Willis, Captain, Military Intelligence 39, 40, 41, 42, 62, 63, 64, 66, 67
Winn, Captain R. C. 86
Winter, Jay 73
Women's Peace Army 142
Wood, Captain, Military Intelligence 39, 57, 142

Ypres 77, 87

Xenophobia 153

Zonnebeke 78, 87, 88, 115
Zuzenko, Alexander 139, 143, 149

www.ingramcontent.com/pod-product-compliance
Lightning Source LLC
Chambersburg PA
CBHW040256170426
43192CB00020B/2821